Tiger in an African Palace

and other thoughts about
identification and transformation

Richard Fardon

Langaa Research & Publishing CIG
Mankon, Bamenda

Publisher:

Langaa RPCIG

Langaa Research & Publishing Common Initiative Group
P.O. Box 902 Mankon
Bamenda
North West Region
Cameroon
Langaagrp@gmail.com
www.langaa-rpcig.net

Distributed in and outside N. America by African Books Collective
orders@africanbookscollective.com
www.africanbookcollective.com

ISBN: 9956-791-70-9

For JDYP

In specialibus generalia quaerimus

I am most grateful for permission to use an artwork by Hassan Musa as the cover illustration for this collection of essays: *There are no tigers in Africa*, assembled textiles, 170 x 236 cm, 2010 © Pascal Polar Gallery, Brussels.

The artist explains,

This work is inspired by a painting of Delacroix's, 'Indian woman bitten by a tiger'. The idea was to take up the theme of 'Tigritude' developed by the Nigerian Nobel Laureate for Literature, Wole Soyinka, who declared, 'A tiger does not proclaim his tigritude, he pounces'.

Soyinka was responding to the notion of 'Negritude' put forward by Léopold Sédar Senghor and Aimé Césaire. He believed that it was not enough to make demands; it was necessary to act. The sort of negritude people want to impose on us is like a bitch that hangs around on the street until she sees someone suspicious coming towards her; then she flees into her owner's compound where she sets to barking. It's a matter of getting some tigritude to counter the essentialism of negritude.

The problem for Soyinka's solution is that there are no tigers in Africa!

TIGER IN AN AFRICAN PALACE

*and other thoughts about identification
and transformation*

Contents

Figures

Copyright acknowledgements

INTRODUCTION
Identification and transformation

The welcome invitation to select some essays for republication by an African press[1] encourages the cosy benefits of selective hindsight being brought to bear on the trajectory of a strand of my past work. I have chosen eight essays, written over thirty odd years, that reflect my ethnographic interest in what are, in several senses, the middling societies of Cameroon and Nigeria. That's to say societies of medium scale and 'in-between' character, living at the confluence of Saharan and Atlantic West Africa, that have felt the divergent pulls of trading systems, world religions, and Empire-building initiatives. This Atlantic-Saharan tension may never been stronger than during the past two centuries of concurrent modernizations which have witnessed the foundation by conquest of an Islamic Caliphate, and its own subsequent conquest, outlawing of the 'legitimate' slave trade, colonization and decolonization during a period which included two World Wars, and a half century of formal independence for Cameroon and Nigeria accompanied by ethno-regional tensions and increasing religious polarization.

Anthropological theorizing has also changed between the decade of my formation in the 1970s at University College London (UCL), the 1980s spent mostly as a lecturer at the University of St Andrews in Scotland, and the quarter century since then of my career at SOAS,

---

1. Thanks are due in this respect to Francis Nyamnjoh for both the enthusiasm of his initial urgings, and his patience while I struggled with the technical challenges of delivering my promises. I would not have been able to deliver on them at all without the advice and practical help of Jim Henderson, Gustaaf Houtman, Catherine Lawrence, and Dominique Remars. I gratefully renew all the acknowledgements made in the original chapters, and offer the collection to JDYP, colleague for more than two decades, whose influence runs through it.

University of London. Rereading my papers, not a favourite pastime, to choose those included here, inevitably with occasional passages that no longer need saying or hardly bear saying, has reminded me what these changes have been. Searching for a thread to guide my selection, I eventually settled on a developing interest in the interplay between two processes that are mutually productive: identification and transformation, or equally transformation and identification. Depending on broader circumstances, these can produce trajectories of convergence, divergence, or – for a time – stable parallelism between identities and the interests they seem to entail. Identification involves finding substantive sameness in the world: in loose terms, sameness of something either with other contemporary elements, or with itself at a previous moment, or with some future envisaged state; transformation I see as the changes that occur in the search for sameness under a particular set of circumstances, sometimes most powerfully when change is resisted. To be clear: claims to substantive sameness furnish stronger prompts to activity than do claims about similarity, which may be understood as more or less metaphorical. I take the process of identification to be about degrees of 'sameness' and not about all of the broader class of 'similarity'. This may all seem unhelpfully abstract, so it is simplest to explain it by means of the eight essays that led me there.

My interest in transformations preceded that in identities (or, more accurately my realization that the two were mutually entailed) and took a predictable form for its 1970s time in the analysis of kinship. In conception, the first essay reprinted here predates my doctoral fieldwork having been written to redeem a first year of postgraduate study that had otherwise gone awry in pursuit of a research project that proved unviable. The first part of its original version was about a now forgotten dispute concerning the different models – respectively group- and individually-biased – used to explain kinship and politics in African and New Guinea Highland societies. In the year I returned from my first African fieldwork, an article by Ivan Karp (1978) said anything that was worth saying on these issues, relieving me of any wish to pursue them further, and leaving me with most of what became the final published reanalysis of the Tiv ethnography. I returned to develop the second half of my paper only after I had written my doctorate and was finding my feet in a first lectureship. The essay begins with a reanalysis of the classic segmentary lineage organization for which the Tiv are well-known to anthropologists and suggests that, prior to its suppression by British colonial authorities, marriage by the exchange, ideally but not always practically, of sisters was an essential procedure for producing patrilineal descent. Men exchanged wards against wives, so the wives of a group of patrilaterally related men had substantively replaced their 'sisters', that is to say either their actual sisters, or the wider category of sister surrogates that was made up of the patrilaterally-related women classed as 'sisters', who were at particular men's disposition as wards, or even women received as wives in respect of 'sisters' but in the event used as wards. Looked at this way, any group defined by agnatic relations was reproduced both through men, and through the wives envisaged as having replaced, hence for this purpose being the same as, those men's sisters and daughters. These ideologically patrilineal groupings were reproduced in the most direct fashion, that is through both their male and female descendants; and evidence of the retention of knowledge about the identities of the wards married out against specific wives suggests Tiv also conceived of their particularly strong version of agnatic descent in this way; or, at the least, that they did so on important or marked occasions. In trying to pursue these ideal arrangements, Tiv had to improvise and found themselves competing with one another to achieve temporary advantage, but the outcomes of their doing so were broadly egalitarian over time because of a tendency for any position of advantage achieved by big men to be eroded during their lifetime (as a result of ageing, expenditure and the number of their offspring) rather than being inheritable by their sons. The 'segmentary lineage system' was not without effects, it was after all part of the way Tiv represented their politics to themselves and so influenced their actions, but an analytic account of politics needed to take account of those patterns of competition at lower levels within lineage groupings that Tiv accounts downplayed in the interests of playing up solidarity towards outsiders. Such competition typically involved patrilaterally-related men wanting to control wards, take wives, and turn wealth into prestige by mastering the major cults of the Tivland. Those who succeeded demonstrated power; and power and witchcraft translate the same Tiv term, *tsav*,[2] a capacity of the person potentially dangerous to both dependents and competitors.

---

2. Raymond Boyd and I have more recently looked into the deep history of this term through its relation to the Hausa *tsafi* (Boyd and Fardon 2014).

The remainder of the paper explored a regional comparison in two directions: the first demonstrated the wide prevalence of marriage by exchange prior to its suppression, and asked what made the Tiv case remarkable among these other instances. The evidence was thin, because the institution had been suppressed before much professionalized ethnography was undertaken, but suggested that Tiv ability to expand both territorially and in population was explicable in part by their incorporating women (and hence, particularly for a polygynous society, increased capacity for social reproduction) from their neighbours. I would now want to emphasise more strongly that they were expanding into the territories of societies that had already been weakened by living at the supply end of the Atlantic slave trade that had peaked in the eighteenth century, and which were further disrupted by the violence preceding and accompanying the onset of the Fulani jihad around the turn of the eighteenth century. A majority of societies practising exchange marriage were not expansive, in fact most were better described as enclaved, which showed that this marriage institution was flexible, useable under differing circumstances. The second direction of my comparison took in more hierarchical societies, lying to the southeast of the Tiv, the area whence they claimed to have originated, in which marriage lords controlled a high proportion of rights in wards in their chiefdoms. Seen from a Tiv perspective, these marriage lords had overcome the structural snares that prevented the inheritance of advantage between generations, so that (with lots of fascinating variants) they were able to transmit rights in wardships unequally to one or more of their sons; at the same time, descent mechanisms that looked like matriliny developed to make the status of ward heritable between generations for women. The existence of mixed systems, with both exchange marriage for commoners and marriage lordship for royals, suggested that there had taken place a historical transition between the two under some circumstances (and not necessarily only in the direction of increasing hierarchy). I did not explore as much as I might have done what historical conjunctures encouraged transformation, but I noted the significance of the ways in which additional females entered the marriage system, notably as slaves among the well-documented Bangwa who had been geographically positioned to take advantage in this regard of the preference for males in the trans-Atlantic slave trade. In looking for 'social evolutionary' mechanisms at the root of hierarchies and inequalities, I was influenced by the structural Marxist discussions of my years at UCL (Friedman 1979), as well as ideas about 'pluralism' and inequality that were forcefully conveyed by M.G. Smith (e.g. Smith 1974).

The investigation in Chapter 1 had started from reanalysis of a classic instance in West African ethnography, set that reanalysis within a regional comparison, and made some of the right noises about moving from comparison as methodology to a more systematic understanding of the historical interrelations within systems of kinship and servility. Producing such an historical account was, and remains, a challenge, since the transformations that the application of kinship theory to regional comparison suggests can occur are difficult to tie to datable changes in the organization of actual societies. Thirty years on, we cannot anticipate substantial enhancements to our direct ethnographic understanding of these historic circumstances. Systems of marriage by exchange have for a variety of reasons – including both official policy and, for shorthand, 'modernizing' changes that would anyway have occurred to practice – fallen into disuse, so observation of these arrangements in Cameroon and Nigeria is impossible (assuming revival is unforeseen). Among the last words about exchange marriage, from a relatively remote set of informants, Hermann Gufler has provided a rich historical reconstruction of the twentieth-century evolution from an exchange to a bridewealth system among the Yamba (Mbem in my original essay) and some Mfumte (previously referred to together as Kaka) (see, Gufler 2003 chapter 2), but this is not to foreclose the possibility of an enhanced theoretical understanding.

David Graeber drew upon the Tiv exchange marriage as an instance of his wider argument about the consequences of the articulation of debts between types of social order that pursued different material logics in relation to rights in people (Graeber 2011). The argument is well-taken, since the articulations between Atlantic and more local systems of servility in West Africa (as well as Saharan systems) have to be taken into account when analysing any particular instance. An even more striking case for his argument, noted already, would have been the accumulation of rights in women in the Bangwa kingdom as a result of the differential demand preferences for people between Atlantic circuits, which needed young men as labourers, and local calls upon the full range of capacities for social reproduction of young women. Although not specifically on the subject, the most substantial ethnographic theorization of the symbolic logic of marriage lordship is implied in Jean-Pierre Warnier's ethnography of the kingdom of Mankon which argues both for the central role of the Fon, or king, in bodily reproducing the society, and the implications of his status, and that of his nobility to a lesser degree, for the permanent subaltern status of a large category of men who could never have married because of the scale of elite polygyny (Warnier 2009, 2012). This range of examples, from the small-scale of the Yamba to the immense kingdom of Bamum, can only gain in historical interest by being envisaged as a set of transformations on themes that are widely shared: ideas that include procreation, power, and personhood.

Although its date of publication makes it appear later (because it spent some years awaiting publication in French), the second chapter here dates from around the time of revision of the first. Writing it helped me to understand better why my interest in the marriage practices of the Tiv and their neighbours had provided such a poor specific preparation for researching kinship among Chamba! The invitation to write the paper came from Elisabeth Copet-Rougier whom I had known during the time she spent at UCL collaborating with my PhD supervisor Phil Burnham. She was by then working alongside Lévi-Strauss's successor at the Collège de France, Françoise Héritier, who was exploring the wider implications of Lévi-Strauss's theories about 'semi-complex' systems of marriage (significantly, *alliance*) that she had applied in her own researches among the Samo of Burkina Faso. According to Lévi-Strauss, semi-complex marriage systems were to be distinguished from their elementary counterparts because they forbade direct reciprocity in marriage exchanges, just the presumption on which sister-exchange marriage is ideally based. Under a semi-complex system each marriage establishes prohibitions against subsequent marriages, and in some semi-complex systems, of a sort that particularly interested Héritier, the prohibitions are so numerous that, by making most partners unmarriageable, they effectively amount to a system of preferences by default. Reciprocity in marriage exchanges could occur only after the passage of several, often three, generations when the prohibitions having as it were lapsed it became possible for a partner to move in the direction opposite to that of the marriage which had set up the prohibitions. At least in ideal terms, semi-complex marriage systems, like those of the Samo, were based on inter-generational debts in a way that direct exchanges, like those of the Tiv, were not. In practice, this immediacy of reciprocity is less clear cut even in exchange marriages systems, since not all obligations could be balanced in the same generation; this, however, would be treated as an anomaly demanding ad hoc rectification rather than a normal feature.

The distinction between elementary and semi-complex marriage systems has another aspect according to Lévi-Strauss: he claimed that semi-complex marriage systems occurred in societies with a specific type of kinship terminology (1966, 1969). Known as Iroquois systems in the literature (after their North American instances), the main characteristic of these terminologies in the adjacent ascending generation is for parents to be merged terminologically with their same sex siblings (so that mother and mother's sisters are all called 'mother', and father and his brothers are both 'father'), but not so merged with their opposite-sex siblings. How these 'collateral' close, senior kin, father's sister and mother's brother, are termed varies. One pattern is for the terminological phenomenon of merging lineal kin to co-occur with skewing of collateral kin terminology: where 'skewed' means that one of the parental opposite sex siblings is terminologically demoted a generation. In an Omaha system it is the father's sister who is demoted, and in a Crow system this happens to the mother's brother. Yoking together a category of marriage practices with a formal type of kin terminology, as Lévi-Strauss does, has been unhelpful according to some recent commentators, because comparative ethnography finds each occurring without the other (Trautmann and Whiteley 2012). This is helpful corroboration of my own reservations that were based on the misfit between some of the theory's suppositions and the Chamba ethnography I had by then amassed.

In formal terms, the kinship terminologies of the Chamba and several of their neighbours in Adamawa[3] have precisely the Iroquois features just described, that is to say parents' same-sex siblings are terminologically merged with them, while their opposite-sex siblings are not. They additionally have Crow-Omaha characteristics, since the terms for parents' opposite-sex siblings are 'skewed' (in the Crow direction, in this

---

3.   Adamawa was named after its nineteenth-century founder, Lamido Modibbo Adama, whose successors created the 'lamidate' within the Sokoto Caliphate. In different spellings it became the name of a state in Nigeria and a province in Cameroon, as well as the term for a related group of languages largely spoken within them, including Chamba Leko. As we see in later essays, the association of Adamawa with Fulani conquest makes it a controversial term.

instance, by promoting patrilateral [FZ children] and demoting matrilateral [MB children] cross cousins). On the basis of kinship terminology, they ought to fit into the semi-complex type of French alliance theory. Hence, the invitation for me to contribute a regional study to the ongoing series of seminars held in Paris that were eventually collected as four volumes of papers (Héritier-Augé and Copet-Rougier 1990-94). But did the marriage practices of the Chamba and their neighbours also correspond to the semi-complex set of marriage prohibitions supposed to go along with the kinship terminology? If so, in practice were marriage alliances scattered according to the pattern that the theory predicted? These questions proved difficult for me to pose, let alone answer.

My attempts to investigate marriage patterns in the senior generations of Chamba who were not Christians or Muslims had been frustrated by the very high reported rate of divorce and the reluctance of my informants to rake over their marital histories for the benefit of an inquisitive, and relatively young, researcher. In part this was because the marriage histories I did collect were often troubled. Rather than marriage leading to 'alliance' in the English language sense, it more often seemed to lead to rancour. Moreover, when explanation was volunteered for the extension of kinship terminology used of close kin to wider classes of relations, that explanation, particularly of skewing, took its cues predominantly from clanship and not from alliance/marriage or indeed traceable descent. For instance, there are two main categories of women whom someone's father might address as 'sister': those who belong to the same generation and same patriclan as himself, and those who belong to the same generation and same matriclan. The first are called by a specialized term for father's sister (*mala*); the second are addressed as 'mother', because they belong to the father's matriclan. More broadly, a person could also address as 'mother' any other female member of their father's matriclan, including those not addressed as 'sister' by their father, a group which would include in genealogical terms father's sisters' daughters. The logic of this arrangement issues from shared clanship and informants cannot explain it by reference either to marriage or to descent traced step-by-step. Quite simply it is knowledge of clanship that cues the extension of kinship terms: if my father's matriclan is, for instance, the bushcow clan, and I meet a woman from that clan previously unknown to me, then I may address her as 'mother' because her clan bore me, and she may address me as 'child'.

So, I concluded that, at least in terms of my contemporary fieldwork experience, the Crow kinship terminology and the semi-complex set system of marriage prohibitions did not appear to cohere, and it seemed unlikely that they would produce the scattering of marriages predicted. But, and it was a big but, what if I was studying Chamba marriage at a moment when the system was in disarray, and it had been more coherent previously, particularly with regard to women's first marriages? For want of direct evidence, this is the kind of counter-factual proposition about which it is difficult to say anything much. The Crow skewing characteristic of Chamba kinship terminology was found widely among others of the societies that were, to varying degrees, absorbed into the Adamawa Emirate, and there were consistent indications that these societies may have more matrilineal in their past organization. Were these characteristics evidence for once regionally shared characteristics of kinship and marriage?

These suggestions seemed to me to take my argument as far as even a relaxed attitude towards evidence allowed. What I did not attempt then, and still find difficult now, is to suggest how these two varieties of regionally distributed kin systems relate to one another. Wendy James has concluded from her recent survey of writings on both semi-complex alliance systems and systems of sister exchange that the two are not so different at a theoretical level as alliance theory suggested (James 2012). In order to function practically, both essentially involve inter-generational debt, the absence of which was supposed to be the feature distinguishing the elementary from the semi-complex. If the debt is normal then it should not be construed theoretically as an accidental feature. This strikes me as a cogent argument that James demonstrates amply from her East African ethnography, where Omaha features of skewing can be argued to recall debts in an exchange marriage system.

A similar argument cannot, however, be made for the exchange and marriage lordship systems analysed in Chapter 1, because these did not occur, so far as I can tell, together with either Crow or Omaha skewing of their kinship terminologies. Trying to envisage transformational models of historical transition between the 'sister-exchange cum marriage lordship' practices (Chapter 1), and 'semi-complex systems of alliance with Crow skewing' (Chapter 2), would also have to involve accounting for transformations in kinship terminology. The regional comparisons presented here, although they concern societies that are at least contiguous and to a degree interpolated, only go so far as to envisage two series of mutually exclusive, transformational possibilities. My hunch is that may well also describe historical actualities. The first models a variation in organizational forms between egalitarian sister-exchange systems (of variable dynamism), mixed systems with the addition of marriage lordship for the elite, and a predominance of marriage lordship to the point of excluding sister-exchange. The other, supposedly 'semi-complex' instance, takes the variations in comparative Chamba ethnography to model a more general possibility of transformations between organizational forms based on matriclanship, double clanship, and patriclanship. There is reasonably strong evidence for Chamba that this was a historical series, though we have no evidence for it being reversible: that is of patriclan-based systems reverting to exclusive matriclanship. What we lack both theoretically and comparatively, and hence in terms of any hypothesised history, is the basis of transformation between these two sets. Presumably, an organization of the second series, having arrived at a more hierarchical organization might adopt marriage lordship, say from its neighbours. This might have been feasible, perhaps, for the elite of the emigrant Bali Chamba, though I am not aware they fully made that transition. But other transitions between types are difficult to conceive in the abstract, and if this reflects a historical reality it is because these transformations could not occur short of some kind of societal collapse. That is, these two series of conjunctures between marriage, kin terminology, descent and kin-category membership were alternatives over the longue durée, and that for any population transformation between types in the different series took place only following social collapse and re-engineering, for collectives, or transfer between systems, for individuals. This notion is made tricky to investigate – both in my two comparisons and in the various theories on offer – by the uneven attention writers typically pay to aspects of the conjunctures of features noted above.

As an instance, my comparison of so-called semi-complex systems was attentive to kinship terminology because alliance theory predicted a correspondence between a type of terminology and a type of marriage practice. By contrast, I had devoted little attention to kinship terminologies when analysing the other (sister exchange and marriage lordship) series, because no theory suggested they were crucial; a particular terminological feature caught my attention only because it underlined the importance of identifying counterparts in particular exchanges (see below). I was wrong in this neglect, because I might have noticed a consistent tenor to anthropologists' comments on kin terminologies in these kinds of societies. Here are the Bohannans on the Tiv, 'Tiv kinship terminology is simple, sparse, and, in reference to linguistic features, largely descriptive' (L&P Bohannan [1953] 1969: 58). Tiv kin terms, they go on to explain, are so imprecise that genealogically close relatives may be referred to by personal names in order to identify them, and this use of personal names extends even to parents (ibid). Tiv kinship has but three important terms: *ter*, which can be modified to indicate seniority, may be used of any male lineal ascendant, particularly but not exclusively in the agnatic line (hence F= FF= FFF = MF = FMF = MMF etc., and B = FB = FBS = FBSS = MB = MBS = MBSS); the corresponding term, with similar range, for any female lineal ascendant is *ngaw*. The third of these terms, *wan*, is used of a descendant, whether of Ego – without discrimination, an own child, or grandchild – or of anyone termed *ter*, *wan-ter*, or *ngaw*, *wan-ngaw*. Individuals who are potentially both *wan-ter* and *wan-ngo* are called *wan-gban*, which as I noted in my original analysis, is reportedly the strongest of all affective terms of kinship, and one which merges full siblings with the offspring of completed exchange marriages.

The terms 'simple' and 'sparse' appropriately describe this terminology, particularly when the discriminations made are compared to those in the elaborate kinship terminologies of the Adamawa series, which not only make the general Iroquois distinctions between lineal and collateral relations, but do so with Crow skewing. Are the Tiv exceptional in this regard, and is that perhaps related to their egalitarian ethos? I think not; here is Robert Brain describing the small set of terms used bilaterally among the Bangwa, '... Bangwa kinship terminology ... by African – even by European – standards is very sparse' (Brain 1972: 47). There is a term for child, another for sibling. The term used for father also connotes patron and marriage lord. The closest relationships are traced matrilaterally to a network of kin, while relations between patrikin are relatively weak, even children of the same father who live apart being addressed by what Brain describes as a 'general throw-away term for relative' no closer than European cousinship. 'Kinship terminology reflects the minimal feelings of brotherhood between agnatic or cognatic kin. Relationships in Bangwa are primarily ones of contract [...]' (Brain

1972: 49, 51). So it would appear that 'sparse' kinship terminology coheres with a dominance of transactional concern with 'alliance' in these systems. This impression is supported by Farnham Rehfisch reporting, or reconstructing, a Mambila kinship terminology formally similar to that of the Tiv (1972), although as David Zeitlyn's more recent study of Mambila kin terms in their practical use argues (2005), ideally we should compare not schedules of kin terms, which may have been assembled on different bases, but rather the uses of kin terms in speech. My supposition, were we able to do so, would be that the Mambila speakers recorded by Zeitlyn used specific kin terms in address and reference less frequently than did the Chamba speakers with whom I carried out research. Moreover, I would anticipate that the declining relevance of Chamba clanship (to areas like marriage and historic Chamba religion) would have had an impact on the frequency of Chamba use of kin terms for those more distant related. But this is the realm of plausible guesswork. I have spent some time revisiting these first two chapters in part because they are the oldest and hence most in need of updating, but looking back I think that it was important that my thinking about identity developed, as it were, bottom-up from reflections on kinship and the person, rather than top-down from concern with the nation state, a perspective more familiar from the literature.

The third chapter derives from a paper I wrote for a conference on comparison at the University of St Andrews, organized by Ladislav Holy who had founded anthropology as a discipline there the year before I joined in 1980. The essay was particularly important to recuperating confidence in the way I had wanted to write up my materials on Chamba history, that is to say as a rejoinder to the conundrum of the common ethnicity of people who varied widely in many respects: socially, culturally and linguistically. In theoretical terms, this chapter is about a concept doing double duty and becoming compromised in the process: the subtlety with which anthropologists of the time were looking at ethnicity was not just missing from their comparative anthropology but would present an impossibility there. Cases for comparison might be labelled ethnically, but they could be defined only by reference to whatever was being compared. Thinking through Ladislav Holy's emphasis on folk models, as applied to ethnicity, was an influence here, since with Milan Stuchlik his very recently published book made a particularly strong case for the self-defining character of human activity, arguing from that position an irreconcilability of folk and analysts' models that I found difficult to accept (Holy and Stuchlik 1983). It was unclear to me how a folk model could be formulated other than analytically: my writing about Chamba ethnicity was an abstraction from actions observed or reported, normative statements offered in particular contexts, and representations Chamba made (to pick terms that correspond to those of Holy and Stuchlik's book title). But my intention in making a written assemblage of these was to provide an account of how Chamba actors were provided by the past with the materials of self-conception; and this might be more obvious to me than it was to local actors, whatever my ignorance otherwise, because my access to historical and comparative materials was greater than theirs. From this vantage, and with no claim to originality, it seemed to me that while acting on the basis of their understandings, contemporary actors were nonetheless called forth by historical processes. The same could be said of anthropologists' understandings of what ethnicity was, or indeed on any other occasion that 'folk' conceptions were bracketed and examined from a wider perspective.

How could ethnicity be both the basis and subject of comparison? My answer was that this could happen only if the same term was conceptualized differently in the two cases. Like religion, ethnicity was one of those things analysts knew when they saw it, but had difficulty defining in abstract, general terms. By analogy with an argument made in anthropology by Rodney Needham (1975) that had recently been applied to the definition of religion by Martin Southwold (1978), I suggested that the anthropologists' concept of ethnicity was polythetic, that is to say in order for something to be an instance of ethnicity it had to share a number of characteristics on an, in principle, open-ended defining list. These would not necessarily be the same characteristics in each case; in all likelihood they would only overlap, like so many intersections of a Venn diagram. Added to this was the complication that when anthropologists wrote in terms of 'ethnicity', they were often self-consciously trying not to write in terms of, say, tribe or race. So, ethnicity was a polythetically delineated class from which subtraction took place to remove inappropriate members: a formulation that sounds obscure in principle but is straightforward in practice.

This was the first of several occasions when I returned to my theoretical and empirical understandings of Chamba ethnicity. As I remarked above, when a doctoral student, I had been advised strongly against writing a thesis which had at its centre the conundrum of a self-designated people, the Chamba, who differed widely in language, and forms of culture and society. I was advised instead to concentrate on the positive. This ran counter to my sense of the effort that Chamba agents had to invest in constructing a shared ethnic identity despite their variety; this would have proved impossible had Chamba agents not been drawing upon historical resources that made shared identity plausible to them under contemporary circumstances. An identity could be neither entirely imposed nor invented from nothing. Whereas I wrote up my thesis as a comparative account, the monographs incorporating the same materials, augmented by subsequent fieldwork, were written within the framework I set out in this essay (Fardon 1988a, 1990).

Two later essays written in the mid-1990s, after I had completed a pair of Chamba monographs, and republished here as chapters 4 and 5 here, explored ramifications of my emerging sense of this same problem. What did ethnicity as a particular experience of modernity in Africa imply for the individual? How did large ethnic narratives articulate with one another?

To respond to the first question, I leant heavily on Ian Hacking's account of human types and asked myself how far ethnic subjects were novel types of human identity to which people were encouraged to gravitate (for both positive and negative reasons). In part, I was addressing the declining importance of a sense of relational personhood, based in kinship, that had been a large part of the subject of my second Chamba monograph on religion (Fardon 1990). I was also responding to the, albeit uneven, resurgence in importance of 'traditional' chiefship which was becoming amply apparent, as was the fact that 'traditional' chiefships were typically conferred on the most 'modern' of candidates, the exemplary individuals. The second essay asked about the larger narratives of which ethnic identities were parts, and particularly what kind of constraints there were for proponents of smaller ethnic identities joining an already congested field of identities from a situation of relative powerlessness. What, in general terms, were the circumstances for people to 'construct', 'imagine' or 'narrate' their identities, as theories of the time had it? I took my cue from imaginative literature, specifically the brilliance of Italo Calvino, because the tale I wanted to tell was itself about telling stories, particularly about the collective biographical self, and so could draw upon Calvino's impish sense of the individual biographical self. One intention was to talk about ethnicities not individually but relationally, by highlighting the narrative assignations which reflected and processed the inequalities brought to any engagement. The instance of the Adamawa Emirate and the 'conquered' peoples of Adamawa, and how the consequences of that relationship persisted through the periods of the Sokoto Caliphate, European colonialism, and Cameroonian and Nigerian Independence, pointed to the inequalities, including narrative inequalities, of more and less powerful ethnicities. So, another aim of this essay was to explore aspects of inequality that I had cited but not theorized properly in the paper written a decade earlier (Chapter 3 here).

I was asked to speak to wider audiences about anthropological understandings of ethnicity on a number of occasions towards the end of the 1990s, and the version republished here as Chapter 6 was the most succinct of the summaries of my own views of anthropological theories produced then. (I say 'my own' advisedly, since not all anthropologists might have agreed with my view of their field.) Around the same time I had been thinking about counterworks between local and global, or more generally larger and smaller forces in relation to localities (Fardon 1995), and this theme provided a staging post to the concerns of final two chapters.

The two twenty-first century papers included here were written after a period working, among other projects, on region-wide transformations in the figurative sculpture and masquerade of the Chamba and some of their neighbours (Fardon and Stelzig 2005; Fardon 2007). Many of these peoples had figured in the earlier papers on kinship and marriage (Chapters 1 and 2), and these comparisons were widened further in the catalogue for a survey of the arts of the entirety of the Benue River Valley (Berns, Fardon and Kasfir 2011). My thinking about comparison had in the interim also been influenced by working with the ideas of the exiled Czech anthropologist, Franz Baermann Steiner, in whose thought relatively arcane comparative, historical ethnology and contemporary issues of ethnic identity were made to speak to one another (Adler and Fardon 1999). Reflecting on scale and movement, he had arrived at the aphorism from which Chapter 7 sets out, a neat expression of the mutual entailment between identification and transformation which I exposed diagrammatically by taking his reference to Leonardo da Vinci literally. My intention was to highlight the identity work required to appropriate exogenous inspirations. The appearance and persistence of a tiger in an African palace in the Cameroon Grassfields struck me as a site at which to think about some of the general conundrums that might be involved in this particular case. What did the tiger come to signify? As a big cat was it simply a super-leopard, or a stripy lion? Was its exotic origin acknowledged and seen as part of its appropriateness as an image of power? The Grassfields chiefdom of Bali Nyonga claimed to have originated from the north, in a movement led by displaced elements of the Chamba (the ethnic thread which had drawn me southwards). The members of what became a very mixed community adapted their palace culture to Grassfields expectations about royal display, retaining only a few attributes strongly marked as 'northern', while keenly taking up architectural, sculptural, performative and so forth conventions typical of their setting. Their kingdom also found itself increasingly receptive to imports via Europe (through the market, or as gifts from visitors), and these objects of prestige (jugs, foghorns, armour, portraits and so on) were included in treasure displays. Particularly striking was the presence of tapestries, or rugs, printed with animal images on bright red backgrounds that were prominent in the major annual ceremony of Bali Nyonga. Of three Indian animals – elephant, lion and tiger – to judge by its adoption as a royal insigne, the tiger made the greatest impression. Notwithstanding a mildly obsessive search at the time of writing this chapter, the exact origin of the imported tiger, and of the other rugs in Bali Nyonga remained unsolved. I have subsequently found another sighting to support my hunch that these rugs may have been not uncommon as trade items. This report comes from the Lere chiefdom of the Moundang, to the north of what would have been the zone of initial Chamba Leko exodus, and from people in rather similar circumstances: a sizeable chiefdom of speakers of an Adamawa Eastern language, where the example of the Fulani had also led to the development of a durbar-style ceremony, like Lela, complete with white flags (on which, see Fardon 2006). Olive Macleod passed through Lere in October 1910, roughly contemporary with the documentation of Lela in Bali in 1908, and left this description of the 'Lamido's' palace.

> The walls were hung with spears and bows, and duiker horns that acted as pegs. Two immense pillars blackened with the juice of some tree, supported a

canopy, though the only seat, a hard divan, was at the other side of the room. A European rug of garish red, stamped with a giant yellow tiger, covered it. (1912: 49)

En route to Lere, the party had been met by horsemen in an impressive example of what also appears to have been a widespread custom that mixed respectful greeting with salutary warning:

... a large body of horsemen appeared on the brow of the hill, headed by the Lamido, Chief of all the Moundang. Horses and riders were magnificently apparelled. The robes were of every hue – red, blue, purple, green, and silver threads, and, united to the sheen of horse-armour and the glint of spears, the effect was one of magnificent glittering confusion. They thundered down on us at a gallop, pulled up within a horse's length of where we stood to receive them, saluted, and wheeled round to escort us in triumph to the town – the whole party riding to the spirited strains of a drum and aligata band. (1912: 42)

Alfred Adler's fine monograph on the Moundang concentrates more attention on the older historic connotations of kingship, an office he calls by its Moundang name of *gon*; however, the accoutrements of this militarized version of kingship, including the white flags issued, in principle, to those empowered to pursue *jihad*, can be seen in his illustrations (1982, particularly Figure Va), and his dynastic history of the Moundang kingship reveals that the king met by Olive Macleod and her companions grew up amongst Fulani (1982: 73). Like the Bali Chamba chiefdoms of the Cameroon Grassfields, those of the Moundang were subject to a range of external influences from both Atlantic and the Saharan West Africa. The modest point of my chapter was to demonstrate the substantial labour involved in transforming external materials – whether Saharan or Atlantic, or indeed from West African neighbours – into local identity. Identities are, undeniably, established within fields of differences, but it is possible to emphasise this to the detriment of recognition of the work sameness: of selection, reinterpretation, performance and so forth, that goes into acting within these fields. Hence my closing reference to the need for a 'labour theory' of identity to supplement the 'exchange theory'.

The final paper collected here (Chapter 8) responds to an invitation to think about identity in the context of cosmopolitanism. To do so, I went back for a last time to think about the identity of the Chamba in the national states in which they live, Nigeria and Cameroon. European-focused debates about cosmopolitanism have a strong tendency, despite protests to the contrary, to take the national state as a norm and cosmopolitanism as a (frequently, but not invariably, positive) supplement to national culture. Starting from the premiss that African states should not be treated as anomalous on account of being multi-ethnic and populated by citizens who are multilingual (often extravagantly so), I wanted to question an implicit assumption that the importance of ethnic identity in African states is somehow inimical to cosmopolitanism. Of course it can be, and instances of ethnic intolerance and inter-ethnic violence are numerous, but this is not invariably the case, and there are occasions when it makes equal sense to see African states as cosmopolitan, and to recognize that some aspects of their functioning are typical of a cosmopolitan mode (similar to the USA perhaps or some multi-cultural compacts, like that in Britain, which involve compromises, entitlements, and considerable expense). Taking the Chamba case, which in this respect is also reminiscent of the larger-scale Yoruba, the insistence on ethnic sameness may also be an attempt to downplay the importance of religious difference, between Christians and Muslims, which are increasingly taking over national politics.

It feels appropriate to end on this affirmative note. Forty years have passed since M.G. Smith sent me to the library at UCL to decide where I wanted to carry out fieldwork. Since then Chamba history, politics, religion and art, in different parts of both Nigeria and Cameroon, have been the main preoccupation of my descriptive monographs and the grounding for many of my more exploratory anthropological essays, some of which are collected here. I cannot imagine, personally or intellectually, what life might have followed from a different choice: other problems, other places, other friends … But I am grateful for the choice I made and for all the kindness met along the path I took.

Chapter 1

Sisters, wives, wards and daughters
A transformational analysis of the political organization
of the Tiv and their neighbours

Part I The Tiv

The reanalysis of classical ethnography has become an anthropological industry. Since segmentary lineage models enshrined so many of the assumptions integral to what we have learned to call the structural-functional paradigm, they have been subjected to trial by this form of interrogation particularly often. Africanists will be aware that the statuses of Evans-Pritchard's model of Nuer social organization and of Fortes's of Tallensi remain controversial within anthropological circles long after their publication. Another of the classical analyses of a segmentary lineage organization, that made by Laura and Paul Bohannan of the Tiv, seems to have escaped the same degree of controversy.[1] The reason is

---

1. A re-analysis of Tiv data has been published by my colleague David Riches (1979). The thrust of his argument, (that the Tiv lineage system constitutes a representational model and that this model is inadequate as an explanation of social action) is one with which I am in broad agreement. Beyond this our analyses diverge (as David Riches has confirmed). Riches's analysis stresses the autonomy of the politico-territorial and lineage systems; my analysis attempts to redescribe political activity through an examination of marriage, kinship and local competition.

not without interest: the Bohannans' analyses have been ensured relative immunity from criticism by the general acceptance that their model of Tiv social organization so evidently corresponds to some of the ways in which indigenous Tiv social theorizing represents Tiv society. In other words, and quite explicitly, the Bohannans' analytic model is also a Tiv folk model.[2]

This model, shared by the Bohannans and the Tiv, leads the Bohannans to propose two very broad generalizations about Tiv political and social organization (generalizations to which, I suspect, the Tiv might themselves be party).

> The social organisation of the Tiv is simple. It is, in fact, so simple that it is difficult to understand. It utilises a single principle of organisation – the agnatic lineage structure, based on the principle of segmentary opposition. (P. Bohannan 1965: 523)
>
> In political organisation the Tiv are in no way typical of the area in which they live. (L. Bohannan 1958: 33)

The two generalizations are sides of a single coin, since it is their segmentary lineage organization, and especially the *simplicity* of that form of organization, which make the Tiv so *atypical* of the area in which they live. I am going to suggest that both generalizations are inaccurate. The inaccuracy, I shall further suggest, can be attributed to notions derived from structural-functional theory in general and the segmentary lineage model more particularly, which led the Bohannans to pre-select their data, and to attribute importance to some items of information while denying it to others. It is commonplace to note that observations, and the reports which organize them, are guided by explicit and implicit theories; of course, reanalyses claim no immunity from this condition under which we work. So, the references which I make to structural-functional theory in general are designed only to corroborate my understanding of the ways in which the Bohannans deduced their model of the Tiv. More important, this paper is addressed to some of the Bohannans' arguments which should concern historians of West Africa as well as anthropologists. I want to claim that, by

---

2. As Paul Baxter has been kind enough to point out to me, this point was remarked by Emrys Peters some years ago (1967: 279n.). The relation between folk and analytic models of segmentary lineage organization has been critically explored by Ladislav Holy (1979). Any discussion of the segmentary lineage organization as a political organization is necessarily indebted to M. G. Smith's seminal paper (Smith 1956).

ignoring historical process, the Bohannans have obscured both (1) the extent to which Tiv indigenous social theory must be understood as a result of discontinuous development, including the impact of colonialism, and (2) the extent of the similarities between the Tiv and some of their neighbours which can be accounted for, at least hypothetically, on the basis of divergent development and transformation. In short, I want to suggest that the Bohannans' analyses have removed history in any specific sense from the relations between the Tiv, their neighbours and, latterly, their colonial administrators.[3]

My reanalysis is organized in two sections which address separately those two related generalizations which the Bohannans make about Tiv social and political organization. In the first part of the essay, I try to show that Tiv social organization is neither simple nor solely based upon the lineage principle of organization (which is not, of course, to suggest that lineage values are irrelevant to Tiv social organization). To do this, I remind the reader of the general background of Tiv geography and history and briefly represent the Bohannans' segmentary lineage model of the Tiv. After showing some ways in which the Bohannans' model derives from structural-functional premises, I move on to show how much we have to complicate this model of Tiv social organization when we take account of marriage practices, the interrelation between kinship and clanship and the various institutions which I treat together under the heading witchcraft and cult organization. In the second part of the essay I suggest that, once we have formulated a more comprehensive model to describe it, Tiv political organization no longer seems atypical of the area in which it arose. Rather more controversially, I argue that Tiv social organization has much in common with such apparently disparate organizations as the formally gerontocratic villages of the Mambila, the ritualized chiefdoms of the Kona Jukun, the complex state organization of Bamum and others beside. These forms of government can be seen as transformations of a single type of organization. Fuller information should one day allow historians and anthropologists to explain why the trajectories of the different societies differed as they have. Here, I have to content myself with a few tentative suggestions and even more unanswered questions.

---

3. Although concerned with long-term processes, the Bohannans' analyses of Tiv expansion and Tiv social movements tend to reiterate the structural-functional assumptions of stasis and regularity (see Bohannan, P. 1954, 1958).

It cannot be repeated too often that reanalysis of classic ethnographic instances is both necessary and, indeed, inevitable if our knowledge is to be cumulative. Nowhere in this essay is any accusation levelled against the accuracy of the Bohannans' ethnography, on the contrary that re-analysis can be pursued so largely on the basis of their ethnography stands as the most persuasive testimony to its scope and excellence.

The background

The Tiv deserve an important position in the ethnography of West Africa on other than theoretical grounds. They were 'by far the largest pagan group in Northern Nigeria' (Bohannan, L. and P. 1953: 9); population estimates put their numbers at 600,000 in 1933, rising to 800,000 twenty years later (Bohannan, L. and P. 1953: 9). More recently a population estimate in excess of 1,500,000 has been suggested (Dorward 1974: 458). Notwithstanding this large population, and the lack of any centralized governmental institutions in the pre-colonial period, the Tiv have maintained an homogeneous culture and a strong sense of ethnic identity.

During the colonial period the singularity of Tiv social institutions posed a problem to colonial administrators, whose paradigm of indirect rule derived from their experience of implementing that policy among the Hausa emirates. Dorward has documented in detail the 'working misunderstanding' that characterized relations between the Tiv and the British and which manifested itself in periodic changes in the status of the Tiv, until they emerged as a type between 'Hamites' and 'Pagans' (Dorward 1974: 463-5; also 1969, 1971). The various attempts by the British to impose a workable system of government on the Tiv, based on their latest theory of Tiv society, demonstrate the quicksilver quality of Tiv organization and the absence of easily discernible structures of government. The development of the segmentary lineage model in the 1940s seemed to offer to the Bohannans the solution to the impenetrability of Tiv social organization, since it predicted this very absence of readily identifiable political processes.

The Tiv live in central Nigeria in the plains watered by the rivers Benue and Katsina Ala. They are primarily farmers, growing staple crops of yams, millet and sorghum, augmented by cassava in some areas (see Bohannan, L. and P. 1968). The Bohannans' fieldwork (1949-53) found about a quarter of Tivland (but not Tiv population) to the north of the

Benue. Prior to British rule, Tiv were expanding at a rate of four to five miles per generation against the Udam people to the south, where the pressure on land was high, and even faster in the north and east, where population density was low and there was little opposition to impede progress (Bohannan L. and P. 1968: 8).

Tiv legends claim that they occupied their present territories from the southeast, where they were far fewer in number and lived as hill-dwellers (Bohannan, P. and Akiga Sai 1954: 296). To the south of the Tiv are found a number of small 'semi-Bantu'-speaking tribes called Udam by the Tiv.[4] Laura Bohannan notes that the Tiv and Udam share 'linguistic and cultural traits' with the 'Cameroons Bantu' tribes and specifically mentions marriage by exchange of women amongst these similarities (Bohannan, L. 1958: 33). The dating of the Tiv expansion is not altogether clear. An attack on the Tiv by the Chamba in the early decades of the nineteenth century does not appear in the traditions of the Iharev and Masev segments of the Tiv, from which Dorward reasons that the expansion north was already underway by this time (Dorward 1971: 17-20).

Tiv relations with the people they neighboured – the Idoma, Jukun and Chamba, as well as the Udam – seem to have fluctuated between hostility and coexistence; cultural borrowings from these peoples appear to have been slight and not to have affected the core of Tiv institutions. Despite substantial demographic and ecological variations, it is possible to talk about the main themes of culture and social organization in pan-Tiv terms, as long as it is recognized that some variation on these themes occurs in different areas.

The segmentary lineage model of the Tiv

The model of organization which the Bohannans have proposed presents a pan-Tiv social structure based on the concepts of descent recognized in Tiv culture, around which much of the Tiv categorization of social space has been constructed.

All Tiv believe themselves to be descended from an eponymous ancestor located some fourteen to seventeen generations back in their genealogies. Legends of origin and the cultural and linguistic

---

4. The peoples called *Udam* by the Tiv would nowadays identify themselves as Ogojan, a label with a geographical rather than a cultural or linguistic significance (Adrian Edwards, personal communication).

homogeneity of the Tiv tend to add credence to such a view in broad terms. The majority of Tiv groups, for whatever purpose they are formed, are defined in the idiom of common descent. Three distinct forms of grouping are distinguished by their different appeals to the Tiv genealogical charter.

The first group to consider is the *nongo,* literally 'line' or 'queue', which 'may be used to enquire after or describe the component segments of any lineage'. The span of the 'line' to which *nongo* refers can be determined only contextually; the concept manifests the quality of total relativity of the classic segmentary lineage model. The *nongo* concept is crucial to the Bohannans' model; a Tiv describes the *nongo* relevant in a specific context by citing the name of a prominent man of the grouping involved. *Nongo* refers to span rather than depth, to living members of the group rather than to the ancestor who defines the segment in opposition to a similar segment consisting of the descendants of his brother. This designation lends the *nongo* referent an ambiguity with respect to the descent group-ings, defined ancestrally, and the political groupings, defined territorially. As Laura Bohannan (1958: 42) explains, this ambiguity 'gives an idiomatic appearance of unity to the lineage and politico-territorial segments' and is 'essential to the strength of Tiv political loyalties'.

The agnates significant for a particular person are called his *ityô.* The referent of *ityô,* like that of *nongo,* is defined contextually. The *ityô* differs from the *nongo* in being defined by depth rather than by span. Its usage is further restricted since

> ... *ityô* cannot be used to describe the component segments of a lineage. It is a personal and particularistic (hence exclusive) term of identification, stating some individual's place among Tiv by identifying that lineage, filiation to which gives him his political citizenship, his rights to land and residence, delimits those per-sons who may bewitch him and whom he may not marry, and appoints the place of his memory after his death. Only his being sold into slavery can sever him from that place. (Laura Bohannan, 1958: 38)

A third set of categorizations refers to the 'spatial and social arrange-ments of political segments'. Two concepts are involved: the segment, *ipaven,* and the land which it claims, *tar.* The segment, *ipaven,* is distin-guished from the local descent group, *nongo,* in two ways: it appeals to political rather than lineage values and it does not segment continuously. Below the level of the minimal *tar,* or discrete territorial unit, Tiv usually claim that the *ipaven* does not segment. The term *nongo* may be applied within the minimal *tar,* but it need not refer to a territorially discrete group, and it is unlikely to do so. The *ipaven* must always be represented territorially through its occupation of a *tar;* the relation between the minimal segment and the minimal territory is one-to-one.

Tiv settlements consist of clusters of huts, which the Tiv call *ya,* and their ethnographers term 'compounds'. The size of the compounds varies with land availability and averages seven to eight huts in the south with seventeen to eighteen inhabitants, while in the north and northwest compound size tends to be greater. A maximum compound membership of eighty persons was found in the south, whereas a maximum of 139 persons is recorded from the north (Bohannan, P. & L. 1968: 1920). Pacification has lessened the defensive value of large stockaded compounds such as the *ugar* of southeastern Tivland, where fighting continued with the Chamba and the Udam (peoples of northern Ogoja) into the late nineteenth century (Dorward 1971: 23-4, 1974: 462). The Bohannans (1968: 102-5) give a clear example of this process. Before the arrival of the British, the Iyon had constituted a *gar* (singular of *ugar*) of eight compounds in the south of Tivland bordering the Uge. Pacification allowed the stockade to be abandoned, and by 1950 the Iyon, who numbered about a thousand, had occupied an area of roughly two square miles. If a further migration had taken place the Iyon minimal *tar* probably would have split.

The genealogical charter which relates the politico-territorial units in a segmentary system is based on that relating the *ityô,* or agnatic descent groups proper. But eliciting genealogies from Tiv segment by segment (in terms of *uipaven)* and eliciting them father by father (in terms of *ityô)* may yield different posited patterns of relations. This is so because relations between *uipaven* are adapted to reflect the current territorial relations between segments and their relative strengths: 'Tiv feel that size and order of segmentation, depth and span of segments, ought to correspond and find difficulties in a genealogy which does not make them correspond' (Bohannan, L. 1952: 309).

The *nongo* referent's ambiguity is in part responsible for masking this disjunction between the two modes of genealogical reckoning. It allows contextual adjustments and compromises to be made which ensure that the substantive and ideological relations between the segments remain aligned. The three sets of categorizations thus depend to different degrees on the pure concept of descent: the *ityô* is the closest to an ideal descent group, the *nongo* additionally recognizes the factor of personal influence, and the *ipaven* takes into account occupation of an exclusive territory. The pertinence of the three sets of concepts is determined situationally and their interrelation, as Laura Bohannan has elegantly demonstrated, adapts to the prevailing power relations with an ease that depends on the three sub-systems of relations, with their different appeals to descent constructs, never becoming immutable or self-contained as systems or in their articulations one with another. Fluidity is most marked at the lower genealogical reaches; relations through women cease to be relevant at the third ascending generation where 'step-by-step agnatic genealogies' lose their pertinence (Bohannan, L. 1952: 313). This level of the genealogy is mostly concerned with 'domestic' grouping (Bohannan, L. and P. 1968: 25). The rate of adjustment of genealogies declines in the middle reaches which describe groups activated for ritual and marital purposes. The relations between territorial groupings described in the upper reaches of the genealogy are relatively static.

This sketch of Tiv segmentary lineage organization hardly does justice to the elegance of the Bohannans' argument. However, my object in this essay is not to deny altogether the pertinence of the segmentary lineage concept, but to question the position it should occupy in a sociological explanation. For the Bohannans, the segmentary lineage constitutes the key to the structural order of Tiv society. Other Tiv institutions such as peace treaties between non-equivalent genealogical segments, markets, age sets and friendships, which cross-cut the vertical political relations between descent groupings, are introduced as secondary factors in the model of Tiv political organization. They 'ameliorate the force of the lineage principle, thus, in fact, making it possible for the principle to work' (Bohannan, P. 1965: 537). This argument seems to reiterate Evans-Pritchard's famous paradox of Nuer organization in a slightly altered context.[5] How in principle are we able to make such judgements? Or, more concretely, why did Paul Bohannan decide that the lineage principle was dominant to such an extent that, even when it was not dominant, other institutions were functioning to permit it to be dominant? At first sight this might seem a paradoxical argument, and a digression will be necessary to unravel the issues involved.

---

5. That the prevalence of matrilateral kinship and matrilocal residence is permitted by the supremacy of the agnatic principle (Evans-Pritchard 1951: 28).

A theoretical digression

In retrospect we are able to discern a number of features which characterized the period of the structural-functional paradigm in anthropology. A lack of specific interest in history and a corresponding tendency to produce closed homeostatic models of artificially isolated societies constitute one set of characteristics frequently commented upon. A consequence of this general orientation was that political relations tended to be conceived as relations between territorial units with a relatively permanent existence, and that politics was equated with law and warfare prosecuted within and between these units. In her analysis of 'Political aspects of Tiv social organisation' Laura Bohannan adopts just such a definition of politics. This definition leads her to see the *utar* and *uipaven* (minimal territorial units and their associated segments) as the smallest political groups. Of groups of a lower order than the *ipaven* she writes elsewhere, 'Such segments within-the-hut are primarily of domestic rather than political significance' (Bohannan, L. 1952: 301).

This definition has some curious effects if applied to the Bohannans' own fieldwork cases. The minimal segments studied by the Bohannans ranged in membership from 169 to 1,047 inhabitants, 'although it seems likely that those over 500 would have split into two minimal *utar* if colonial political power and severe land shortage could have been overcome' (Bohannan, L. and P. 1968: 35). Below the level of the *tar,* compounds are scattered without any very precise relation to the genealogical charter and, although statistically most adult men live in the *tar* to which their *ityô* gives them access, no prescriptive rules determine exactly where and with whom they must live (Bohannan, L. and P., 1968: 36). The sub-*ipaven* level is the arena of the maximum density of multiplex relations and the focus for competition in ritual and secular terms, yet it is presented as peripheral to a model of political organization. However, once processes emanating from the sub-*ipaven* level have been allowed expression in the splitting of the *tar* (territorial unit), the relations between the two new unit entities are admissable as political relations in terms of the model. In trying to avoid foisting upon the Tiv concepts alien to their way of thought the Bohannans seem implicitly to have accepted a Tiv ideology which denies political content to relations at the sub-*ipaven* level. The Bohannans, therefore, have to formulate different models to account for relations above and below the minimal territorial unit. Implicitly, the Tiv ideology of agnatic solidarity becomes assimilated to an analytic judgement and, beyond this, to an explanatory 'principle'.

Alternatively, Laura Bohannan (1958: 65) defines political activity as the 'sphere of relevance of that aspect of social organisation which also determines territorial loyalties': but allied to her judgement that there 'is no social structuring of inter-compound relationship(s)' (Bohannan, L. 1958: 52), the cut-off point for the political is still at the *ipaven* level where residence ceases to be predictable. Not only political organization but social structure too becomes a function of relations between per-during territorial groups (compare Evans-Pritchard's similar statement about the Nuer, 1940: 262-3). If, as Laura Bohannan claims, the system functions 'through the absence of an indigenous concept of "the po-litical"' (1958: 65) the case for refusing to impose an analytic concept of 'the political' becomes a doctrinal one. But, having accepted that the genealogy is a political idiom at the super-*ipaven* level, it seems un-likely that at the sub-*ipaven* level, where it attains its greatest flexibility, it ceases to carry political import. This becomes tantamount to equating politics with the absence of choice. However, it could be argued that, even if the Tiv do not conceptualize politics in Western terms, they do have powerful idioms in which to discuss the notion of power. At the super-*ipaven* level the tribal genealogy is adjusted to reflect the prevailing power relations between groups; at the sub-*ipaven* level the interpersonal supernatural idiom of *tsav* appears to conceptualize the ambiguities of the Tiv notion of power.

In 1965 Paul Bohannan wrote that Tiv organization 'utilises a single principle of organisation – the agnatic lineage structure based on the principle of segmentary opposition' (1965: 523, quoted fully at the be-ginning of this essay). It is this view that makes Tiv social organization exceptional among the societies which are its neighbours, and renders the cohesion of such a large society lacking centralized institutions of government anomalous. However, twelve years earlier the Bohannans had written that marriage by exchange of women 'was basic to Tiv social organisation and to the interweaving of kinship and lineage values with those of magic' (Bohannan, L. and P. 1953: 70). This difference may represent some inconsistency in the Bohannans' definition of social or-ganization or a change in their view over time; whatever the case, no synthesis of kinship, lineage, marriage and magic has, to my knowledge, been attempted. The separation of the concepts of *nongo, ityô, ipaven* and *tar* in their differing relations to the concept of pure descent is a masterful piece of ethnographic description and translation, but it is not altogether clear in what sense these concepts can be said either to organize political action or to constitute a political organization. A lengthy quotation from Paul Bohannan (1954: 13) may illustrate this point:

> In all local areas of Tivland, different and varying depth and span of lineage are associated with units within which court cases must not be called, units within which fighting of any sort must not take place, within which fighting with clubs must not take place ... But these criteria do not systematically coincide with any other criteria for singling out lineages ... Tiv 'use' their lineage system to adjust these matters [e.g. theft, vengeance etc. R.F.], but in no case do these matters affect the structure of the lineage system. The lineage system is constantly expressed in terms of marriage, political action, crime and [in the old days – and still occasionally] warfare. But it is conceptually independent of any of these activities.

The Bohannans' model is asking a lot of the lineage system and, in the process, is in danger of arriving at circular arguments. Not only is the segmentary lineage system the basis of social organization and the idiom of inter-group relations, reacting flexibly to changes in the relative strengths of the groups; but, while standing apart 'conceptually' from the affairs of everyday life, it is 'used' to adjust the disturbances to which social systems are prone. At the same time it provides the framework for political action and, in Laura Bohannan's formulation, is the major aspect of social organization involved in the political process.

The paramount position accorded to the segmentary lineage by the Bohannans systematically understates the importance of other Tiv social institutions and, through failing to define the political process in terms independent of the Tiv genealogy, actually inverts the processes of political action. For present purposes, I define politics simply as competition to control or influence the outcome of events, without making any *a priori* judgement about the resources which may be employed in the process. On this basis, there is no particular reason to give analytical priority to the segmentary lineage system. M. G. Smith (1956) demonstrated that a number of conditions must be fulfilled for the segmentary lineage system of a society to be coterminous with its political system. In formal terms it is necessary for all political action to be pursued through the processes of fission and fusion of a series of unilineal descent groupings arranged according to a segmentary charter. If the segmentary lineage system does not organize all political action then there is no good reason to allot it a privileged position in analysis. Among the Tiv, and indeed among all people with segmentary lineage systems, cross-cutting institutions and nascent forms of office are found. In terms of a definition of political action independent of the genealogical charter, these pervasive institutions cannot be considered secondary.

In the following paragraphs I shall attempt to look at Tiv social organization in a way diametrically opposed to that of the Bohannans. Instead of looking at the system from the top down (in terms of descent from Tiv) as the Tiv tend to do, I shall try to locate a core of basic procedures in Tiv social organization and see whether they can be held to reproduce the macro-level features of the society. Seen thus, the problem of Tiv social organization revolves around the absence of state formation. Over a hundred years of expansion into the Benue valley, accompanied by rapid population growth, wars and proximity to trade routes (all those features which are usually held to explain the formation of the state) apparently left the Tiv an uncentralized yet strongly self-conscious ethnic category. Ethnographically this outcome is quite unusual.

Marriage by exchange

The homogeneity of Tiv culture and persistence of Tiv identity are quite remarkable features, considering their decentralization and the high degree of differentiation found among ethnic groups of 'middle belt' West Africa far smaller in size than the Tiv. The segmentary lineage model might suggest that Tiv exclusiveness is an expression of the lineage system at full strength, opposing all Tiv to all others. This is undeniably true, but it only illustrates one bit of Tiv ideology in terms of another bit. More persuasively, Tiv exclusiveness can be seen as a by-product of the practice of marriage by exchange of women. By a fiction, which we shall examine below, marriage by exchange of full sisters could be interpreted as a form of descent through both the men and women of the patrilineage. Substantively, marriage by exchange ensured that Tiv society was endogamous with respect to its own women. This fact emerges clearly from the writings of Akiga Sai, himself a Tiv, and may be corroborated from other sources.

Recounting an early movement away from the 'bush tribes' (the small tribes to the south and east of present day Tivland) prior to the eruption of the Tiv into the Benue plains, Akiga vividly describes the refusal of the Tiv to recognize reciprocity in women with non-Tiv, and the fracas that resulted.

The Tiv married women from the neighbouring Bush Tribes, and had children by them, both sons and daughters. When their sons grew to manhood and their daughters reached puberty, the Bush People cast their eyes upon them, and demanded that the Tiv should now give them their daughters to marry in return. When they refused to do this, the Bush Men were angry. 'What!' they cried. 'Why are these Tiv becoming so assertive? We used to give them our daughters to marry, thinking of our children who were yet unborn; why will they not give their daughters to our sons?' (Akiga 1939: 21)

This hostility, Akiga claims, led to the Tiv entering a symbiotic relation with some Fulani, who offered them protection from the slighted 'bush tribes'. The amicable break-up of this association is recounted in familiar terms.

But the Tiv did not like the Fulani marrying their daughters. When the elders saw that this was their intention, they were not all pleased. 'For,' they said, 'this is just the thing which we have already refused to allow, and here it is again! We do not let the Bush Tribes marry our daughters, so why should the Fulani be scheming to take them?' (Akiga 1939: 22)

A further movement by the Tiv away from the Ugbe and Iyonov elicits only the phlegmatic remark from Akiga that it was occasioned by 'trouble over the question of women' (Akiga 1939: 49). Rupert East, Akiga's translator, confirms the contemporary pertinence of Akiga's historical remarks in a footnote. He comments that it is 'almost unknown for a Tiv woman to marry outside the tribe, although men, especially in the border clans, will take non-Tiv wives' (East 1939: 21n.). Laura and Paul Bohannan record a similar phenomenon in the former Eastern Region of Nigeria, where Tiv had expanded and settled among the Ogoja tribes (known to the Tiv as *Udam*). Although Tiv men 'usually' married *Udam* women, they refused to allow their women to marry *Udam* men (Bohannan P. and L. 1968: 5).

Here we have a fairly well documented fact: Tiv women were enjoined to marry within the tribe but Tiv men married women from non-Tiv tribes when the opportunity presented itself. In short, Tiv expansion was in part fuelled by drawing in women from their neighbours, while Tiv exclusiveness was maintained by endogamous marriage for their own women. This effect at the level of the tribe depended on core procedures enjoined at the micro-level of Tiv organization. Therefore it is necessary to examine traditional Tiv marriage in some detail.

According to the Tiv, the most important form of marriage, both statistically and ideologically (as the paradigmatic form), was marriage by the exchange of women. Complex in practice, this institution ideally consisted of an immediate and exact reciprocity in which two men exchanged their sisters as wives. On the assumption that the women bore the same numbers of children in equal sex ratios, an exact reciprocity would complete the exchange within one generation. This ideal representation was used by the Tiv to explain the institution to Europeans (Bohannan, P. 1957: 72) and was implicitly applied in how they represented it to themselves. Secondary elaborations of this simple procedure may be regarded as attempts to implement the ideal in an imperfect world.

In practice, two sets of exchanges were necessary to carry out exchange marriages: one set of transactions distributed wards among the men taking part in exchange marriages; a second set of transactions was necessary to exchange wards for marriageable women (Bohannan, L. and P., 1953: 69-71). To distribute wards or *angôl* (plural of *ingôl*), Tiv formed small groups of kinsmen – 'those who eat one *ingôl*. I shall refer to these ward-sharing groupings as *ingôl* groups. Within the *ingôl* group, wards were allocated to men who became their guardians. This status carried the right to exchange the ward against the ward of a member of another group. Further complications leading to more secondary elaborations were necessitated by: incomplete transactions, the death of one or other exchanged ward, conflicting standards held by the Tiv on the distribution of wards within the *ingôl* group, inequality in the numbers of children borne by women in paired marriages, exogamic restrictions, competition between agnates to control wards, and so on.

In exchanges external to the *ingôl* group, the ideal of exact reciprocity entailed either the replacement of a wife dying prematurely or the return to the widower of his ward and the annulment of the paired marriage. The same consideration of reciprocity necessitated the transference of some of the children of the paired marriage to the *ityô* (patrilineage) of a man suffering a relative deficit in progeny, should the fertility of the wives involved in the exchange prove to be unequal. In practice these rules were not adhered to rigidly. If the death of a paired wife followed a lengthy period of marriage, or if the difference in fertility between two women proved not too great, the exchange was considered good (East 1939: 103). On the other hand, barrenness in one of the women always constituted grounds for adjustment of the exchange.

Incomplete exchanges appear to have been rife; not only did the ideal of exact reciprocity complicate the completion of single exchanges, but further elaborations to make the system workable had the effect of linking transactions and making their successful conclusions mutually dependent. The existence of debt in the system rendered exchange marriage a fertile area for dispute. Prohibitions on marriage or the existence of an outstanding debt could lead to one of the paired wards acquiring through the exchange not a husband but another guardian, who would then use her to engage in further exchanges or debt repayment. The Bohannans report the case of a woman who 'passed through five hands, and travelled a good hundred miles before reaching a man with whom and a place in which she eventually settled as a wife' (Bohannan, L. and P. 1953: 71).

The abolition of exchange marriage by the colonial administration, on the grounds that it offered scope for too many disputes, makes precise reconstruction of individual cases difficult. The Bohannans remark on the virtual impossibility of eliciting undisputed case histories at the time of their fieldwork (Bohannan L. and P. 1953: 70-1): and the high proportion of cases in Paul Bohannan's *Justice and Judgement among the Tiv* concerned with wards and marital disputes, despite (or because of?) the abolition of exchange marriage, bears witness to this fact. For the purposes of the present analysis, only two facts need to be established: the ideal simplicity of marriage by exchange and the processual elaboration and high degree of optation which necessarily accompanied its implementation.

Turning to the internal constitution of the *ingôl* group, we must broach the question of entitlement to membership. Membership of all Tiv descent groups, including the *ingôl* group, was determined by the form of the individual's parents' marriage. The logic of this system is revealed in the rules governing the affiliation of the offspring of completed exchange marriages; divergent rules stem from the failure of exchange marriage to be realized in some respect. The children of a completed exchange marriage joined the *ityô* (patrilineage) and *ingôl* group of their father. The sons sought wards within their father's *ingôl* group, the daughters became wards within that group. Incomplete or 'bad' exchanges, in which transference of offspring between the paired marriages had to take place, led to corresponding changes in entitlement to group membership. Transferred children joined the *ityô* and *ingôl* groups of their mother's marriage guardian. For the purposes of filiation this man, rather than the children's genitor, became their sociological father, pater.

Forms of marriage other than by exchange defined different, but predictable, entitlements to group membership for the children. *Kem* marriage was a traditional form operated alongside exchange marriage, although later use of the term to denote the forms of bridewealth marriage followed since the abolition of exchange marriage has led Akiga to deny its antiquity (Akiga 1939: 100; Bohannan, L. and P. 1953: 72, 1968: 232): 'The word *kem* means to give a number of small things until they grow to a big total' (Akiga, 1939: 120). *'Kem* marriage consisted in the acquisition of sexual, domestic and economic rights in a woman, but not the rights to filiate her children to the lineage of her husband' (Bohannan, L. and P. 1968: 232). Filiation of children to the husband's patrilineage could be acquired by making separate payments for each child in brass rods. But the procreative powers of a woman (a Tiv woman) could not be bought; their only equivalent was the same rights in another woman (Bohannan, L. and P. 1968: 232). By the same token a child was not affiliated to the *ityô* of his genitor; he had also to seek wards in the *ingôl* group of his mother's marriage guardian, or become a ward in that group in the case of a girl.

Filiation of children to a woman's guardian's or father's *ityô* and *ingôl* groups might also follow from other variant forms of marriage or institutionalized cohabitation. These forms seem to have been practised to greater or lesser extents in different areas within Tivland. 'Bearing children at home' described forms of marriage in which rights *in genetricem* were not ceded to a woman's husband. The objective of the woman's father or guardian was to filiate her children to his own *ityô,* since 'it is foolish for a man to die without sons when he can "beget sons through a daughter"'(Bohannan, L. and P. 1953: 74-5). Such strategic marriages appear not to have been acceptable throughout Tivland. Under 'sister' or 'companion' marriage, the partners to the affair were called sibling spouses (*wangban kwase/nomsu,* sibling wife = woman/husband); for further discussion of the term *wangban* see my section on kinship terminology. This form of marriage did not normally entail the transfer of rights *in genetricem* to the husband/lover, although the woman might be taken back to her husband's compound and, if she was potentially marriageable, a *kem,* or purchase, marriage might subsequently be arranged. In the case of a particularly fertile companion relationship, the right to filiate a single daughter might be given to her genitor by the mother's father (Akiga 1939: 129). In western and northern Tivland there occur institutions of elopement which may involve lovers belonging to the margins of single large exogamic categories. The fates of such liaisons are varied: the union may be regularized, or the lover may ritually renounce his interest in his mistress, or the relation may continue after marriage whenever the woman returns to her father's compound. The uncertain relations between some of these forms and regular unions meant that the lineage membership of children might be in dispute (Bohannan, L. and P. 1953: 75; Edwards, personal communication).

To break out of the reciprocity entailed in exchange marriage (and which is also implied in the variant non-exchange forms) Tiv could attempt to establish exclusive rights in their daughters. The most radical breach of the system of internal redistribution of wards within the *ingôl* group was achieved by the acquisition of a wife by brideprice, in cattle, cloth or brass rods, from outside the tribe (Bohannan, L. and P. 1953: 71, 1968: 235). Since Tiv recognized no reciprocal rights in women acquired outside the tribe, the female offspring of a foreign wife were the concern of her husband and his male descendants alone. A second type of marriage which avoided the external phase of reciprocity of the exchange marriage form was known as *iye:* 'a term applying to an arrangement between two lineages, generally of adjoining *utar,* to allow the mutual capture of wives (i.e. marriage by elopement) without revenge' (Bohannan, L. and P. 1953: 71). The exact status of the offspring of such a union is unclear. Some Tiv informants claimed that rights to filiate offspring were transferred by virtue of the overall reciprocity recognized between the two lineages. Others believed that a later exchange should be arranged to regularize the union (Bohannan, L. and P. 1953: 71).

How closely normative and statistical patterns of recruitment to *ingôl* groups corresponded is difficult to ascertain, as it must rely on evidence collected after the abolition of exchange marriage. By the time the Bohannans carried out their fieldwork (1949-53) *ingôl* groups were still formed to distribute wards prior to bridewealth marriage. The smallest group consisted of a single man who used his wards for his own purposes. The largest group had sixty-five adult male members and was about to split. Commonly, groups consisted of twelve to twenty-five members, although groups of forty were not unusual (Bohannan, L. and P. 1953: 73). East does not cite figures for *ingôl* group size but states that such groups would normally have a genealogical depth of three generations, consisting of the descendants of a founder and those junior siblings to whom he had given marriage wards (East 1939: 109). Adrian Edwards was told in western Tivland that rights in *angôl* were shared by the descendants of a common great-grandfather, although groups had previously been larger; in eastern Tivland (Turan segment) rights were retained under the control of full or half-brothers (Edwards nd: 14). It seems likely that the size of *ingôl* groups would have varied quite widely, reflecting such factors as the availability of non-Tiv wives and the prestige of the directors of the group.

Reports of the actual distribution of wards under the exchange marriage system are not wholly consistent. It seems to have been the case that the age of marriage was late for most men; Akiga (1939: 106, 123) states this to have been so, and Downes (1953: 16-17) wrote that 'In the old days a youth had to distinguish himself by some act of prowess in the chase or in war before he could seek a wife, in any case he did not marry at an early age.' The absence of successful delegation of authority in Tiv society adds circumstantial evidence to the suspicion that competition for the scarce resource of marriage wards must have brought to a head many of the ambiguities latent in Tiv social organization. A fictionalized example used by Akiga to illustrate the formation of an *ingôl* group deserves quoting at length.

> If a man had five sons and two daughters, the sons had the use of the *angôl* in order of seniority. The elder sons took them first, and the younger sons had to await their turn. When the elder sons begat daughters they took some and gave to their younger brothers who came next after them. But the youngest would still be left. He might be well on in years before his turn came to take an *ingôl,* and all this time he would be still a bachelor. This was the reason why men who lived in former times did not marry early. But when daughters were eventually born to the other brothers they went on giving them to him, one after another, so that in the end he had a host of *angôl.* From this the saying has arisen, 'The youngest gets the most *angôl'.* When the youngest son had obtained wives by exchange, and they had borne children, he took one of his daughters and gave her to his brother who had previously given him the *ingôl,* because she was of the same stem as his mother, and his brother exchanged her for a wife. (Akiga, 1939: 106)

Some of the Tiv ideas about the way in which kinship relations should impinge upon the organization of the *ingôl* group are illustrated in this passage. It is the duty of a father to provide a first wife for his son but, should the father fail in this respect, Akiga visualizes the duty devolving upon a man's other siblings. Initially access to wards is determined by the seniority of the siblings, but over time it is possible, and apparently common, for a younger sibling to acquire more wives than his older brothers. Significantly the system is represented to suffer from a shortage of women. The age of marriage for men is represented to be late, and polygyny is highly valued. The extreme rarity of pawning girls in the past may be attributed to the 'demand for exchange women' (Bohannan, P. 1965: 527). Two conclusions follow from these considerations. Within the ward group, paternal and fraternal obligations must necessarily compete. Failure to fulfil these obligations, and to meet individual aspirations, must lead to attempts to acquire wards and wives outside the *ingôl* group. I shall look at the second point first.

Akiga justifies the donation of a marriage ward by a younger sibling to his older brother by the fact that this ward belongs to the same 'stem' as his mother. This would imply that a quasi-descent line is recognized consisting of those women acquired by the group by exchanging their sisters and the daughters of these women. This is a concept which we shall find more widely recognized among some of the neighbours of the Tiv with similar marriage systems. The corollary of the existence of a quasi-descent line of women substituted for the sisters of the group is that women acquired without the mediation of one of the group's wards are not the concern of the group and are not subject to redistribution within the *ingôl* group (Bohannan, L. and P. 1968: 235). The possession of such a wife is indicative of man's 'ability and success financially', and he may be constrained to share her daughters only if his agnates force him to do so through threats of witchcraft (Bohannan, L. and P. 1968: 235). The acquisition of non-Tiv wives is enjoined by individual prestige-seeking, and this prestige-seeking consists, in part, of an attempt to convert wealth into wives and, in part, of an attempt to convert secular success into publicly recognized supernatural prowess.

Although at the super-*ipaven* level Tiv genealogies must depend on the regular association of the principles of descent and the equivalence of same sex siblings, at the sub-*ipaven* level paternal and fraternal obligations must tend to compete if wards are not numerous. The *ingôl* group, ideally the means for an equitable distribution of wards, must become the locus of competition between close agnates, since the twin obligations to sons and brothers produce a situation in which the number of wards men desire, and to whom some are entitled, must exceed the number of wards available to all but the most fortunate groups. Only 30 per cent of marriages were polygynous by the time of the Bohannans' fieldwork (Bohannan, P. 1965: 527), but some men were able to acquire large numbers of wives. Laura Bohannan (1960) writes of a man who had fifteen wives, and Paul Bohannan of another who was able to assert his will to acquire an eighteenth wife, despite his son remaining wife-less (Bohannan, P. 1957: 169-72). Within the agnatic group, we may ask which of the two relations (paternal or fraternal) would normally be preserved at the expense of the other. Adrian Edwards has given explicit attention to this problem and sums up his findings in the phrase, 'Kindly fathers, ungrateful sons, hard brothers' (Edwards 1983: 464). More expansively he states, 'When talking about the father-child link, Tiv emphasise a father's indulgence and kindness, and the frequent ingratitude of children … Between brothers, however, conflict and mistrust are explicitly recognized. "A man does not fear his father, he fears his elder brother"' (Edwards nd: 17).

This complex of attitudes within the agnatic group is intimately linked to the Tiv concept of *tsav*, very roughly 'sorcery', the practice of which is believed common between brothers but rare between fathers and sons. We shall look at Tiv supernatural beliefs in a moment, but first I shall examine the wider mesh of kinship and clanship in which the individual is involved and the relation of this web of kinship to Tiv marriage practices.

Kinship and clanship

In addition to incorporation in his father's *ityó* (at least if he was the child of a completed exchange marriage), a Tiv man was also related through various matrilateral ties to five other patrilineages, creating a complex scheme of 'individuation' within the lineage (to borrow Fortes's phrase). In order of importance these patrilineages were: the mother's *ityó* (her son's *igba)*, the father's mother's *ityó*, the father's father's mother's *ityó*, the mother's mother's *ityó*, and the *ityó* of the mother's secondary marriage guardian (Bohannan, L. 1958: 38). (The secondary marriage guardian was the man to whom a woman's guardian handed over responsibility for her welfare on her removal to her husband's compound.) A man's *ityó* affiliation depends, as we have shown, on the form of marriage contracted by his parents. Even if a man was the child of a full exchange marriage, he could still belong to his mother's father's *ityó* if adjustment of the offspring of the paired marriages had taken place. According to the Bohannans, 83 per cent of the adult members of the *ityó* live in the territory associated with that segment (Bohannan, L. and P. 1953: 21; Bohannan, L. 1958: 40). However, this figure masks a variety of forms of attachment and options about residence. A man's *ityó* need not be that of his genitor, while at least four types of attachment of 'lineages within the hut' (below the level of the minimal political segment, *ipaven)* have been recognized:

> (1) attachment which results when the descendants of an unmarried woman stay in the house of her father and become numerous, thus making an attached segment-within-the-hut; such people have no 'agnatic lineage' (*ityó*) except that to which their segment-within-the-hut is attached ... (2) Attachment which results when the descendants of a married woman come to live in the home of her father and become permanent residents; these people have 'agnatic lineages' ... other than those to which their segment-within-the-hut is attached, but these are only nominal ... (3) Attachment which results when strangers or affines live permanently among a lineage ... a fourth principle [is that] ... the attached segment-within-the-hut may be the descendants of a woman whose relation to the agnatic lineage was that of marriage ward to guardian rather than a biological kinship link. (Bohannan, P. 1954: 11)

Members of such attached lineages-within-the-hut would presumably be counted as agnatic co-residents in the Bohannans' figure of 83 per cent patrilocality, and from the Tiv actors' point of view as well (since the *ityó* to which they were attached acted as their lineage in politico-jural affairs).

The situation of an individual attached to a lineage other than by patrifiliation to the *ityó* of his genitor following completed exchange marriage differs from that of a member of an attached lineage-within-the-hut. The various types of linkage represented institutionalized means for the differentiation of individual life chances. A man's formal rights to citizenship issued from his affiliation to a patrilineage, but securing these rights in practice demanded the support of other lineages to which he traced attachment. The most important of these ties to lineages other than his own were traced to the mother's patrilineage, *igba,* and the father's mother's patrilineage, *igba ter.* The task of these groups, especially the first, was to assist the individual to withstand the supernatural attacks which his attempts to achieve prestige among his patrikinsmen might provoke.

Since three relationships were essential to the maximization of life chances, it is apparent that in Tiv society, although it has been dubbed egalitarian, men were not really born equal. At one extreme was the status of domestic slave, acquired following either the sale of the individual as an undesirable by his agnatic kin, or the capture of prisoners in war against a foreign tribe. Such individuals had no *ityô*, and inability to take part in exchange marriage made the status heritable through both parents (Bohannan, L. and P. 1953: 45-6). Slightly better placed were those people who were affiliated to an *ityô* but lacked the support of an *igba* or *igba ter* to make good their claims within that group. Such a status might result from failure of the marriages of both the father and paternal grandfather to conform to the ideal of completed exchange marriage. Logically, the next improvement in status fell to those individuals whose father's marriage did not for some reason give them the support of an *igba*, but whose grandfather's marriage compensated for this disability by defining a relation to an *igba ter* (FM's *ityô*). The *igba ter* would be able to fulfil some of the functions which ideally should be discharged by the *igba*. The status of a man who lacked support of an *igba* has been summarized by Paul Bohannan (1954: 12): 'Such a man can never obtain full legitimate control of five or six most important magical forces *(akombo a tamen).* In Tiv parlance, he remains a "youngster" *(wanye).'*

Continuation of the logical progression of statuses brings us to the status of a man who, while having recourse to an *igba* by virtue of his father's marriage, lacks an *igba ter*, because of the circumstances of the union between his grandfather and paternal grandmother. Quoting Paul Bohannan again (1954: 12), 'This is of less importance [than lacking an *igba* R.F.], but it is still said to be sufficient to keep him from obtaining control of such magical apparatus as *swem, swende, biamegh* and others of utmost political importance. The fact can in some cases be used by his adversaries to check his ever becoming a man of influence and power.'

The most favoured status in the system accrues to those men whose *ityô* membership is secured through exchange marriage and who also have *igba* and *igba ter* to come to their aid, by virtue of the form of marriage contracted by their father and paternal grandfather. But even this status is not homogeneous. In order to benefit fully from the support of the *igba*, territorial proximity and size are vital. For this reason Tiv prefer to contract marriages with members of socially distant lineages so as to maximize the genealogical opposition between *ityô* and *igba*. Even within the status of children of exchange marriage, it seems, a further category distinction was made. Downes claims that the *ihambe*, an *akombo* or cult to ensure the fertility of women, was set up for the wife by full sister exchange of the head of the compound (Downes 1971: 82; see also Akiga 1939: 117). Further, according to the same source, the *biamegh*, a major cult, could be erected only by the son of a true sister-exchange marriage (Downes 1971: 61). Whether or not the status of child of a sister-exchange marriage was particularly differentiated, it is clear that Tiv society traditionally recognized a fluid system of rank and that this system depended on the conjuncture of the twin considerations of marriage and descent, in which the former was determinant.

The Tiv rank system was fluid because, by and large, diffuse prestige could not be turned into control of a corporate office nor transmitted intact to a man's descendants. Disabilities of birth, apart from slavery, could be eradicated in three generations, depending on the forms of marriage which were followed. Thus, members of an attached lineage-within-the-hut suffered no jural disabilities through not being attached to the main agnatic stem through agnatic linkage. Attachment of a lineage could not be said to take place until the third generation but 'In the third generation, it doesn't matter so much which particular lineage acts as agnatic lineage for a man, so long as it can be clearly distinguished from his mother's agnatic lineage *(igba)* and his father's mother's agnatic lineage *(igba ter)* (Bohannan, P. 1954: 12).

Attachment of a lineage-within-the-hut can take place in the same length of time that it takes to wipe out individual jural disability. After three generations rights to wards and to enter cults become equivalent to those of men attached to the agnatic stem patrilineally; jural disability is therefore transient. The same point may be made about success. The successful man is likely to acquire more wives than average from outside the exchange marriage system. But in this process the jural status of his children by these wives is downgraded through their lack of extra-patrilineage support. Tiv egalitarianism is therefore a function of a competitive process, and a number of institutions serve to undermine both unusual success and disability. Part of this process must be explored through the Tiv understanding of power and the supernatural.

Witchcraft and cults
Adrian Edwards has identified two unusual features of Tiv cosmology: the absence of an ancestor cult and the centrality of witch beliefs (Edwards 1984). The central concept in the complex of Tiv

witch beliefs is that of *tsav*. *Tsav* cannot easily be translated, but the Bohannans claim it has four referents in Western thought '(1) witch-craft substance, (2) power, (3) talent, (4) ability' (Bohannan, L. and P. 1953: 84). As a substance *tsav* may be detected as a growth around the heart, the shape of which reveals whether the owner used *tsav* for or against the common good during his life. In its other aspects, short of administration of the sasswood ordeal, *tsav* is detected in the living by accepted rules of inference. Possession of developed *tsav* is an attribute of powerful and successful men, as well as those of advanced age. *Tsav* is necessarily demonstrated by success, since it is believed prerequisite to success. The power of *tsav* may be increased by the consumption of human flesh, which the *mbatsav* (night society of men of *tsav*) can obtain only through bewitching and killing their own agnates, a category which seems practically to be restricted to the members of their own compound (for instance, in the cases reported by Bowen/Bohannan, L. 1955, 1960). In the final analysis all death is attributable to the action of *tsav* in some form or other, and it is this rider which gives *tsav* a morally ambiguous character. For, while *tsav* in the wrong hands is dangerous to the social good, the ability which *tsav* gives men to achieve mastery of the most important cults or fetishes (*akombo*, sing. *ikombo*) and to direct the affairs of their local group makes this facet of personality vital to the well-being of the community. By relegating their creator God, *Aôndo*, to a role in which, although he may be supplicated to bring rain, little interest in human affairs is imputed to him, and by insisting that the dead have power after death only through curses uttered during their lifetimes, Tiv have insisted on a world open solely to human control through the supernatural qualities of the living. It is in this circumstance that witchcraft beliefs become the central tenet of Tiv cosmology and the patrilineage the domain of supernatural competition conceptualized in terms of *tsav*.[6] If the genealogy is the dominant political ideology at the super-*ipaven* level, at the micro-level of organization *tsav* dominates.

---

6. Adrian Edwards has emphasised the amorality of core Tiv beliefs and the disintegrative effects of ritual. Tiv elders are also witches. *Akombo* medicines controlled by elders operate as masks for witchcraft. Even *swem*, the oath pot replenished with ashes from a mountain in Cameroon, is operated by wizards and controls witchcraft only through the binding force of oaths made upon it. The optimism of Tiv culture is redeemed by an 'outer circle' of beliefs in sprites and shape-changers (Edwards 1983).

Whether or not the society of *mbatsav* had any real existence is difficult to say; early writers such as Abraham (1933) seem to imply that it did exist as a night society practising witchcraft; the Bohannans stress the identification of the *mbatsav* with the community's elders rather than with a secret society. In their role as elders the *mbatsav* are responsible for the mastery and control of the cults of the community, *akombo*. *Akombo* are a type of fetish: constructions of pots, plants, figurines, ashes and stones variously combined, for the erection of which Tiv pay men who have achieved mastery of the particular cult. Innumerable *akombo* are set up and propitiated for all manner of reasons, at birth and during pregnancy, for hunting, for good crops, to deter thieves, to avert illness and so on. Each *akombo* is set up for a specific reason, has its own manner of propitiation and set of proscriptions on conduct. For example, the *akombo-ikungu* is propitiated for fertility; infraction of its rules is manifested in epilepsy, which necessitates 'mending' the *akombo*. But without the cooperation of the *mbatsav* (either through their bewitching an individual or removing witchcraft protection from him) *akombo* cannot be responsible for death.

Mastery of *akombo* sets an individual on the way to becoming a *shagba*, or man of prestige. The culmination of this process involved the mastery of the great *akombo* of communal importance, which could not be erected without the mystical sacrifice of human life. Such *akombo* included the *ndyer* or tree drum, the *imborivungu* and *biamegh* propitiated for fertility, the *po'or* bin, which was propitiated for success in hunting, and a number of others. The details of these cults do not really concern us here; it is probable that they were not identically defined in every area of Tivland. The principle that life had to be sacrificed for the erection of the great *akombo*, which were, however, essential to well-being, and that life could be taken only within the agnatic group, ensured ambiguity in Tiv morality. In practice this meant that to live in the compound of a powerful man could be both dangerous and beneficial, depending on the use to which he put his powers (*tsav*). As the Bohannans note (1953: 91), 'There is thus a practical necessity for the leadership which is ideally absent.'

The role of the *igba* (mother's patrician) can now be stated more clearly. The obligations of the *igba* to the individual are not those of duty – '*ityô* do things for a man because they must, *igba* because they will and like' (Bohannan, L. and P. 1953: 24). The *igba* provide a man with material support in food and livestock, they may come to help him set up particular *akombo*, and they will challenge a man's agnates if they believe them to be bewitching him. In return, a man will not fight his *igba* in time of war but attempt to arrange peace as a messenger and go-between, and if life is intolerable among his agnates he will seek refuge among his *igba*, where he will be welcomed. In marked contrast to the *ityô*, which is a domain of intrigue, supernatural competition and rivalry even between brothers and especially over the control of wards, the *igba* is a domain of mutual aid and empathetic relations. Yet the vast majority of men choose to live among their agnates and to expose themselves to the dangers which lie there. It is in this sense that Tiv society is egalitarian, for although there are hereditary differences in life chances in the *ityô*, and although a man will eventually die as a result of the *tsav* of his agnates, only by remaining within his *ityô* can a Tiv attain equality with his fellows. The price of safety in the *igba* is adopting the rights of a woman (in line with the matrilateral link which relates a man to his *igba*) and abdicating the struggle to attain and maintain equality.

Kinship terminology

The opposition of relations traced through men and through women can be demonstrated by an examination of Tiv kinship terminology. Tiv terms of consanguinity are bilateral and separate lineal and collateral relatives. Assuming Ego to be the child of a full sister-exchange marriage, the terminology maps a series of categories of kin defined in terms of common descent.

Ego's great-grandparents, grandparents and parents are merged as either *ter*, male lineal ascendant, or *ngo*, female lineal ascendant. Collateral relatives may be referred to as descendants of the lineal relatives: *wanter* and *wanngo*, child of a male or female ascendant. A third bilateral zone of consanguineal relations demarcates that category of relatives with whom Ego is able to trace a blood relation through more than one link. Full siblings are the paradigmatic example of such a relation, as also are the children of paired full sister exchange marriages (since in this case MBch=FZch). The term applied to this category of relations is *wangban*. The fourth zone of relations is that of Ego's descendants, called *wan*, child. The four zones thus have primary referents of ascendants, descendants of ascendants, double consanguineals and descendants. These terms are subject to extension and modification; *ter*, father, can be modified according to seniority relative to Ego's father, and *ngo,* mother, can be extended to include a 'woman socially associated with any female ascendant', such as a woman involved in the same marriage cycle or having the same marriage guardian as a female ascendant' (Bohannan, L. and P. 1953: 59).[7]

The second operative contrast in the terminology is between relationship traced through a female link and that traced through solely male links. 'Two men whose only kinship link is through a common father's father's father will say neutrally, "We have one father"; to indicate close and friendly association, they say, "We have one mother," pointing out, if questioned, that one woman bore their common ancestor' (Bohannan, L. and P. 1953: 58). The term *wanter,* 'child of a male ascendant' is used within the *ityô,* patrilineage, as a term of reference. But this term is considered 'rude' used of anyone with whom a common paternal great-grandfather is shared and is not normally used within the minimal exogamic lineage, since it emphasises the purely jural aspect of agnatic relationship (Bohannan, L. and P. 1953: 59). The greatest contrast to this term is found in the term for double consanguineal. Whereas modifiers may be used with most kinship terms to indicate sex or relative seniority, employing a sexual modifier with *wangban* alters its meaning to 'lover', for *wangban* is 'the strongest affective term of collateral kinship' (Bohannan, L. and P. 1953: 60).

There is, therefore, a gradation of emotional load which may be imparted to kinship relations and a degree of choice in the type of sentiment which may be invoked in any particular relation. This gradation runs from double consanguineal, to 'one womb', 'one mother', 'one father' and so on, with 'descendant of male ascendant' standing at the other end of the spectrum. The jural relations at the male end of the continuum express the rights and obligations located within the domain of competition, with its attendant supernatural dangers, rank system and struggle to achieve equality. The relations at the female end of the continuum express mutual rights and obligations as well, but these are located in the domain of empathy and are assessed on an affective basis rather than through the cold calculations of reciprocity and duty. Since equality cannot be achieved in the female domain, such considerations are not relevant there.

---

7. Supporting our earlier contention of the calculation of female 'stems' by the Tiv.

Conclusion

At the beginning of this essay I noted the prominence which the Bohannans gave to the Tiv segmentary lineage in their analysis of political organization and criticised this emphasis on a number of grounds. Models based on the 'principle' of patrilineality both tend to circularity and systematically understate the importance of other institutions by defining politics in terms of descent groups and everything other than descent groups as deviations from the model. The segmentary lineage model also made Tiv political organization a local anomaly, totally unlike that of their neighbours. In the next part I shall address this second point. First, I must sum up the argument so far. In the absence of vertical flows in the Tiv segmentary lineage system of either a material or metaphysical kind, the system had constantly to be regenerated from the sub-*ipaven* level, a process which the Tiv systematically obfuscate by conceptualizing their social system in terms of descent from Tiv himself. The generation of a form of endogamy assures exclusiveness at the level of the tribe, while equality is maintained through a fluid system of social inequality, which is normally inheritable for a maximum of three generations. By allotting to a rival patrilineal category the role of *igba,* the extent of hierarchization within the *ityó* is severely circumscribed and inequality is made a transient phenomenon while the major struggle is to maintain equality. The simplest way in which the system could be centralized would be through monopolization of rights in women, as happened in some systems akin to that of the Tiv. Indeed, we may suppose that at the borders of expansion against foreign tribes, the taking of female prisoners or purchase of foreign wives temporarily may have permitted such a process. But institutions at the micro-level systematically turned over such advantages through a definition of quintessential Tiv-ness based on marriage by exchange, which was the sole means to acquire, for the child of the marriage, the support necessary for full participation in the supernatural side of prestige-seeking.

The appearance of *tsav* at the sub-*ipaven* level expresses the failure of authority to be delegated and the failure of social life to conform to the ideals of the genealogical charter relating larger units. As Adrian Edwards has written, 'The association of authority with witchcraft reflects not any ruthless effectiveness on the part of the elders but rather the refusal of Tiv society to grant a charter of legitimacy even to such limited structures of power as it possessed' (Edwards, 1983: 371). The basic procedure, that men should exchange their sisters as wives, leading over time to the formation of deep lineages descended from the founder and (through her exchange partner) his sister, proves impossible to carry out in practice. Secondary elaborations are required. Groups are formed to organize the distribution of 'sisters'. Degrees of approximation to full exchange are recognized, depending on the closeness of the relationship between the ward given and the mother of the donor, which result in quasi-descent lines associating women of the same 'stem'. Alternative forms of marriage describe a system of fluid social inequalities for their offspring. Unequal sex ratios in the *ingôl* group necessitate complex debt structures within the group, while ambiguity in the definition of rights to wards within the group overturns the ideal unity of the male sibling group. Institutions of best-friendship and age sets are resorted to for help. Wider ramifications lead to markets becoming focal points both for the settlement of disputes and for the ambitions of big men; treaties guarantee peace between non-equivalent genealogical segments, and so on. Surmounting these transactions is a genealogically defined ideology of tribal separateness, which defines the differentiation of the larger-order lineage groups 'as if' relations through women were not important and implicitly converts the marriages of all ancestors into the full-exchange type. The ideals of Tiv social organization are made normative by transforming the actions of the ancestors. The only form of immortality to which a Tiv can aspire is to take his place among the structurally significant ancestors, and this ambition can be achieved only through engaging in the struggle for equality within the patrilineage.

Part II The transformations

In the first part of this article I set myself two objectives, each of which took its cue from a generalization made about the political and social organization of the Tiv by their principal ethnographers, Laura and Paul Bohannan. I proposed to challenge the related views (1) that the political organization of the Tiv could adequately be described as a segmentary lineage organization and (2) that their organization was atypical of the area of middle-belt West Africa in which the Tiv live. Confining my attention to Tiv ethnography, I argued in Part I that a persuasive case could be made for a more complex account of Tiv political processes which recognized the salience not only of descent but also of marriage, kinship and local competition for the achievement of personal prestige through manipulation of marriage strategies, mastery of the major *akombo* or cults and claims to the possession of legitimate *tsav* or supernatural power. Tiv society still retains remarkable features on this view of its political processes, but they are not those of complete atypicality. Instead, it becomes apparent that, while sharing many of its core institutions with neighbouring societies, Tiv culture combines them in a unique manner. The uniqueness of the combination becomes visible through the effects of Tiv social organization, the more important of which I would itemize as:

1. The persistence of Tiv culture and identity in a region of generally fragmented populations.
2. The capacity for expansion of Tiv society.
3. The capacity of Tiv society to absorb so many circumstances conducive to the development of hierarchy yet to remain, by and large, acephelous.

Point 1 must be related not only to the segmentary lineage ideology which relates all Tiv to Tiv himself by descent, but also to the fiction by which all ancestors' marriages are implicitly converted to the full exchange type so that descent is claimed through male agnatic ascendants and also through their sisters who acted as the exchange partners for these ancestors' wives. This consideration is practically reinforced by the virtual endogamy of Tiv society with respect to its own women. The competitive processes which emanate from attempts to control the direction of female wardships may also account for some of the Tiv's extraordinary rate of expansion, since alternative forms of marriage encouraged importation of foreign wives by Tiv men. The absence of hierarchy in Tiv society was shown to result from routine consequences of the kinds of competition in which Tiv men engaged. Competition for the control of wards engendered sibling rivalry, which I have suggested is the mainspring of Tiv dynamism. Personal success tended to be transient in the senses that (1) it was tied to the rather unstable conception of *tsav*, a power of moral ambiguity verifiable only on the evidence of current attainments, and (2) Tiv society has slight mechanisms for the hereditary transmission of advantage and probably tends regularly to undermine achieved inequalities. Successful men would acquire wives outside the exchange marriage system, and the children of those wives would be disadvantaged in political competition, since they were not equipped with the full complement of descent statuses necessary for competition on the most advantaged terms. These disadvantages were just as transitory as the advantages which might accrue to Tiv individuals; all (except slave status) could be extinguished within three generations, given a series of favourable marriages.

In this second part of my argument I shall try to add weight to the Tiv evidence by demonstrating the different political organizations which may result when minor modifications of rulings or mutual arrangement are wrought among the core institutions of Tiv society. In other words, I shall be looking at examples of societies which are superficially different from the Tiv but share similar institutional forms and, thus, may be seen as transformations of the institutional matrix identified among the Tiv. I shall concentrate particularly upon the distribution of the institution of exchange marriage and kindred forms of this institution. This strategy is adopted on methodological grounds, since these highly defined forms are relatively easy to isolate as distinct traits. First, I shall document the wide distribution of exchange marriage systems, before their colonial suppression, in middle-belt Nigeria and Cameroon. One case, that of the Mambila, will be examined in some detail, to demonstrate a different and less dynamic form of organization based upon what are essentially Tiv-type core institutions. My other instances will demonstrate various ways in which hierarchy may be introduced into a Tiv-type matrix of institutions. Most basically, this transformation involves redefinition of the rules governing (1) access to and control of sisters and wives, wards and daughters, (2) redefinition of the descent relations between parents and children and (3) reconceptualization of the *tsav*-like powers of those who hold authority in the society. In all cases of hierarchization the character of the rank system evolved appears to have depended upon the way in which access to supplies of female slaves was controlled and exploited. More specifically, the extent to which hierarchy could be sustained depended directly upon the assertion of hereditary rights of wardship in the female children of the wards at the disposal of marriage lords. This assertion is, of course, a direct and specific inversion of the ideal of the full exchange of sisters through which men renounce rights in the children of their sisters in favour of rights in the children of their wives. Transformations of exchange marriage systems into marriage lordship systems rest upon the denial of full reciprocity between the male parties to the transaction. Transformation from marriage lordship to exchange marriage would entail the reassertion of full reciprocity between the parties to a marriage. Although my description of these transformations is formal rather than empirical, I suggest that such developments are likely to have occurred historically; and this supposition is reinforced by ethnographic instances of mixed systems in which exchange marriage and marriage lordship are preferred forms of marriage for different classes in the same society (see the Kona and Wiya below).

Exchange marriage systems

Before its suppression by both British and French colonial governments, marriage by exchange was widely practised in present-day Nigeria and Cameroon. C. K. Meek's article, written in 1936, remains the only extensive survey of exchange marriage systems. Basing his statements on data gathered in the 1921 Decennial Census, Meek was able to list twenty-one societies in Nigeria which had practised, or were practising, marriage by exchange. Numerous other groups are said to have practised the institution before 1921 but are not included in the list, while other groups of the then Mandated Territories (now included in the independent republics of Nigeria and Cameroon) were excluded from the census for administrative reasons (e.g. Mambila, Batu or 'Tigong', Kentu). If all these groups are taken into consideration, Meek is able to adduce about thirty societies (here depending on the definition of units) of 'middle-belt' Nigeria which had practised marriage by exchange.

The peoples practising exchange marriage can very roughly be separated into two groups. The first group, to the north of the Benue, consisted of a number of small societies existing on the margins of the large states of Kano and Bauchi. They included the Butawa, Kudawa, Jere, Buji (Sangawa), Rebinawa (Ribina), Anaguta, Seyawa and Gurkawa (Meek 1936: 65, 1925,1: 204, located from the map in Meek 1925, II; see also Gunn 1954: 27, 29, 32-3). Gunn records the results of a colonial investigation of exchange marriage among the Jerawa group at Ribina in 1927 but, apart from this, few data appear to be recorded from these groups. Gunn's account of the Jerawa is sufficient to show the similarity of their form of exchange marriage to that institution

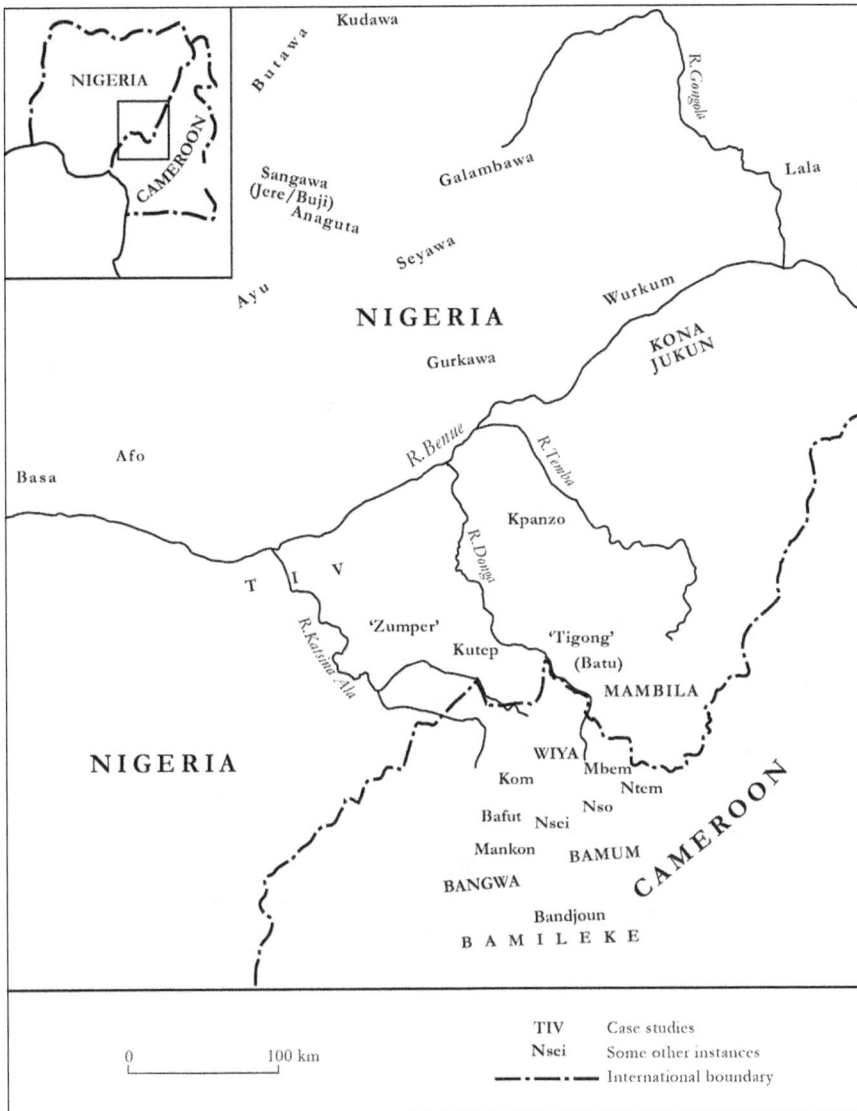

Figure 1.1. Distribution of exchange marriage and marriage lordship systems: eastern central Nigeria and west Cameroon

among the Tiv. Wards might be exchanged against other wards, who were not necessarily married off but might be involved in a series of exchanges before they reached their husbands. Sisters' daughters might be accepted as deferred exchanges if no direct exchange had taken place at the time of the marriage. Among both the Jerawa and Buji, wives were bought from neighbouring peoples (the Angas and

Birom respectively) to augment the supply of women within the tribe. This northern group of exchange marriage systems will not concern us further in this article,[8] but does demonstrate the wide provenance of an essentially similar institution.

The outriders of the southern group of exchange marriage systems are the Basa and Afo, around the Niger-Benue confluence, and the Wurkum, to the east of these peoples. (Meek 1925: 204, lists the Idoma as well as the Afo, but Idoma does not occur in the 1936 listing, and Armstrong 1955, does not mention the existence of exchange marriage among the Idoma.) Tiv traditions point to an area to their southeast as the lands from which they began their migration into the Benue plains (Bohannan, L. and P. 1953: 12; Akiga 1954: 296). The small tribes to the southeast of the Tiv are described by them as the 'bush tribes'; they share various cultural traits with the Tiv, including, in some cases, marriage by exchange. Among these groups we may number: the Mambila of Adamawa, for whom we have comparatively full descriptions (Meek 1931; Rehfisch, especially 1972), the Batu and Abo groups of 'Tigong' (Meek 1931: 204, 1936: 65), the Kentu, Kutep and Kpanzo (Meek 1936: 65; Garbosa 1960: 93), and the Mbem, Munkap, Mashi, Memfu and Ndabile (Chilver and Kaberry 1968: 29, 31; Kaehler-Meyer 1953: 109), small groups of the northwestern Bamenda Grassfields. Finally, we may note that the Banen (excluding the 'Nyokon' section) south of the Bamileke and Bamum peoples of Cameroon also practised marriage by exchange (Dugast 1953: 148). In the present limited state of our knowledge concerning most of these peoples it is impossible to interpret the gross distribution of this trait.[9] However, it is clear that if Tiv traditions of migration from the southeast are accepted, then they would once have formed part of this band of peoples practising marriage by exchange.

In addition to these peoples among whom marriage by exchange was the preferred form for the entire population, we may also identify at

---

8. Barrie Sharpe has pointed out to me that marriage lordship does not occur among this 'northern group', where transformation to 'secondary marriage' systems may have taken place. For a recent analysis of secondary marriage systems see Muller (1982).

9. I cannot, in the confines of the article, consider West African peoples (such as Senufo and Mossi), who live away from the immediate vicinity of the Tiv. Even farther afield, for a well-documented example of exchange marriage from the Sudanese/Ethiopian border area, see Wendy James (1975, 1979).

least two peoples among whom marriage by exchange was the preferred form for commoners but not for chiefs. In both these cases the chiefs practised a form of marriage lordship and refused to recognize reciprocal rights in women with their subjects. This organization was found among the Wiya, a Grassfield group whose chiefs claim Tikar origin (Jeffreys 1962), and the Kona Jukun, who lived to the east of the Tiv and west of the Shebshi Mountains (Meek 1931, 1936: 65-9).

In the last category of peoples we shall be considering, marriage by exchange is relegated to an internal aspect of transactions carried out between marriage lords. In these societies, rights in wards have become more or less heritable and are the vehicle through which enduring differences of status are transmitted. Although I shall draw particular distinctions between them, the Bangwa (and western Bamileke, of which they are a section; Brain 1972), the eastern Bamileke (Hurault 1962) and the Bamum (Tardits 1970, 1973, 1980), and others of the Grassfield Cameroon chiefdoms, belong to this general category.[10]

To illustrate the series of transformations in core procedures among the peoples enumerated above, I shall briefly describe the institution of exchange marriage among the Mambila, then discuss the mixed systems of the Kona Jukun and Wiya and, finally, relate these two types to the most centralized marriage lordship systems.

The Mambila

The Mambila live to the southeast of the Tiv on that part of the Adamawa Highlands named, after them, the Mambila Plateau. Fortunately, their social organization is relatively well documented (see Rehfisch 1960, 1962, 1969, 1972; Meek 1936).

Mambila live in villages, internally divided into hamlets and compound clusters. The population of a village is between 200 and 2,000 people, while a hamlet consists of a number of compound clusters each made up of from two to six compounds. Hamlets are associated with one or more corporate cognatic descent groups called *man*; the same term is used to refer to bilateral kin networks. The *man* is named

---

10. Claude Tardits lists eight Cameroon societies, other than Bamum, in which the chief exercised the right to reclaim as wards the daughters of women he had given in marriage (Ntem, Wiya, Nso, Nsei, Bafut, Mankon, Bawok, Kom; Tardits 1980: 660 n.; see the map to this article for distribution). Within the limited ambitions of this essay, Bamum and Wiya have to serve as examples of such chiefly perquisites.

after its founder, who is located between two and five generations before the oldest living group member, and has an average of seventy members. There is an agnatic bias, in a statistical sense, to the *man*, but no status discrimination attaches to those members who use female links to demonstrate their descent from the group founder. In practice, not all members of the *man* can demonstrate a pedigree all the way to the founder, but co-residence and an assumption of descent are sufficient to claim membership.

Another descent group, *memin*, regulates access to marriage wards. Rules of recruitment to the *memin* operate in the same way as the rules regulating recruitment to the Tiv *ingôl* group. The offspring of a stable exchange marriage or a slave marriage belong to the *memin* of their father; the offspring of a bridewealth marriage belong to the *memin* of their mother's father. The *memin* has ten to fifteen members and is named after its oldest male member and leader. The constitution of the group depends on the types of marriage followed by its earlier members. Since exchange marriage was the favoured form, and the majority of stable marriages tended to be of this type, the *memin*, like the *man*, must have had an agnatic bias. The *memin* is not a segment of the *man*, since not all *memin* members necessarily take up residence in the same *man*.

Exogamic prohibitions led to a scattering of marriages, which were mostly contracted outside the village. Locality was a prime organizational principle and, traditionally, no leadership was recognized other than that of the oldest member of the hamlet. Among the Mambila, witchcraft is operative between fellow villagers and can be used or transmitted within a bilateral range of kin (Meek 1931,1: 550). Rehfisch has described competitive gift exchange from the Mambila. Partners, who may not be kinsmen or members of the same hamlet, hold feasts to which they invite their 'guest' and his co-residents to consume beer, food and, especially, meat. Exact tallies of donations are kept and should be reciprocated when the host becomes guest in his turn. The feasts are said to have the twin functions of supporting the Mambila status system and enhancing the solidarity of the village (Rehfisch 1962: 101-2).

The Mambila, in common with the Tiv and the other societies which we know to have practised exchange marriage, recognized a set of rules of exchange which allowed affiliation of children of completed exchange, or slave marriages, to the descent group of their father. In all the examples which have come to my notice, alternative forms of marriage, not entailing the transference of the right to filiate children, were also recognized. Such data as exist also suggest that all the exchange marriage systems were 'ward hungry' and tended to attract women from neighbouring societies with whom reciprocity was not recognized.[11] The structuring of access to wards imparts a patrilineal and patrilocal bias to most of the societies which practised exchange marriage. Cumulative patrifiliation was generated to the extent that marriage by exchange was the norm. Although there seems no logical impediment to it, there appears to be no instance of exchange marriage in which rights were normally vested in maternal uncles, which would have led to matrifiliation and, probably, matrilocality.

If we compare the Mambila and Tiv a nuber of differences emerge. The core procedures are quite similarly defined, but the Mambila lack the segmentary ideology which surmounts the micro-level processes of Tiv social life. The thoroughgoing gerontocracy of the Mambila seems to have lessened the tensions in the co-resident group and limited competition between co-residents. The *memin*, or ward sharing group, is similarly constituted to the Tiv *ingôl* group, but the co-residential *man* has a cognatic charter for membership. This would seem to imply that rights to wards could be pursued without co-residence, which, again, would seem not to be the case among the Tiv, where the co-resident agnatic group is the arena of competition. In this context it is interesting to note that Mambila beliefs claim witchcraft to operate within the co-resident group rather than among co-resident agnates. The greater dynamism of the Tiv system seems to be due, in part at least, to the friction between agnates generated by preferred patrilocality, which led to the splitting of the territorial group and the regular expansion of the Tiv people into space, as Paul Bohannan (1954) has excellently demonstrated.

Intermediary systems: Kona and Wiya

Two peoples occupy a position in this analysis between exchange marriage and fully fledged marriage lordship. Data on neither the Wiya nor the Kona are very full, so I shall be brief.

The Kona Jukun were the only group of Jukun traditionally to practise marriage by exchange, and when Meek recorded the custom among them it was restricted to a small group living between Kona and Yola.

---

11. This may help to explain the fragmentation of the societies neighbouring the Tiv.

As among the Tiv and Mambila, the normal form of marriage was by the exchange of women. In this way full rights were acquired in the offspring of the marriages. An alternative form of marriage was recognized in which only a small brideprice was exchanged against the wife. No rights in children were acquired by the husband, who bought only the wife's domestic services, although he might be allowed by her parents to filiate one son to his own descent group. Under normal circumstances the parents of a girl did not allow her to become a full exchange wife until she had borne a daughter under the small brideprice regime to act as her replacement in her father's ward group (Meek 1936: 66). Members of the royal clan married off all their daughters under the small brideprice regime and thus retained the right to filiate all their children. This custom implied a denial of reciprocity with the commoners of the chiefdom, who could never acquire rights in the children of the royal clanswomen. How the royal clansmen acquired their wives is, unfortunately, not clear. Possibly exchange marriage was practised between sections of the royal clan, or perhaps high brideprice was paid for women to marry the royal clansmen. If the royal clansmen married by payment of small brideprice (for they appear to have had no wards with which to engage in exchange marriage with commoners) this would have led to the interesting position in which the royal clan was recruited entirely through the retention of rights in its out-marrying daughters. If, on the other hand, the royal clan was able to recruit through both its men and women, then it would have steadily gained in strength at the expense of the commoners. Unfortunately Meek's notes are not sufficiently full to pursue these speculations.

The Wiya, in the northeast of the Bamenda Grassfields, have a fairly typical Grassfields organization, with a chief, palace officials and retainers, and a number of secret societies. Like the Kona, the Wiya recognized distinct types of marriage for different classes of the members of the chiefdom. However, only the chief, rather than the entire royal clan, renounced exchange marriage. The peculiar form of marriage practised by the chief has been documented by M. D. W. Jeffreys (1962: 99-100):

> After the coronation the question of providing the chief with new wives arises. The *tala sigogot* [council – R.F.] will notify the people that the chief is searching for new wives. The chief will send through the country his heralds to select a number of immature maidens in the various villages. These heralds travel with powdered camwood made into a red paste. Whenever a herald sees a beautiful

maiden he will rub the doorposts of her home with the camwood paste. This sign indicates that here lives a girl worthy to be the wife of a chief. Such maidens are known as *kinto*.

The chief does not pay dowry for these wards, nor do all the palace maidens become the wives of the chief. A number are given to village heads or court officials or are bestowed upon the boys who do palace service at the time of their departure from the palace. At least the last category send the first daughter of their marriage to be a palace ward.

It was possible to marry a chief's daughter by presenting him with two female slaves. Any children she bore belonged to you and not to the chief. It was not possible to marry a chief's daughter on the exchange system which governed the rest of the tribal marriages in the old days. The reason that one could not marry a chief's daughter on the exchange system was because, to be able to do so, would imply that you were of the same rank as the chief.

Usually, the chief's daughters did not marry. They chose paramours and any children born belonged to the chief.

These quotations are part of a description given to Jeffreys by a Wiya informant. A number of points emerge clearly.

The strategy followed by the chief of the Wiya represents a systematic attempt to cultivate wardships by abstaining from exchange marriage, and this strategy is made possible, as Jeffreys's informant says, by the recognition of a difference of rank between the chief and the commoners which attaches also to the daughters and wards of the chief. Thus it is impossible to marry a chief's daughter on the exchange marriage system and her equivalent is two female slaves. Normally no exchange is accepted for a chief's daughter and, as we have seen from examining exchange marriage, in such systems refusal to accept direct reciprocity implies retention of rights to filiate children. The direct recruitment of palace wards by the chief, without payment of compensation to their fathers, is a feature we have not met in these marriage systems before now. The chief's ability to recruit in this manner represents a further breach of the rules of reciprocity governing marriage: not only does he retain rights *in genetricem* in his own daughters, but he also appropriates the daughters of his commoners. The increment in wardships allows the chief to use the donation of wives as a technique of political control, by redistributing them to sub-chiefs and headmen, and to palace servants.

The normal form of marriage for commoners among the Wiya was marriage by exchange. Various expedients were recognized to facilitate the operation of the system. A slave might be given in exchange for a wife by a man with no sister to exchange; later, a daughter of the marriage would be given to the wife's father to make good the exchange. Marriage without exchange might be practised by commoners. In this case the husband was allowed to retain a single son of the marriage but all other children were filiated to the wife's father or guardian (Jeffreys 1962: 211). Both these elaborations, we may recall, are also features of non-hierarchical exchange systems.

It is possible only to speculate about the development of the Wiya marriage system. However, the following facts seem to be pertinent. Wiya traditions (Jeffreys 1962: 174) maintain that chiefship was established among them by immigrants of Tikar origin from the west. From our earlier survey of the distribution of exchange marriage we know that the peoples to the north of the Wiya for the most part lacked centralized governmental institutions and practised marriage by exchange. The Tikar, on the other hand, have centralized chiefships but do not practise exchange marriage. The inference – and it is no more than that – would be that Wiya organization represents an amalgamation of the two existing organizations in the context of an indigenous acceptance of immigrant chiefship. This acceptance may in turn have rested on the military superiority of the immigrants or their ritual supremacy, based on the ownership of a chiefship with ritualized functions, or both.

Marriage lordship: Bamileke, Bangwa, Bamum

The Bamileke and Bamum peoples to the south of the Wiya possessed systems of marriage lordship in which few rights in women were ever transacted directly (i.e. by exchange marriage) and a large proportion of rights in wards were controlled by chiefs. In terms of the argument I have been proposing, these peoples represent the most centralized forms of the series of interrelated marriage systems we have been examining.

Bamileke chiefdoms, of which there are over a hundred, are widely distributed within the Cameroon Grassfields. Hurault (1962) has described the organization of the chiefdoms of Bandjoun and Batie. Another group of nine Bamileke chiefdoms on the western edge of the Grassfields bordering the Mamfe forests has been described by Robert Brain (1972). Since no attempt at exhaustive coverage is made in this article, I shall limit attention to these two groups of Bamileke and for convenience refer to the chiefdoms documented by Hurault as the Bamileke and the group described by Brain as the Bangwa.[12] There are a number of differences in the organization of these two groups.

Bamileke chiefdoms vary in size from a few hundred inhabitants to several thousand. The polities are multiply centralized. The chief controls a number of secret societies, stands at the head of a hierarchy of offices occupied by servants and sub-chiefs and also directs the marriages of a large proportion of the women within the chiefdom. Small patrigroups are formed around the inheritance of offices, skulls, property and rights in marriage wards. Hurault (1962: 30-2) insists that these groups are not genuine patrilineages. Except in the case of the inheriting son, relationship to a patriline is not traced after two generations. Inheritance practices lead to the formation of new patrigroups within two generations, when the skull of a non-inheriting son allows the group to establish an independent skull line. Skulls are also inherited in the matriline. But in the case of the matrilineage there is no membership cut-off after two generations. Entitlement to membership tends to tail off when one or two male links attach a person to the stem of the matriline.

The difference between matrilineages and patrigroups is intimately connected to the forms of marriage recognized by Bamileke. The form of a person's parents' marriage affects his entitlements within his patrigroup but not within his matrilineage.[13] Two forms of marriage were traditionally recognized: *tangkap* and bridewealth marriage. *Tangkap* marriage ceded rights *in uxorem* but not rights *in genetricem* to a girl's husband. Bridewealth marriage ceded both the wife's domestic and sexual services and the right to filiate the children of the marriage. Thus the membership of the patrigroup was determined by two factors: the tie to the skull line, which continued for two generations, and the form of the marriage contracted by a person's parents. The daughters of *tangkap* marriage became the wards of their mother's marriage lord. Rights to wards, titles and lands were inherited impartibly by testament. Thus each patrigroup

---

12. More accurately, Hurault's Bamileke are representative of the eastern Bamileke and Brain's Bangwa of the western Bamileke.

13. Among the Tiv, we noted the existence of a notional quasi-descent line associating the children of an exchange partner in terms of descent from the ward exchanged for their mother. Where perpetual rights in wards are recognized there is a practical necessity for a more clearly formed notion of matrilineal descent to keep track of these rights.

represented a petty centralization. The head of the group controlled the patrigroup's material resources, including women, and access to the group's skull cult. Non-inheriting sons moved out of the hamlet occupied by the inheritor to found their own hamlets on land granted by the ward chief on behalf of the paramount chief.

Before the suppression of the institution by the colonial government, as many as 80 per cent of Bamileke women were married under the *tangkap* system. Between a tenth and a seventh of the marriage wards were under the direct control of the chief, who was able to use this pool of marriageable women to cement his relations with the various classes of his chiefdom (Hurault 1962: 40). Wards might be given to his servants, or to his sons, or to the commoners of the chiefdom. In whichever case, the wards would be married under the *tangkap* system, and their daughters, or at least some of them, would revert as wards either to the chief or to his successor.

There are a number of differences between the *tangkap* institution found among the Bamileke and that found under the same name among the Bangwa to their west. Like the Bamileke or Wiya, the Bangwa have chiefs whose power depends in large measure on their control of marriage wards. But, unlike any of the peoples we have discussed so far, the Bangwa recognized partible rights in wards. Four marriage lords have rights in Bangwa women (Brain 1972: 124). The most important of the marriage lords is the *tangkap*, the direct agnatic descendant of the original donor of the *ma'ngo*, or matrilineal ancestress of the ward. Every *ma'ngo* is said to have been a slave bought by her original *tangkap*, who then gave her in marriage. The rights of the original *tangkap* are inherited by his patrilineal descendants in perpetuity, and the status of ward is transmitted matrilineally from the *ma'ngo* to her descendants. Three other marriage lords have non-perpetual rights of wardship. These are the *mbe nkembetü*, the MMF, in his status as donor of the individual's grandmother, the *mbe tetse*, MF and donor of the mother, and the *mbe nzo*, the father of the ward. These non-perpetual rights in wards lapse entirely after three generations; the amount of bridewealth received decreases with each succeeding generation.

The Bangwa system of marriage lordship uses a different method to achieve the same purpose as the Bamileke system: the retention of wardship rights by the community chiefs. The Bamileke marriage lords are forced to give their wards in marriage without accepting bridewealth, so as to replenish their pool of wards (by maintaining rights in female offspring of the marriage); the Bangwa *tangkap* are able to accept bride-wealth, since their rights in the descendants of their wards are perpetual. Bangwa ideology permits this transformation by the insistence that all the ancestresses of the wards were slaves.

In common with the Bamileke, the Bangwa recognize inheritance through testament. Siblings with small shares in the patrimony move out after their father's death to seek their own fortunes, relinquishing any further claim on the patrigroup property. On the death of these displaced siblings their children gain independent access to the patriline ancestors through their father's skull, and the splitting is complete. The kinship relation between paternal siblings who disperse is relegated to *betat*, 'a general throwaway term for relative' (Brain 1972: 49). As their ethnographer observes, 'Such a system is not one of corporate segment-ing lineages; it resembles more a multitude of little "dynasties" of vary-ing depth and relatively constant span' (Brain 1972: 94).

The choice of inheritor by testament has the effect of riddling the patrigroup with tensions. As Brain has noted, the patrigroup of the Bangwa is smaller and less corporate than the same group among the Bamileke (Brain 1972: 93). Patrikin tend to disperse as a result of con-flict and witchcraft accusations. Despite the variety of ties which relate the chief to the sub-chiefs of his chiefdom, 'The chief, with the con-sent of his motley collection of subchiefs, transformed a complex ge-nealogy into one magnificent agnatic family tree for political purposes' (Brain 1972: 94).

The empathetic links of a man with his matrilateral kin are also more diffuse than among the Bamileke. The term *atsen'ndia* denotes, in addi-tion to the mother's matriline, a matrilateral network, involving at most one male link. As among the Tiv, witchcraft is an idiom of power, but its use is largely appropriated by the chief and his night society. Not only the paramount chief but all titled men have witchcraft in order to rule. Like Tiv *tsav*, Bangwa witchcraft is ambiguous: all death is attributable to witchcraft but witchcraft also protects the country (Brain 1972: 20).

The peculiar features of the Bangwa marriage system, and western Bamileke systems in general, seem to result from economic factors. Living on the western edge of the Grassfields, the Bangwa were impor-tant middlemen in the slave trade. Women bought from the east were kept within Bangwa country; men were usually sold along a chain of middlemen to the west. The women retained in the community by chiefs and traders were used as gifts to chiefs, payment for society fees and death dues. When these female slaves were given in marriage, rights in their children were retained and continued to be the property of the descendants of their original owners (Brain 1972: 98). The difference between the *tangkap*/ward systems of the eastern and western Bamileke would therefore appear to rest on the slave origin of many of the Bangwa marriage wards.

A final variant of marriage lordship illustrates a different alignment of the principles we have been examining. The Bamum (Tardits 1970, 1973, 1980) occupy part of the western Grassfields. As among the Bamileke, rights in women were largely controlled by the *mfon* (chief) of Bamum. At the turn of the century Foumban (the Bamum capital) had a population of about 20,000, grouped in 500-600 *nzu*, nucleated groups of descendants of a founder in the male line plus their wives, unmarried daughters and the descendants of their slaves. The Bamum State was a larger organization than those we have been considering so far. Certain of the *nzu* were under the direct control of the *mfon*, and the heads of such lineages, *nzi* (apart from those *nzi* descended from the companions of the first *mfon*), were attached to the *mfon* by ties of 'quasi-filiation'. New *nzu* were founded in each reign by the sons and daughters of the *mfon*, as well as by his brothers and sisters if they were not already set up. All lineages were founded by a royal grant of land, slaves and women. Further lineages were led by the companions of the first chief who had accompanied him at the time of the foundation of the chiefdom in the late seventeenth century, by twins who were sent to the capital to undertake palace service, and by captives who had been of service to the chief, fugitives and slaves. If status was initially determined by birth, service to the *mfon* could lead to a person being granted created noble status. Such created nobility were attached to the chief by an ideology of agnatic relation (as among the Bangwa).

The formation of collateral lineages, normally attached to that of the *mfon*, led to a gradual territorial expansion of the chiefdom as the lineages founded in each reign displaced those of the former reign from the centre (Tardits 1970). The problem of rival agnates at the centre of power was solved in Foumban in a more thoroughgoing way than among the Bamileke, by the systematic formation of new lineages and the recruitment of non-royals as servants. At every level of the society redistribution of marriage wards took place. The chief received women in respect of earlier gifts by himself or his predecessors and in token of fealty from subject princes. In sum, he controlled the disposition of several thousand women. The majority of the women were given to the created nobility, who had come to constitute about half the population. Further redistributions were made by the *nzi* to the members of their lineage groups and from the family heads to their sons and servants. Marriage did not generally carry the right to disposition of female children and, as the major polygynist and marriage lord, the *mfon* retained control of a large proportion of marriageable women.[14] In the past this supply was periodically augmented by the chief's right to distribute women captured in war. As Tardits (1973) has shown, the chief was permanently a net creditor in women with respect to his subjects.

Conclusions

At the outset of the second half of this article, I claimed that Tiv organization was not exceptional but represented one possibility which can develop from a core of basic procedures. The crux of this argument depends on the acceptance of an alternative model of the Tiv, which both relativizes the importance of the segmentary lineage and redefines its role within a model of political organization. Marriage by exchange was shown to be a determinant of descent, and access to wards one of the foci of competition between agnates at the *sub-ipaven* level. Witchcraft and descent are both political ideologies among the Tiv but operate at different levels of organization. A contrast between relationship through men and women defines opposed domains of competition and non-competitive solidarity.

Societies practising exchange marriage were shown to be widely distributed, but exchange marriage alone was apparently incompatible with a centralized form of government. The Mambila social organization, like that of the Tiv, rests on a conjuncture of descent constructs and exchange marriage. But, unlike the Tiv, the Mambila live in cognatically organized local groups which are directed by their elders. Competition and witchcraft accusations appear to have been less

---

14. The scale of royal polygyny, the origins of royal wives and the destinies of royal wards are admirably detailed in Claude Tardits's recent study (1980, especially chapters 14-16).

prevalent than among the Tiv, but it may be an indicator of intra-village tension that witchcraft is supposed to be operative in the local community regardless of kinship status, rather than only between co-resident agnates as in the Tiv case.

The Wiya and Kona represent types of intermediary systems in which exchange marriage remains the normal form of marriage for commoners but nobles or royals do not enter into direct reciprocity with their subjects.

In the thoroughgoing systems of marriage lordship (Bangwa, Bamileke and Bamum) we see various conjunctures of descent constructs and marriage forms. The patriline remains the domain of competition, and various strategies are devised to move non-inheriting agnates away from the agnatic group. Manipulation of rights in wards becomes a buttress of hierarchy in these systems, and the marriage lords themselves become the objects of ambiguous witchcraft beliefs analogous to the Tiv *tsav*. Relationship through women is still conceptually opposed to the overtly political relations of the male domain, but this domain is differently defined in the three cases. With the advent of perpetual rights of wardship in women, there emerges the practical necessity for a way of keeping track of them. In the Bamileke case the tracing of perpetual, impartible rights in women can be satisfied by a relatively simple matrilineal descent construct. Bangwa recognition of partible rights in wards necessitates tracing a network of matrilateral relatedness.[15] In both cases, patrilineal descent is truncated by the removal of competing agnates. The descendants of siblings other than the main inheritor of the patrimony tend to establish independent patrilines with their own skull lines. The Bamum state utilizes organizational resources similar to those available to the Bamileke and Bangwa but on a far larger scale. The capacity of the chief to direct the circulation of wards and manipulate fictive agnatic relationship is correspondingly enhanced.

If we now return to our starting point, it is possible to ask what further light can be shed upon the particularities of Tiv organization. Evolution in the direction of marriage lordship would probably have been the line of least resistance to Tiv centralization in the pre-colonial period. But we have seen that a complex of counteracting mechanisms to this tendency existed in Tiv society. Most of these mechanisms can be related to the

---

15. In neither case am I suggesting that matrilineal descent constructs can be *reduced* to these practical functions. I am suggesting that, whatever their other effects, they must minimally discharge these exigencies.

failure of Tiv society to by-pass low-level agnatic competition. However, the very failure to control low-level competition or crystallize transient inequalities through the assertion of perpetual rights in wards imparted a dynamism to Tiv social organization that cannot but have contributed to the success of the Tiv eruption on to the Benue plains in the two centuries before the imposition of colonial rule. The Cameroonian chiefdoms developed institutions to remove non-inheriting agnates; the Mambila embraced cognatic recruitment to their villages; but the Tiv lived out the more difficult option of a culture that enjoined both agnatic competition and agnatic co-residence.

Finally, it may be well to question the extent to which the transformational analysis proposed here represents a privileged cross-section of an historical process. As things stand, this is not a question which can be answered; we simply do not have sufficient information at our disposal. But now that the worst excesses of conjectural history have been purged from reconstructions of African history, it seems worthwhile to join other recent commentators in proposing that transformational analyses, and the hypotheses which can be developed from them, are one species of grist that anthropologists can submit to the historians' mill.

ACKNOWLEDGEMENTS

This article has come out of the drawer on numerous occasions and accumulated enormous intellectual debts in the process. An early version was presented to a departmental seminar at University College London in February 1975 at a time when I was the grateful recipient of a Social Science Research Council studentship. I benefited from the comments of those present and from later critical readings by Professors Mary Douglas and M. G. Smith and Drs Rosemary Harris, Phyllis Kaberry and Murray Last. Especial debts are owed to Drs Adrian Edwards and D. C. Dorward for allowing me access to [then] unpublished papers on the Tiv, and to Mrs E. M. Chilver for help with Cameroonian materials. Adrian Edwards has discussed my reading of the Tiv data and unselfishly allowed me to draw on his very substantial first-hand acquaintance with Tiv culture. Recently, Drs Phil Burnham, Ladislav Holy and Paul Baxter have been kind enough to encourage me to clarify the argument of the article. In the midst of so much help the remaining errors represent my contribution.

Chapter 2

ALLIANCE AND ETHNICITY
Aspects of an Adamawan regional system

What can we most usefully understand by alliance? The word in English has a number of senses which overlap with, rather than correspond to, what my dictionary suggests to be its range of uses in French.[1] Alliance can mean marriage, but it can also refer to relationships of mutual support and, in French, the term may refer to those relationships which are created by marriage (a usage which would have to be signalled in English by a phrase such as 'dynastic alliance', which introduces connotations of nobility and high politics). There is a tendency in French, not so marked in English, to elide definitionally the other senses of the term alliance with marriage. Affines in English may become 'allies' in French. There is no English term to cover marriage, the categories of relative constituted by the union, and the relationship created between them. Calling marriage alliance in English centres our attention on the relationship created between the two parties. Even between two languages as closely related historically as French and English, and even when our concern

---

1. '*Alliance: mariage; parenté qui en résulte. Anneau de mariage. Ligue, coalition, confédérations entre Etats ou souverains. Fig: union, mélange de plusieurs choses.*' (*Larousse*). Compare the *Shorter Oxford English Dictionary*: ' the state of union or combination ... union by marriage ... combination for a common object ... community in nature of qualities ... people united by kinship or friendship, in which the priority between senses is reversed.' The importance of literal and figurative senses is almost reversed between French and English.

is with identical words, it seems necessary to begin a discussion by clarifying the connotations of our terms. The literal translation of, what I shall refer to as, marriage amongst the Chamba is 'taking a woman' or 'taking a husband', a phrase which has no necessary connotations of alliance in the Chamba languages and dialects. I am going to argue that for certain communities of Chamba, during a period of at least a hundred years, marriage and alliance were not only terminologically distinct but were even inimical to one another. If by alliance we are going to mean the whole range of French senses implied in the formulations of alliance theory, it seems especially important to pause in order to consider the local significance given to whatever local term or phrase we are translating as marriage and to place that notion amongst other means of defining or creating interrelationships in the societies we describe. This is no more than a particular instance of the more general necessity to take account of the local sense of our theoretical notions, what I take Françoise Héritier to refer to when she writes, of the differential valuation of sexes embodied in kinship terminologies, that to 'read' a marriage system we must know the ideas that went into the making of it.[2] Philip Burnham, in a discussion of Gbaya marriage, also presented to this seminar, applies the point to the local definition of the units between which marriage exchanges are made.[3] As anthropologists we have constantly to temper our desire to generalize with recognition of the specificity of the senses of local terms which we necessarily translate by a single term of our own. This is simply one of a number of tensions to which we hope to supply temporary and enlightening resolution.

A number of the contributors to the analysis of alliance systems have drawn information from West African societies, but the analyses I have been able to read have concerned what have been called Omaha systems of terminology and alliance (those in which matrilateral cross cousins are promoted a generation). My case studies will concern the formal opposite of this: marked Crow terminologies with skewing on both patrilateral and matrilateral sides, and in which marriage prohibitions are sometimes, but by no means always, formulated in terms of

---

2. The quotation apropos marriage systems reads '*Si le critère de la valence différentielle des sexes est bien un paramètre de la parenté, ses effets doivent apparaître dans la terminologie elle-même (…) s'il fut utilisé pour sa construction, il devient indispensable pour sa lecture*' (Héritier 1981: 53).
3. I take this opportunity to thank him for a copy of this paper prior to its publication (Burnham 1990).

matriclanship. In broad terms, the 'Crow' features, with which I shall be concerned, are sandwiched between peoples with 'Omaha' features to the north and south.[4] The institutions are of regional rather than tribal or ethnic distribution and, although I am not aware of a comprehensible way of writing about peoples that allows us entirely to eschew ethnic terms, one of my aims in this paper is to examine the changing relationship between ethnic terms and the distribution of marriage institutions. In the second part of the argument, I shall provide clear historical evidence for relatively recent changes in the systems of kinship terminology and marriage prohibitions amongst peoples of this 'Crow' belt. In common with many recent writers, I shall emphasise that regional rather than ethnic perspectives define appropriate fields within which we can begin to study the development of political and economic processes.

This regionalist critique of writing in 'tribal' terms has been resurrected several times in African studies. It has both positive and negative arguments attached to it, and it cuts both ways: we need both to look to larger units than those defined according to an ethnic criterion, and also to smaller units to the extent that contemporary ethnic units are culturally diverse. On the constructive side, I could mention the recent work of Jean-Pierre Warnier (1985) focusing especially on economic relationships in an area of the Bamenda Grassfields, or Richard Werbner's continuing researches on regional systems of cults in central Africa (1977 and subsequently). Or, we could approach the issue through the critiques that have been made of the uncritical use of African tribal terms in general, some of which have been based upon materials directly drawn from the area that concerns me.[5] The new ideals of competence we can draw from these lessons advise us to adopt regional perspectives, but there are undeniable practical problems involved: analysis is frequently curtailed by the lack of the information that would allow us to push further. However, the limitations of perspective which accrue

---

4. 'Omaha' systems are reported for regions to the north of the Chamba (Moundang, Adler 1982: Part 3, Chapter 1) as well as to the south (Burnham 1980: 90-2; 1990; Copet-Rougier 1980, 1985).

5. I have attempted a summary of the issues elsewhere (Fardon 1987a Chapter 3 in this volume). A. Southall (1970) is a seminal paper in any discussion of African ethnicity. Numerous writers on areas near to the Chamba have emphasised the ethnic heterogeneity of communities and urged clan by clan historical analyses. It has also become commonplace to note the malleability of ethnic distinctions (see Tardits 1981; Adler 1982).

from ignoring regional context outweigh these drawbacks, and even deficiency has the virtue of stimulating others to do better.[6] I shall be using my Chamba materials, themselves of different degrees of completeness, as a baseline from which to argue about the similarities and differences between Chamba groupings and various of their neighbours. My conclusions will be speculative, but I hope not rashly so.

Adamawa as a region

The Emirate of Adamawa (which takes in roughly the middle third of Cameroon and the adjoining areas of Nigeria) makes its way into datable history at the beginning of the nineteenth century. It owes its name to the first Emir of the Fulani (or Fulbe) Emirate Modibbo Adama, hence Adamawa. This name, and its virtual synonym Fombina, or the emirate of the south, remind us that Adamawa enters history as the southerly and easterly outlier of the greater Fulani Caliphate of Sokoto established during the first half of the nineteenth century. The people who had inhabited Adamawa prior to the Fulani conquest first appear in our records as victims of slave raids, as conquered peoples, and as 'pagans'. At least, this is the guise in which they enter early travellers' and colonial reports, which owed much to the vantage point of Fulani hosts, interpreters and informants, self-consciously Muslim and self-consciously dominant. But even at the early period, an exception to the equation of pagan and slave was sometimes made in the case of the Chamba (amongst whom I have conducted about thirty months fieldwork in the last ten years [writing in 1986]). The Chamba, it was recognized, were entitled to the title of warriors themselves. They had slave-raided and founded chiefdoms some hundreds of miles from their homelands and, on the perverse grounds which led military-minded colonialists to grant respect to their new subjects, it had to be recognized that Chamba, or at least some part of them, had fallen to no conquest other than that of the Europeans. It has been largely on the basis of Chamba traditions that scholars have tried to read back 'behind' the pseudo-state apparatus which the Fulani put in place before the end of the nineteenth century so as to discern the type of organization which might have predated the Fulani conquest.

6. Several research programmes are underway on both sides of the Nigeria/Cameroon border amongst the Verre, Koma and Pere. The shortcomings of this article should soon be rectified.

Local scholars, perhaps influenced by restricted European visions of the possible forms of political association, have suggested two models of the organization that was swept away by the Fulani. On the one hand, there is a tribes and chiefdoms model, favoured by Sa'ad Abubakar, which tends to represent pre-jihadic Adamawa as a patchwork of tribes and chiefdoms (undergoing shifting change through migration and friction), on the other hand, is an imperial conception, endorsed by Eldridge Mohammadou (and owing much to the writings of Governor Palmer) which associates the blocs on the map in terms of an imperial alliance associated with the Jukun and related peoples. Both conceptions are open to criticism from the vantage of alternative ways of envisaging regional organisations. (Both scholars, in case my reservations be misinterpreted, have made outstanding contributions to our knowledge of nineteenth-century Fulani history, and it may be their immersion in such forms of polity with their accompanying rhetoric that has lead them to imagine indigenous political organization either in terms of an ethnic patchwork or, in reaction against this, in terms of a predecessor empire.) The comparison of alliance systems may also be a step towards suggesting an alternative perspective on the pre-jihadic history of the Adamawan region.

The Chamba ethnicity and identity

Chamba are a highly differentiated population of speakers of two distinct languages.[7] In the roughest terms, they may now number between two hundred thousand and a quarter of a million. The differences existing amongst Chamba before the nineteenth century were multiplied during that century by the varied reactions of local communities to the armed menace of the Fulani. Some of the Chamba trusted to defence in the hills, political initiatives, compromise and an eye to the main chance for their nineteenth-century survival; other Chamba joined the raiding bands that were setting out towards the south and southwest. Eventually these emigrant raiders settled in the Bamenda Grassfields and below the Benue plains where they founded a number of chiefdoms (see Fardon

---

7. Strictly, the term Chamba is anachronistic used of the nineteenth century. I cannot reiterate the issues involved here, but I should explain that speaking a Chamba language is not tantamount to being ethnically Chamba. Not all Chamba speak a Chamba language and some Chamba language speakers are not Chamba. This accounts for my pedantry in the main text (see also note 18).

1988a). The nineteenth century divided the Chamba into raiders and refugees; it was during the colonial period that Chamba ethnic identity assumed its present shape and membership. In an earlier period, the ancestors of the Chamba lived alongside the ancestors of people who have not become Chamba today. Ethnic differences between these populations may have concerned matters of degree, rather than sharply defined categories of inclusion and exclusion. On the borders of the Chamba were people who are now classified as Pere (Koutine), Momi (Verre), and Koma, some of whom have 'become Chamba', as well as such peripheral Chamba-speaking groups as the Taram, Dirrim, Tolla, and Lamja (Chamba Daka speakers) and Kolbila, Wom and Mumbake (Chamba Leko speakers), who are not usually considered to be ethnically Chamba (see *Figure 2.1*). A full regional analysis would want to take equal account of them all; but I cannot achieve this ideal, since I have to base my account largely on my own research, the longest period of which was spent in the one-time refugee community of Mapeo. So, it is from Mapeo that I begin my survey of the politics and economics of Chamba alliance.

Mapeo

In the mid-1970s, when I lived there for a year, Mapeo was a collection of hamlets lining a dry season road which ran alongside the northern faces of the Alantika Mountains. It supported a population of about two thousand. At the beginning of the century the hamlets had been located half way up the hill-side, and the population may have been as much as twice as large. During the colonial period it had become safe to farm in the plain to the north of the mountains, and many of the Mapeo villagers left to join the hamlets set up close to this newly available resource. In some respects Mapeo is untypical of the central Chamba in ways that can often be traced to the lack of centralization which prevailed there at a time when the majority of the central Chamba communities were organized as chiefdoms. In other ways, for instance in the formal organization of kinship terminology and clanship, Mapeo is much more typical of the other central (non-emigrant) Chamba communities.

Kinship terminology

Like other central Chamba communities Mapeo has a system of double clanship which we can relate closely to Crow features in the kinship

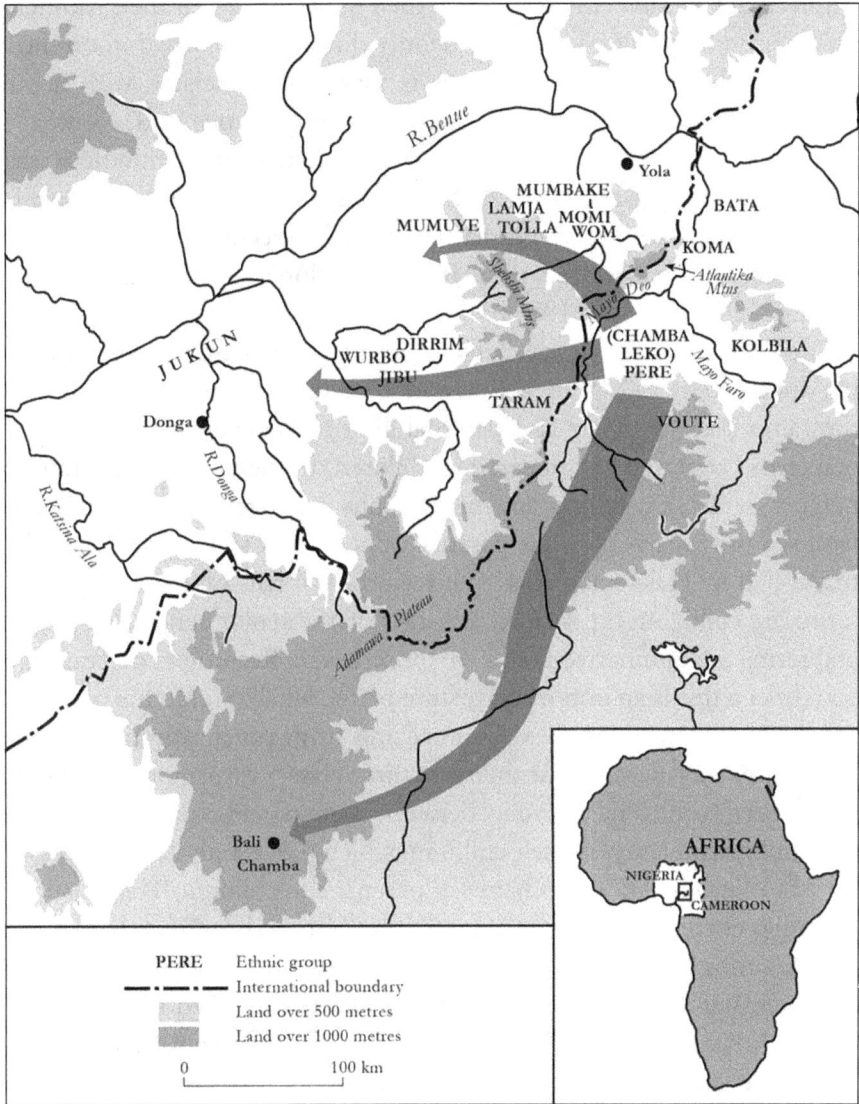

Figure 2.1. The Adamawan regional system and the Chamba

terminology and to a theory of gestation that emphasises the different contributions made by mothers and fathers to their offspring. Summarizing a view which for most informants remains implicit or unconnected, Chamba children derive their substance from their mothers and their individual and spiritual identity through reincarnation on their paternal side; this paternal heritage is especially associated with name and, amongst eastern Chamba, with facial appearance and eventually skull. The most important features of the system of terminology are summarized in *Figures 2.2* and *2.3* Since the kinship terms vary in the different Chamba languages and dialects, I shall concentrate on the formal properties of the system with a few illustrations where necessary (for more detail, see Fardon 1988a).

The Crow features of the kinship terminology hardly need remarking upon (*Figure 2.2*): there is promotion of patrilateral cross cousins to the same class as father and paternal aunt respectively, while matrilateral cross cousins are assimilated to children. In the parental generation, parents' same sex siblings are merged into the parental statuses (albeit with seniority markers) while parents' opposite sex siblings are both distinguished by collateral terms. The reciprocal forms of the first pair of terms are child, but the reciprocal forms of the senior generation collateral terms are diminutive forms of those terms. Regardless of language and dialect, this is an important feature of the kinship referents recorded from Chamba communities. Generalizing from purely formal features (*Figure 2.3*) we can state that there are three classes of seniority relations.

1. There is the   relationship between parents and parents' same sex siblings and any of their children, which the terminology expresses as a lineal relationship between parents and children. This relationship corresponds to the usage of the verb 'to bear' in either of the Chamba languages.

2. Another larger class of seniority relations is marked by the use of reciprocal terms which are modified by diminutive suffixes and, in some cases, also gender suffixes. Terms are formed in this way for four classes of relatives.

   a. Thus we find FZ with a reciprocal term FZ + diminutive, and MB with the reciprocal MB + diminutive. This usage marks these relationships as collaterals in contradistinction to the 'parent-child' class. The verb 'to bear' should strictly not be used between these collateral relatives.

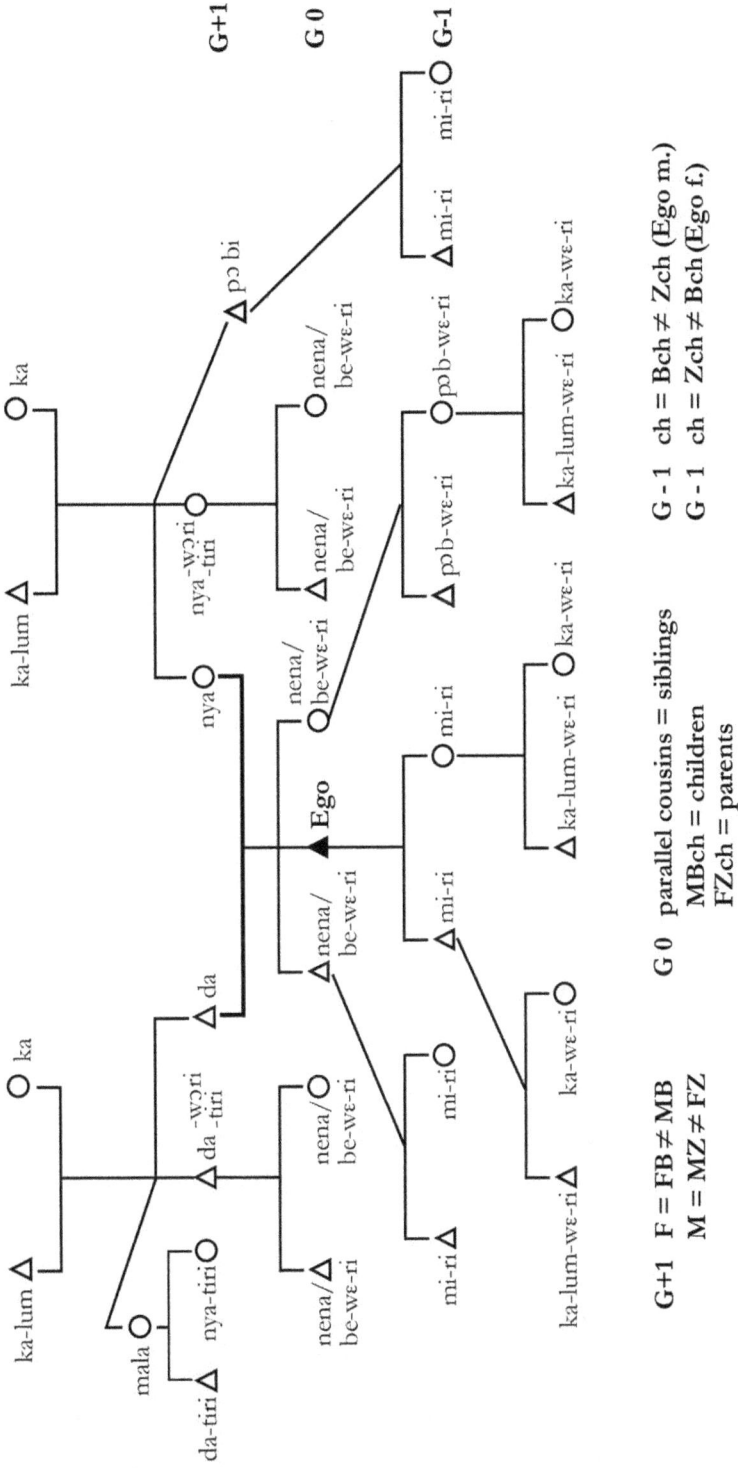

Figure 2.2. Crow skewing in Mapeo Chamba kinship terminology (male Ego)

    b. The relationship terms for the four grandparents and their grandchildren are composed of a root term, with male and female diminutive suffixes. Here again the verb 'to bear' cannot be used directly of the relationship but only by specifying that a grandparent 'bore' my 'parent' who 'bore' me.

    c. The terms for respected affines are composed from a root term, plus masculine or feminine suffixes, plus diminutives.

    d. Finally, relationships of seniority between siblings are expressed in some Chamba dialects by a root term modified for seniority and, in other dialects, through a specialized term for older sibling.

3. The terms for familiar or joking affines, used for MBW and older siblings' spouses, are reciprocal without modification for seniority in keeping with the familiar equality their relationship presupposes. Strictly, these terms negate reference to seniority. In some dialects, the reciprocal use of diminutives between siblings of different sex may also be used to obviate reference to relative seniority.

To move from expression of these terms as genealogical referents to the world of Chamba practice we need to know something about Chamba clanship.

Clanship

Chamba (my point of reference is Mapeo, but central Chamba are similar in these respects) belong to a number of clans (*Figure 2.4*). A man is primarily affiliated to his patriclan (the clan of his fathers and children, paternal aunts, grandparents and grandchildren), and to his matriclan, (where he has mothers, maternal uncles, nephews and nieces, and more grandparents and grandchildren). A woman's affiliations are identical, except that her children belong to her matriclan, while her nephews and nieces belong to her patriclan. This follows from the distinction between lineals and collaterals in the senior generation, and has the important effect of differentiating the male and female vantages on the system of interrelations. A more unusual feature is the manner in which Mapeo clanship is extended (*Figure 2.5*). Individuals have relationships with their father's matriclan, the members of which are all termed senior generation lineals, with the father's father's matriclan, together members of the second ascending generation, and (though less importantly) with the members of the mother's father's matriclan,

Alternate ascending generation +2

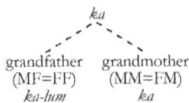

ka

grandfather grandmother
(MF=FF) (MM=FM)
ka-lum ka

Adjacent ascending generation +1

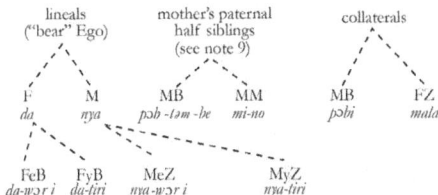

lineals mother's paternal collaterals
("bear" Ego) half siblings
(see note 9)

F M MB MM MB FZ
da nya pɔh-təm-be mi-no pɔbi mala

FeB FyB MeZ MyZ
da-wɔri da-tiri nya-wɔri nya-tiri

Ego's generation O

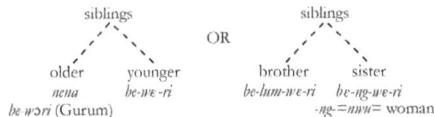

siblings OR siblings

older younger brother sister
nena be-wɛ-ri be-lum-wɛ-ri be-ng-wɛ-ri
be wɔri (Gurum) -ng-=nwu= woman

Adjacent decending generation -1

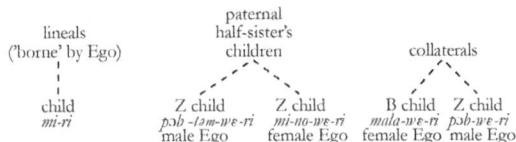

paternal
lineals half-sister's collaterals
('borne' by Ego) children

child Z child Z child B child Z child
mi-ri pɔh-təm-wɛ-ri mi-no-wɛ-ri mala-wɛ-ri pɔh-wɛ-ri
male Ego female Ego female Ego male Ego

Alternate decending generation -2

grandchild
ka-wɛ-ri

male female
ka-lum-wɛ-ri ka-wɛ-ri

Affinal terminology

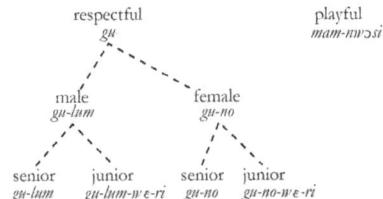

respectful playful
gu mam-nwɔsi

male female
gu-lum gu-no

senior junior senior junior
gu-lum gu-lum-wɛ-ri gu-no gu-no-wɛ-ri

Other terms for relatives by marriage: spouses of 'father',
'mother' and 'grandparent' are designated by the appropriate
opposite sex term for lineal kin: 'father', 'mother' and 'grandparent'.

Figure 2.3. Formal features of Mapeo kinship terminology

whose members may also be elevated to the second ascending generation. Looked at from the viewpoint of the single matriclan, this means
that each matriclan is made up of a category of full members, who
recognize relationships of seniority amongst themselves, and who stand
collectively in the relationships of parents and grandparents towards
attached categories of 'children' and 'grandchildren'. The Chamba term
for matriclan, based on the same root *kun-* or *kon-* in the different languages and dialects, may refer either to the extended or non-extended
unit. Patriclanship is less widely extended than matriclanship. Individual
affiliation is recognized between a person and his or her mother's patriclan, but the relationship is awkwardly handled in the terminology with
compound collateral terms.[8] The emphasis Chamba place upon multiple clan membership goes hand in hand with very shallow genealogies.
Most individuals do not know, indeed do not need to know, more genealogical information than is required to trace their membership to the
clans of their father, mother, father's father, and mother's father. Even
in these cases, an individual may be aware of the clan to which he can
trace affiliation rather than of the name of the person through whom
the relationship is traced. Chamba clanship is creative of kinship in that,
for instance, two men will know that they are siblings *because* they share
membership of the same father's matriclan, but they will probably be
unable to state a genealogical relationship between their fathers. What
Chamba clanship gains in breadth, it seems to lose in depth. In such a
system, the retrospective significance of marriage lies in the way that it
allocates individuals between the clans to which they belong. To put it
another way, the creativity of marriage as alliance occurs a generation
later, when relations of affinity of extremely circumscribed significance
are replaced by the solid ties of clanship. I shall refer to this temporal
structuring of relationships as 'clanification' in distinction to the static
connotations of clanship as a form. It seems truer to Chamba conceptions of the process to envisage clan affiliation in active and processual
terms; clanship is an agency in Chamba affairs.

---

8. In Mapeo, the compound terms *pob-təəm-be* (maternal uncle of the bow) and *mi-no*
(child-female) are used for the mother's patrisiblings. The reciprocals of these terms
are diminutives, confirming that the relationship is not perceived lineally (since it is
the reciprocal 'child' that marks relations between members of adjacent generations
as lineal). *Mi-no-təng- təng* is used of women of the father's matriclan other than Ego's
grandmother and her sisters.

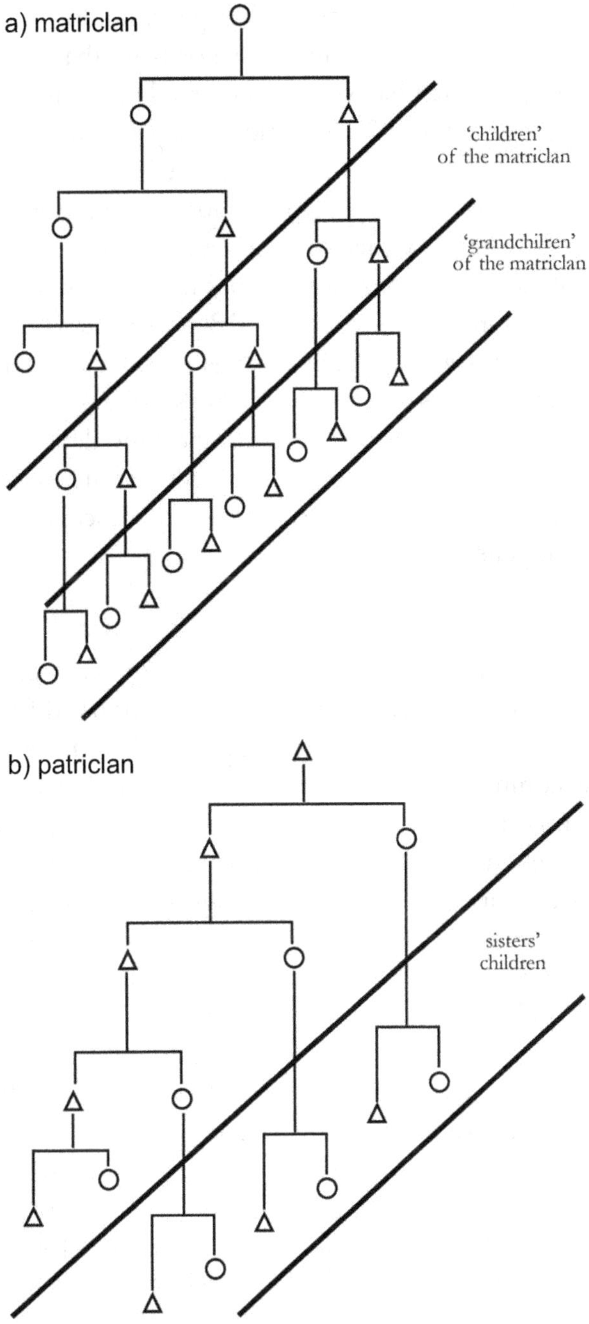

Figure 2.4. Central Chamba extended clanship:
a) the matriclan (*kuni* Daka; *kuna* Leko),
b) the patriclan (*da-membu* Daka; *ba-wa* Leko)

The Crow features of Chamba kinship terminology can be interpreted from the perspective of the individual or from that of the clan categories; and Mapeo Chamba explain their own kin terms in ways that derive from both viewpoints. The elevation one generation of the FZch may be explained in terms of the respect owed to the FZ, or in terms of the categorical relationship of parentation between Ego and the members of his father's matriclan. In practice, we can account for the extension of all the parental terms only by using both arguments.[9] The single generation demotion of the MBch may likewise be derived from categorical matriclanship (Ego belongs to Alter's father's matriclan) or from kinship (Ego is the child of Alter's father's sister). The relationship between the extension of terms and time depends crucially upon clanship, since categorical relations of descent are maintained between a matriclan and all those who can show any descent relation from it in the last two generations.

Marriage regulations in Mapeo

Whereas clanship and kinship terminology are relatively invariant throughout Chambaland, marriage regulations differ substantially. Mapeo marriage regulations are not identical to those of other central Chamba communities, and we shall see later that there may be reasons for this. Throughout Chambaland marriage regulations tend to be rather loosely defined, and subject to disagreement. I cannot imagine a Chamba informant offering marriage prohibitions of the specificity reported from West African 'Omaha systems' (see Burnham 1990; Copet-Rougier 1980, 1985; Héritier 1981) or from East African 'Crow systems' (Beidelman 1967, 1971). The prohibitions are so slight that contemporary Chamba marriage should probably be classed as a complex rather than semi-complex form (Lévi-Strauss 1969). Later, I shall ask whether we are in a position to make the same judgement of earlier marriage regulations.

---

9. The father's full and maternal half-sister's children who belong to Ego's father's matriclan are covered by the local rules that all members of the father's matriclan are to be addressed as grandparents (if maternal uncle or mother to Ego's father), as paternal aunts or fathers (if siblings to Ego's father), or as 'small mothers' or 'small fathers' (if nephews/nieces to Ego's father). The father's paternal half-sister's children are elevated to 'small mother' or 'small father' because of the rule that FZch are respected.

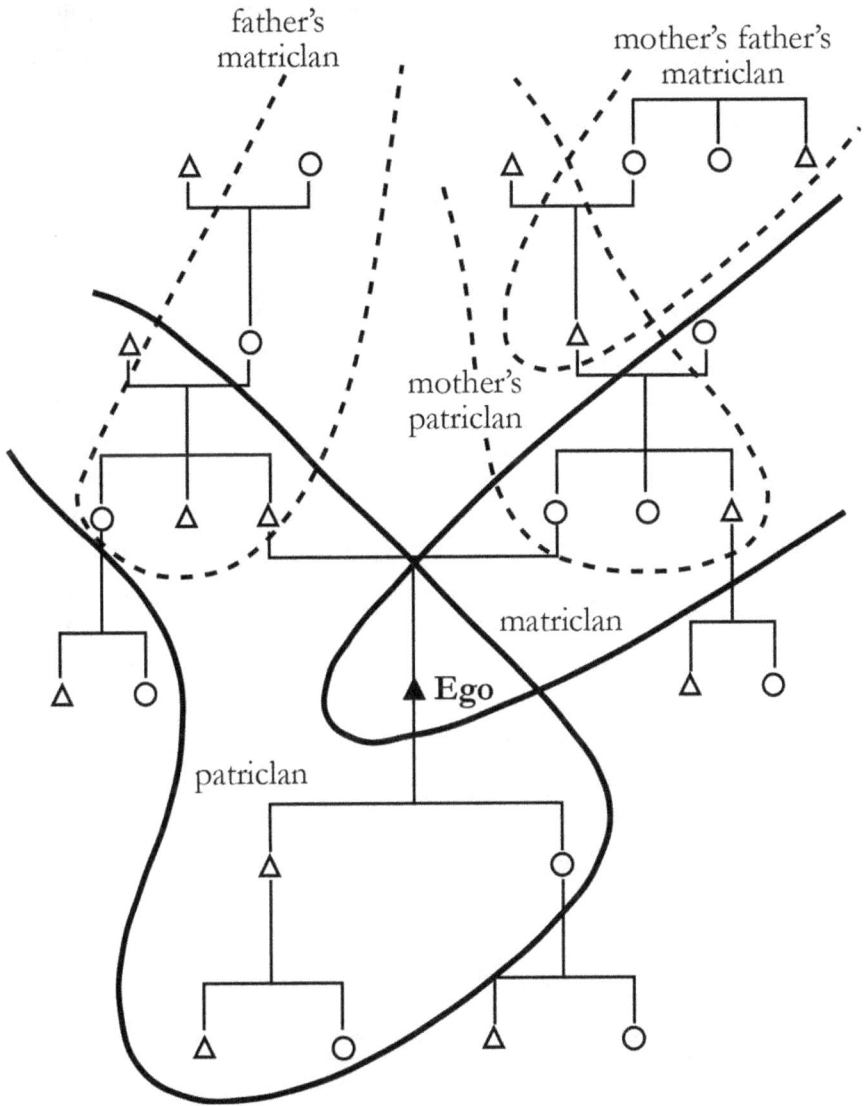

Figure 2.5. Extended clanship: male Ego-centred perspective

In Mapeo, patriclans are strictly exogamous (though some informants claim that they have not always been so and attribute their becoming such to Fulani influence). But since there are about twenty five patriclans within the Mapeo village cluster (and more in the surrounding villages which belong to the Mapeo dialect and culture area within which most marriages take place) this exogamic restriction does not greatly curtail the number of potential spouses for a first marriage. There is no restriction on marrying a woman from the mother's patriclan. Matriclans are less numerous than patriclans (local notions of equivalence reduce the number to about a dozen throughout central Chambaland). Matriclan groupings are important in determining exogamous units in some places, but not in Mapeo where any matriclan woman is marriageable. Although MZD marriage is looked askance by some, I have found an instance of this marriage. In Mapeo, it is also quite permissible to marry a matrilateral cross cousin. Other than these restrictions: men should not take more than one wife from any given patriclan, nor wives more than one husband, these regulations preclude sororate and levirate. Respected affines should not marry. The wives of all close senior generation kin, with the exception of the mother's brother's wife, fall into the category of respected affines, as do the close senior kin of one's own spouse. MBW is a joking affine and potentially marriageable, spouses of older siblings (and therefore spouses' younger siblings) are also joking affines, but marriage would be possible only if an affinal tie to a given patriclan was not replicated. A man could marry his older matrisibling's wife, but not the wife of his full or patrisibling, nor the wife of a younger sibling however related. In sum, few formal restrictions are placed upon first marriage in Mapeo, although the practicalities of meeting a wife would have restricted the size of the marriage pool during the refuge period and prior to the development of markets in the Chamba area. Subsequent marriages will tend to be restricted by the previous marriages of both partners, since no individual should twice marry into the same patriclan. But even in this case, we find that patriclans recognized as single units in ritual affairs may be subdivided for marriage purposes.

Motives for marriage and marriage patterns in Mapeo

The rate of polygyny in Mapeo is not pronounced, although the rate of serial marriage is extremely high. Such figures as I have suggest no particular trend to marriage, but my figures are not extensive.[10] Given that Mapeo has a Crow terminology, it seems reasonable to ask whether we can detect marriage strategies in the matriclan domain. Statistically, marriage into own and father's matriclans occur in proportions that we might anticipate in a random distribution, neither strategy is statistically significant. Mapeo Chamba have definite ideas about both types of marriage.

Speaking of contemporary circumstances, Mapeo informants say that marriage within the matriclan has the advantage that a boy can expect assistance with brideprice from his maternal uncle. There is some ambivalence about intra-matriclan marriage, however, which probably relates to its earlier strategic use in marrying girl slaves. Transference of, especially, young female children between matriclans used to occur because of pawning during food shortage, because of the reportedly unscrupulous desire of some maternal uncles to buy robes or prestige goods, or as blood compensation from another matriclan when a murder had taken place. According to Mapeo Chamba dogma, slavery was transmitted in the matriline but not the patriline, and there are allegations that some matriclan sections are composed of the descendants of slaves. Nowadays, the rumours of slave status are, in most cases, unverifiable and mutually contradictory; given the traditionally non-centralized nature of the Mapeo polity, it seems likely that slave status could not have been enforced if a slave section became numerous, and that the legal statute of many clan sections may have been in dispute prior to the outlawing of slavery. Nonetheless, intra-matriclan marriage may still bear some stigma of its erstwhile significance. Slave status was normatively transient for male children, whose own children would take the status of their mothers. According to informants' recollections, the master of a young slave might marry his own daughter to him, thus tying the children of the marriage to him. In the converse case, male children of a marriage between a woman of slave status and a matrikinsman of free status would be terminologically children

10. The fullest source is Appendix 4 of my unpublished doctoral dissertation (Fardon 1980). Marriage with a member of one's own or father's matriclan was found in about 12-13% of cases. I also record some instances of brideprice and some brief marital histories that support my contentions about the high rate of divorce in Mapeo and the replacement of the earlier system under which brideservice was performed for a first marriage.

of the father's section of the matriclan and, therefore, of free status when discharging the responsibilities of this role in clan affairs. The more persistent inferior status was transmitted between women in the matriline, and even this must have been difficult to maintain in practice given the fragility of marriage in Mapeo. Although rumours of slave status abound and strategies to direct slave marriages are recalled, the uncentralized character of the Mapeo polity, and the ideological refusal to recognize slavery in the localized patriclan sections, suggest that slave marriage would not have been a statistically significant component of Mapeo Chamba marriage patterns.

Like marriage into the matriclan, marriage into the father's matriclan with a classificatory 'small mother' is said to have been enabled thanks to the mediating position of a senior close kinsman, in this case a boy's father rather than his mother's brother. The main disadvantage of this kind of union was that marital difficulties or divorce could threaten the smooth running of the important relationship between a man and his father's matrikin. From the perspective of his father's matriclan, the boy had married his senior kinswoman, and this status could easily become incompatible with his attempts to exercise a husband's authority over her. In both cases of close kin marriage, advantages and disadvantages had to be weighed one against another. The upshot of this weighing in the balance seems to have produced a fairly random distribution of marriages. Mapeo Chamba do not state preferences for particular classes of marriage partner, and no statistical trend emerges from the sum of their choices.

There are several reasons, additional to the absence of stated preferences, why it would be remarkable to find much regularity to the choice of marriage partners. One of these is the very shallow and unspecific way in which genealogical reckoning takes place. A majority of informants could identify by name only those of their own grandparents whom they had known. The name of a grandparent is less important than knowledge of the clan category of shared descent to which affiliation may be traced through that individual. I speak advisedly of shared descent rather than a genealogical continuum, because Chamba tend to envisage descent not lineally but in terms of the qualities shared by members of a patriclan or matriclan by virtue of their co-membership. Recognized patri- or matrifiliation is the criterion of membership in a collectivity allied by a certain types of similarity, which we have seen to differ in the domains of matriclanship and patriclanship. If Mapeo Chamba were to have specific rules or preferences about marriage partners, then these would most probably be expressed in terms of categories of clanship, rather than specified genealogically (which is not a favoured way of talking about such relationships). But there are no clan-based preferences other than patriclan exogamy and the prohibition on remarriage into a patriclan. Although there are numerous forms of alliance recognized between clans and distinguished by name (joking partnerships both between matriclans and between patriclans, relations of common descent between matriclans or patriclans which carry obligations in certain ritual contexts, conventionalized obligations to perform certain types of ritual in concert, co-residence relationships between patriclans, and so on), none of these relationships is the basis for a stated marriage preference. In short, marriage, as distinct from the clanship created by marriage for the progeny of a union, is considered devoid of any positive political importance, while relations between clans are systematically cultivated and attributed overt political importance.

The Mapeo Chamba marriage institution, or more properly institutions, militated further against there being any systematic outcome to the sum of individual marriage choices. Two forms of marriage were recognized (and we would want to count the present form of marriage by bridewealth payment as a third form). The first marriage, apparently both for men and women, was usually in the form of what Mapeo Chamba call 'farming the father in law's farm'. This amounted to a brideservice in terms of farm labour and household construction by the groom and his age mates over a couple of years, as well as the donation of goods in kind. Labour was channelled to both of the parents-in-law, each of whom had a farm cultivated in successive years. The extent of the labour or goods donated differs in the recollections of various informants; the total seems to have been an inconvenience rather than representing a genuine impediment to marriage for men. A second type of marriage translates exactly as 'wife stealing'. In this form a man persuaded a woman to leave her husband and come to live with him. The event is typically recalled by men as a daring raid on a local hamlet at dead of night in company with a selection of youthful patrikin; the women's version of these exploits (supported by the fairly independent position of Chamba women in general) suggests that all the excitement would have not been possible if the lady in question were not willing.

The wife stealer would kill a goat and distribute meat to his patrikin and hamlet co-residents who would then recognize the legitimacy both of the union and of any children born to it. Another small payment was made to the woman for sexual access, and that was that. Or at least it was if the patrikin of the robbed husband made no attempt to recover the woman. Informants recall that patriclans had to function as units willing to protect their rights in women through force of arms if necessary, and a violent reprisal, including the firing of an entire hamlet, had been carried out some years earlier by the patriclansmen amongst whom I resided. Only if the wife stealer belonged to a clan which joked with the affronted husband would a violent reprisal be completely out of keeping with the nature of situation. In this case, again according to normative accounts, an aggrieved reaction would lead to the wronged husband looking even more absurd. We ought to note that Chamba wife-stealing differs from formally institutionalized secondary marriage systems in that the rights of a first husband who had completed brideservice were entirely conditional upon his ability to retain his wife in his compound. If she left then her husband automatically forfeited his rights to her services and in the paternity of her subsequent children, and this forfeiture might eventually be recognized by the woman's parents if they accepted a small payment from her new husband to establish a relationship between them.

Wife-stealing, and the subsequent high rate of separations, reinforced the nexus between patriclanship, locality and exogamy. Since remarriage of men or women in a given patriclan was forbidden, patrikin could not steal one another's wives (although they might enjoy their favours secretly); by and large, this must have favoured the general calm of patriclan life. As importantly, the prohibition on remarriage into a patriclan also prevented a dispossessed husband petitioning for a replacement for his stolen wife. Moreover, and there is undeniable ambiguity here further complicated by the recent replacement of brideservice by bridewealth, there does not appear to have been clear provision for any compensation to be made to the dispossessed husband for his loss of the labour and goods invested in his marriage. Again, it seems to have been the case that the strong came off best, and strength usually, but not always, depended upon the ability of localized patrikin and their co-residents to defend their rights. It is to the colonial restraint of violence following wife-stealing, that Chamba informants attribute the rapid adoption by purchase amongst the Mapeo clans of the cults *jup-yaa* and *jup-dagan*. In their different ways, both cults seemed to assist men's attempts to control their wives. *Jup-dagan* is held to cause illness in a woman or her children. They can be saved only if their mother confesses the name of her lovers to the cult members, who would demand compensation in goats from the adulterous men. A wife stealer would find it necessary to offer at least a goat and beer to the practitioners of *jup-dagan* before consummating his new union in order to avert the suspicion that he was recklessly inviting a blood debt by indirectly menacing the children of his stolen wife's previous husband, and an errant wife would find herself risking the welfare of the children upon whom Chamba mothers dote. Clans that own *jup-yaa* are able to force the wives of a deceased man to pay them a goat before she may marry or have intercourse with another man without both partners risking illness. Together, the two cults are explained as, amongst other things, means for men to protect the increased investment that they now have to make in order to marry their wives.

Given the ramifications of wife theft, it is not difficult to see that amity between patriclans was more likely to be maintained by avoiding intermarriage than by prosecuting it consistently. I can recall no case of wife stealing occurring between the co-resident members of a hamlet, and if such cases arose it seems certain that the wife-stealer would have to leave the hamlet. The relationship of co-residence between members of different patriclans in a single hamlet is one marked by ritual cooperation and, in the past, the men of the hamlet formed a single unit for offence and defence. Although I cannot demonstrate the point statistically, on the basis of cases for which I have the appropriate details, I think that hamlets tended to be exogamous. In Mapeo, there is at least one hamlet which informants say has superseded its constituent patriclans as the unit of exogamy. Certainly, there is no indication that marriages were ever consciously linked in terms of exchanges between patriclans, which might have made them more stable, but might equally have tended to a situation in which linked unions became mutually destabilising. In short, there seems to be scant reason to look at marriage as alliance at all - at least in our popular language understanding of the term.

Where cooperation is important: within the patriclan, between co-residents of different patriclans, between a man and his father's matriclan, we have found either that marriage is not contracted or that Chamba informants clearly weigh its potential risks. More generally,

Mapeo Chamba explain that they try to keep apart men who have sexual interests in the same women, since it is believed that they are bound to argue. Such men are banned from attending cult rites at the same time, since argument there would carry supernatural dangers. The injunction against a woman marrying twice into the same patriclan is also explained in terms of the danger of arguments between patrikin, and full sororate is said to be rendered entirely impossible by the propensity of closely related women to argue over men. Although it might be argued that all these avoidances and separations are symptomatic of an underlying notion of pollution or contagion, my attempts to steer Mapeo Chamba informants into this type of explanation were always arrested by an appeal to the pragmatic considerations of avoiding dispute. This is not to discount an implicit rationale but simply to state that, as their own sociologists, Mapeo Chamba are acutely aware of the discord which marriage and sexual relations introduce to their communal relations.

The upshot of the old Mapeo marriage institutions was a very high divorce rate. To develop this point convincingly it would be desirable to present detailed data on the marital histories of the older men and women of Mapeo (if we accept that the younger people's marriage histories would be influenced by contemporary legal arrangements); but I cannot do this. Older Mapeo men talk about their marriage histories reluctantly: in part because they are potentially vulnerable to ridicule through them, in part because of a sense that the past is past so far as marital relations are concerned, and in part because raking over the status of present spouses is potentially liable to lead to the revelation of information that is much better quietly left alone. I assembled marriage histories for about a dozen middle-aged men whom I knew well (some of which are detailed in Fardon 1980 Vol.2 Appendix 4). Because I realized that informants were uncomfortable about discussing their marriage histories seriously, and since marriage was not a central concern of my research, I did not jeopardize other areas of enquiry by over-insistence. Such information as I have suggests that men in late middle-age might easily have made fifteen to twenty marriages, and only exceptionally did I find a very low number of marriages. Where this had occurred, the explanation lay in the compatibility of the spouses and (probably not unrelated) the fertility of the union. Normally, marriages which were fertile and in which children survived, and in which the wives considered themselves well treated and found their co-wives (if there were any) cooperative, tended to be stable. The majority of marriages were, therefore, not stable. But again impressionistically, it seemed to be the case that marriages either lasted many years or were of extremely short duration. There seemed to be no correlation between the form of the marriage and its longevity; many elders had lived for decades with 'stolen' women who had given them numerous offspring. It was evident that patrikin were reluctant to let a woman go before someone had performed bride service for her (or today paid bridewealth), and in some cases bride service had been carried out more than once for the same woman, but given the inability of patrikin or husbands to control the fate of the marriages subsequently, women retained a high degree of freedom to terminate their marriages. The position of Chamba women in the system of double clanship is germane here. Chamba wives are never really incorporated into a husband's patriclan, other than residentially, and have no relationship with their husband's matriclan. Chamba women bear children for their own matriclan, regardless of their husband's affiliations, and retain their links with their natal patriclans. On the death of her husband, a widow is formally returned to her patrikin, and at their own deaths the bodies of all women, or some relic to represent their bodies if they have died in a distant place, must be given back to their patrikin for burial in the patriclan graveyard. In short, marriage affects the status of Chamba women rather less than women in many other West African societies.

Marriage as alliance?

I have argued that the significance of marriage in Mapeo is best looked at not from the perspective of alliance in the generation in which it occurs but in terms of its implications for the clan affiliations of the offspring of the marriage. Alliance, in the broader sense of the term, tends not to be expressed as marriage but as relationships of different types between or within clans. Ethnographically, Mapeo Chamba tend to envisage their own organization in terms of clanship rather than in terms of marriage. Marriages are often transient and tend to destabilize relations that ought to be more stable. Marriage is not one of the great ceremonies of Chamba life, and even the position of women is relatively independent of it. This does not mean that marriage is devoid of analytic importance (filiation and marriage entail one another). But marriage, as I said earlier, is more likely than not to be an impediment to alliance. I am not concerned to defend an Anglo-Saxon descent model here against French alliance theory; that argument, thankfully, is behind us. But I do claim that Mapeo Chamba organization, indeed all central Chamba organizations, are preeminently readable in their own terms of clanship: not clanship as a set of immutably fixed categories, but clanship as a perspective, a framework of action and as a set of processes, which I have, extending the usage of Alfred Adler (1982), called 'clanification'. In this sense, clanship is also, in the broad sense, alliance, and the ramifications of alliance in terms of clanship prevent marriage from playing an important structuring role per se. Marriage is necessary for recruitment to the plethora of clans to which Chamba trace relationships; but the overriding concern seems to be that marriage does not destabilize pre-existing alliances.

The Chamba, their neighbours and a central Adamawan regional system

In the second half of this essay, I move from Mapeo by way of a brief consideration of a pan-Chamba developments to look at some of the wider regional issues. What happened in Mapeo between the late eighteenth and the mid-twentieth centuries was part of a larger canvas of Chamba, inter-ethnic and eventually international history about which I must say something, if only briefly.

If Mapeo existed as a Chamba community in the mid- to late-eighteenth century, it would have been a small and rather insignificant place on the periphery of one of the most important and ritualized of the Chamba chiefdoms, known as Yeli. The inhabitants of Mapeo paid nominal tribute to Yeli in recognition of the power that the chief there exercised over rain, smallpox and locust infestations. But the location of Yeli made it, and other Chamba chiefdoms along the important Faro-Deo river system, vulnerable to attack in the early years of the Fulani jihad. The settlements of the eastern Chamba were thoroughly disrupted in the early years of the nineteenth century by wars and by the migrations which preceded and succeeded them. Disruptive migrations occurred throughout Chambaland but since it was located in a defensible position directly to the west of the old eastern chiefdoms, Mapeo became the chosen refuge of a large share of the displaced clan sections. Its population grew rapidly, while that of Yeli declined. The ritual link between the two places continued to be recognized, and Mapeo Chamba continued to fear Yeli, but that was about the extent of the relationship between them. If we look at the names of the patriclans presently settled around Mapeo, we find ample evidence of diversity: of the various ethnic groups from which the present clansmen trace descent, of the distant parts of Chambaland from which others migrated, of the titles to which they have made claim and suchlike (see Fardon 1988a for details). In the matriclan domain this diversity of origins is far less evident.

Like other central Chamba localities, the Mapeo local community can be seen in two lights: one viewpoint suggests local, ethnic and linguistic similarity and a conceptual solidarity; the other represents the local community as a heterogeneous assemblage of patriclans of quite different ethnic and cultural backgrounds. Both views have a certain truth to them. In Mapeo, and throughout central Chambaland, the important characteristic of the second perspective is that it is always expressed through patriclanship. Disruptive migrations transplanted patriclan sections from one place to another, multiplied the numbers of clans in any given locality and enhanced the internal diversity of the local community. The patriclan composition of a settlement gives us valuable information on its historical development. Remarkably, the processes of clanification amongst matriclans worked towards different results. Throughout Chambaland, there are about a dozen or so matriclans; local variation is submerged from public view at the level of matriclan sections. Knowledge of the internal composition of matriclans is normatively treated as the private preserve of clan members. Elsewhere, I have shown at length that matriclanship and patriclanship are contrastive spheres in Chamba life (Fardon 1985b, 1988a). Patriclanship is concerned with cumulative historical time, in which a pool of individuals are reincarnated, draw upon a collection of names which is their patrimony and maintain the cultural distinctiveness of their patriclan as well as assuring, if need be through violence, the rights of the clan's members; overtly, matriclanship is invested with mythological values, stresses similarity rather than difference, and does so especially in terms of presuppositions of shared substance that underwrite shared bodily concerns about birth, disciplining, witchcraft and slavery.

Looking at our Mapeo case again, we may say that together: the scale of disruptive migration, the loosening of the Yeli connection, and the failure of an alternative hierarchy to be instituted, enhanced the significance of patriclans, and enhanced most especially their significance as units charged with self-defence and the assertion of the rights of their members against those of the members of other clans. Under these circumstances, it is reasonable to anticipate that the significance of patri-clans in marital strategies would also be enhanced. Thus, in the Mapeo case, we find a Crow kinship terminology with marriage prohibitions defined in terms of patriclanship. Moreover, the marriage tie appears to have been fragile and to have been deemed inappropriate as an ex-pression of alliance. While admitting that social life infrequently corre-sponds to our logical models of it, when we know that a region has seen such drastic change, there do appear to be grounds to ask whether an historical explanation could be suggested. Such evidence as I have from the southern part of Chambaland, which shares Crow kinship termi-nology (especially from the older matriclan chiefdoms of the southern Shebshi Mountains and the southern Alantika Mountains), and I should emphasise that this evidence is no stronger than informants' recollec-tions of past marriage practices, suggests that exogamic restrictions had previously been stated in terms of matriclanship. The plausibility of this report is enhanced when we find similar restrictions amongst the Pere-speaking southern neighbours of the Chamba. Furthermore, there are suggestions that both patriclanship and patri-viri-local residence may represent introductions into a previously matrilineal and matrilocal sys-tem under which marriages were usually both monogamous, in a statisti-cal sense, and stable. It is to consideration of the evidence for regional variation and to the historical context in which that variation occurred that I turn next.

Throughout Chambaland, marriage regulations concerning matri-clanship are continuing to fall into disuse – a development associ-ated by informants with the increasing influence of world religions. But, if my analysis of the Mapeo case has any validity, it is likely that matriclan prohibitions on marriage could have been loosing their strategic pertinence throughout the nineteenth century and perhaps even earlier. My evidence here falls into several parts. I can demon-strate other strategic adjustments of marriage policy from the con-quest chiefdoms founded by Chamba and their allies in the wake of the Fulani creation of Adamawa. We can range these cases in terms of the increasing reliance placed upon patriclanship at the expense of matriclanship as the Chamba left their homelands and incorporated peoples of divergent cultures (see *Figure 2.6*). I can also present evi-dence from the southern part of central Chambaland showing traces

Figure 2.6. The possible transformations of Chamba marriage and clanship

type of community	kinship terminology	clanship	marriage rules	characterization of marriage
Taram, Dirrim; also Pere, Koma?, Voute (18 century)?	Crow	Matriclanship	Matriclan exogamy	Virtually monogamous Very stable
Matriclan chiefdoms: refuge communities	Crow	Double clanship	Previously exogamous matriclans; now diverse	Reported previously stable among Leko; in 20 century fragile among Nnakenyare, where the rate of polygyny for nobles increased.
Mapeo refuge community	Crow	Double clanship	Patriclan exogamy	Very fragile marriage; low rate of polygyny
Patriclan chiefdoms: conquest chiefdoms within Chambaland	Crow	Double clanship	Patriclan exogamy	High level of polygyny for notables; preferential endogamy among 'immigrants', plus wife-taking from 'indigenes'; marriages probably more stable than in matriclan chiefdoms
Patriclan chiefdoms: conquest chiefdoms outside Chambaland	i) Donga Crow	Patriclanship	Patriclan exogamy, plus any descendants of FM or MM	High rate of polygyny for notables. No data on stability.
	ii) Bali Hawaiian	Patriclanship on Grassifeld model	Ideally no marriage with traceable relations over 3-4 generations; but royal parallel cousin marriages found (E.M. Chilver personal communication)	Very high rate of royal polygyny

of earlier matriclan marriage regulations and documenting marital instability similar to that found in Mapeo for the early colonial period. Finally, I can show that many of the Chamba's pre-jihadic neighbours preserved Crow kinship terminology with marriage regulations defined in terms of matriclanship into the twentieth century. This may suggest earlier shared central Adamawan features and go some way to support my contention that some of the adaptability of the Chamba during the nineteenth century derived from their having developed a patriclan organization lacked by their neighbours. In turn, the supposition that Chamba patriclanship was developed in the context of a preexisting matriclan organization makes sense both of the names of the patriclans (derived from locations, other ethnic groups, and offices) and of the generally contrastive relation maintained between the two domains of Chamba clanship. My argument is explicitly hypothetical, but my hypothesis is argued in terms of the evidence that can be mustered and presented no more strongly than as a set of suppositions to explain some ethnographic puzzles.

I begin in the nineteenth century with the chiefdoms founded within Chambaland at about the same time as the Mapeo refuge was swelled by incoming clan sections. The allied patriclans of different Chamba and non-Chamba origins which colonized the northern part of Chambaland pursued a policy of restricting important offices to members of an immigrant group of dominant patriclansmen. Matriclanship retained very slight significance in these chiefdoms' governmental institutions. The immigrants maintained a degree of residential separation from their subjects, who belonged to a congeries of hill-dwelling, Chamba-speaking peoples of the northern mountains and, in keeping with this concern, we find traces of preferential intermarriage between the immigrant patriclans, at least so far as their own daughters were concerned. In the case of one of the smaller chiefdoms, however, I also found recollections of earlier prohibitions on remarriage into a matriclan from which a spouse had previously been taken. Preferentially endogamous marriage strategies were directly related to the immediate political concerns of maintaining domination and, as such, counterparts of the restriction of access to offices. On the face of it, the single reference to a matriclan regulation may be a survival of earlier organization.

In the two areas of chiefdom foundation outside Chambaland events took a rather different course. Donga, the largest of the Chamba-founded chiefdoms in the Benue plains is the only organization from this area for which I have any information. Significantly, Donga retained a patriclan organization, in which many of the clans bear names recognizable from Chambaland, but no trace remained of the Chamba matriclans which had somehow died out between departure from Chambaland and information supplied about a century later. In strategic terms, a Chamba minority attempting to maintain control of a confederation which itself was becoming multi-ethnic would profit from the attenuation of matriclanship. But another consideration needs to be added: the presence of a system of matriclanship analogous to that of the Chamba seems to have been one criterion for identifying people as similar and assimilating them to a Chamba identity. Thus, matriclan attenuation never seems to have happened when Chamba intermarried with Verre, or with Pere, or with Koma; whatever differences there may have been amongst these peoples, they were overridden in the domain of matriclanship. The same mechanism may provide one explanation for the generalization of matriclanship and ethnic identity between the speakers of two different Chamba languages in the first place. Hypothetically, I would argue that ethnic incorporation initially took place through the mechanism of incorporation of incomers into matriclan categories, but that this mechanism later operated in concert with patriclanship and in some places was displaced by it. Hence, in the Mapeo case, we saw a double mechanism of incorporation into matriclan categories and the definition, or redefinition, of incomers as members of discrete Chamba patriclans. In the case of the Chamba raiders, ethnic incorporation, if it took place, did so in terms of patriclanship. Although both mechanisms could lead to incorporation, the outcomes differed. Matriclan incorporation left the overt and formal organization of the community unchanged, since the diverse origins of matriclan sections were publicly concealed. Patriclan incorporation, on the other hand, tended to multiply the number of patriclans within the local community. By these means, the pertinence of ethnic distinctiveness, which in Chamba terms differs from patriclanship only in degree, was consistently enhanced during the nineteenth century.

Donga kinship terminology, notwithstanding the attenuation of matriclanship, retains the formal Crow features of the central Chamba. We still find a distinction between lineals and collaterals in the adjacent senior generation, and a skewing of cross cousins in a speaker's own generation. However, the formal continuity conceals a change in the internal logic of the arrangement, which now derives solely from the promotion of the FZch as a reflection of the status of the FZ; whereas in Chambaland the arrangement was explicable both in terms of this logic and in terms of the logic of extended clanship. By implication the extension of cross cousin terms would have been far less wide than amongst central Chamba. Meek tells us that Donga patriclans (he calls them kindreds) were exogamous, and offers us a striking echo of central Chamba rationales for out-marriage.

> The reason assigned for the prohibition against marriage within the kindred is that such marriages would be difficult to dissolve, should the partners find that they are unsuited to each other. (Meek 1931 1: 342)

Patriclan exogamy aside, Donga Chamba were also barred from marrying any woman with whom they shared a grandmother (either FM or MM) so that, unlike in Mapeo, marriage with the actual cross cousin was not permitted. Otherwise, the choice of a first marriage partner was a free one (although Meek does not tell us whether there were restrictions on subsequent remarriages, or whether the marriages of siblings placed any constraints on the individual). Meek does not tell us how slaves were attached to their owners with the demise of the earlier mechanism of matriclanship. My own superficial researches suggest that this would have been a fluid area. Chamba ethnic status was withheld from subject populations who remained in categorical relations of submission where this was feasible, which was not always because non-Chamba had to be incorporated to augment the strength of the Chamba raiders. Female slaves were usually taken as wives with a consequent rise in the rate of polygyny for Chamba notables.

In the other emigrant Chamba case, that of the Bali Chamba, the change has been more radical. Not only has matriclanship disappeared entirely, but so also has the Crow kinship terminology. Chamba clanship has been effectively replaced by a Grassfields form of positional succession, reflecting the overwhelming numbers of Grassfield peoples incorporated within the Chamba-led alliance. Nevertheless, Chamba language has persisted in four of the five Bali chiefdoms and all five claim to be ethnically Chamba.

Taking Mapeo as a control case for comparison, the Chamba conquest chiefdoms introduce to us systems of marriage and clanship that are typologically marked by patriclanship. Matriclanship is either absent or attenuated, while there are at least suggestions of preferential patriclan marriage strategies. The older chiefdoms to the south and west of Mapeo present typological features in which matriclanship is more important. Thus, we find consistent references to earlier matriclan, or matriclan section, exogamy. Frobenius, the earliest investigator in 1911, claims that all Chamba matriclans were previously exogamous, except for that of the blacksmiths which was endogamous (Mohammadou 1984: 35, 95-6). I was told of earlier matriclan regulations in the central Chamba chiefdoms (Gurum and Yebbi), and Meek records previous matriclan exogamy from more easterly Chamba (at Kubi, an outlier of Yeli). In Yeli itself, I was told that the royal matriclan was exogamous, although other matriclans were not; and in the chiefdoms to the north of Yeli, ruled by members of a royal patriclan, we find a negative endorsement of the importance of the exogamous strategy of the royal matriclan, since no member of that clan was allowed to marry into the community.[11] Similarly, the royal matriclan of Sugu did not allow its girls to marry into the neighbouring chiefdoms of Gurum and Yebbi, although in this case, the restriction is explained locally by the simmering hostility between these chiefdoms, on account of which the girls would have been 'treated like slaves'. In virtually all cases, these marriage regulations now exist only as recollections.

Contemporary data on the stability of marriage may also mislead us about an earlier set of circumstances. The adoption of bridewealth payment, in preference to the regime of brideservice plus gift-giving, and the legal endorsement of the marriage bond has made divorce a more rule-bound business than once it was. Meek remarks the instability of marriage amongst particular groups of western and northern Chamba (Gandole and Lamja) during the 1920s (Meek 1931 1: 380). Another colonial official, E.S. Lilley, in a report of about the same date, refers to the prevalence of marriage by elopement amongst western Chamba and emphasises the fragility of the marriage bond (Nigerian Archives Kaduna NAK 1921). Frobenius had earlier likened the marriage bond amongst the westerly Chamba to no more than a premarital affair amongst eastern Chamba (Dakka and Tschamba in his terms) (Mohammadou 1984: 95). The most convincing corroboration of the fragility of the marriage bond is a report commissioned from the colonial officer T.G.B. Welch into Chamba wife-stealing described as

---

11. Old Yeli is now so small (seven compounds) that no conclusion can be drawn from marriage data collected there. The endogamy of the smith matriclan (reported by Frobenius but not now practised) may mirror the prescriptive exogamy of the royal matriclan (which is still practised). The power of the royal matriclan was closely related to the physical presence of its members in other local communities. This explains the significance of the ban on marriage with members of the royal matriclan to the north of Yeli.

'the only blot on the Chamba record leading to violence' (NAK 1935). Although Welch does not remark it, in all probability a rise in rates of polygyny amongst Chamba officials in the chiefdom concerned (Gurum) had played some part in the increasing rate of wife-stealing.[12] Welch's report is astute (certainly more useful than the solicited opinion of the local missionary that wife-stealers should be flogged and put in prison [Fleming letter in NAK 'Chamba Marriage File']). Welch notes that matriclan exogamy had died out and that elopement might take place with married or unmarried girls. The only deterrent to wife-stealing was self-help, there being no other means to secure a refund of bride payments. Divorce was recognized *de facto*, and a husband would need to give his newly acquired wife's kin no more than a pot of beer and a chicken. Chamba tended not, however, to steal wives from close relatives of their parents or from men who belonged to the 'group' (not further specified, perhaps local group) from which a woman had been taken in first marriage. Again, we find evidence of a Chamba realization that marital and sexual relations endanger established alliances which have to be shielded from the instabilities of matrimony. With some insight, Welch in summary attributes wife-stealing to three factors: low brideprice, the social recognition of irregular unions (for Chamba, irrespective of marital status, the publicly known *genitor* is also the *pater*), and the independence of Chamba women. The second two reasons would certainly apply in Mapeo today.

What might the Chamba experience tell us about the regional systems of alliance existing in Adamawa before the jihad? The way in which change occurred during the nineteenth century may be indicative also of the earlier period. Chamba chiefdoms departed further from their pre-jihadic styles the more distantly they were established. From what we know, physical and cultural distance correlated quite closely. Thus, Chamba-led confederacies appear to have been able to absorb members from certain of their neighbours without fundamentally changing their

---

12. There is reason to believe that the scale of polygyny had been increased under the reign of Gang Maken (c. 1897- c. 1925) who was responsible for centralizing the chiefdom during the German colonial period. Patriclan exogamy is currently reported from Sugu, the southern neighbour of Gurum, by some informants. In the Chamba chiefdom that was most closely allied with the Fulani, Dalami, informants deny that matriclans or patriclans are currently exogamous. I have conducted interviews but no intensive fieldwork in these communities.

system of double extended clanship. Such peoples were distinguished by name in the domain of patriclanship but absorbed into the existing categories of matriclanship. The twin processes of 'clanification' were sufficient to assure 'Chambaization'. This seems to suggest that the pre-jihadic forms of organization of the central Adamawan peoples were distributed in a way that may have resembled what linguists are beginning to understand of their languages and dialects: that is to say in the form of chains with occasional discontinuities. I think I can demonstrate this, at least for some of the closer neighbours of the Chamba. It is also likely that the predominant marriage organization of the area was based upon matriclan regulation of exogamy and remarriage and occurred with a kinship terminology marked by Crow features in the classification of cross cousins. More hypothetically, divergence from this model may suggest areas of endogamy in the past (although we have to be careful here, first because peoples can intermarry with divergent rules, and, second, because change evidently took place during the hundred odd years between the Fulani jihad and our earliest reports on social organizations in the area, so that it is not wise to assume that either these reports or current recollections of a 'traditional' organization necessarily refer to pre-jihadic forms of organization).

I have suggested that Chamba organizations tended to change when they had to assimilate peoples with different clanship and marriage systems. While processes of Chambaization still took place, incorporation was predicated upon patriclanship alone. Within Chambaland, the nineteenth century witnessed a reshuffling of population, the general effect of which was to strengthen patriclanship; but in order to explain why the initial Chamba reactions to Fulani inroads were organized in patriclan idiom, it seems necessary to assume that the development of a patriclan framework of organization was underway well before the nineteenth century. The delineation of two clanship domains *may* have been one difference between many of the central Chamba and most of their neighbours. Whether or not this was the case, there can be little doubt that patriclanship *became* a dominant idiom only during the nineteenth century. Previous marriage prohibitions appear to have become eroded without patriclan exogamy becoming a general norm; marital instability *may* have been aggravated by these developments. That said, the wide distribution of 'wife-stealing' suggests it also was not a nineteenth century innovation.

Prior to the jihad, the southern neighbours of the Chamba were the Pere and Potopo (called Koutine by the Fulani and in colonial reports), who were joking partners of the Chamba and with whom they intermarried.[13] Like the central Chamba, the Pere have Crow skewing in their kinship terminology and are organized into extended matriclans, divided into internal sections and then shallow lineages traced from a common grandmother. Although the Pere have no patriclan organization, elements of putative Pere origin found among some of the southern Chamba, as well as among the emigrant Chamba, are treated as a patriclan: amongst the emigrant Bali Chamba and the Donga Chamba variants of the name Pere persist to denote patriclans which are now thought to be Chamba in origin and culture. This supports our suppositions about the easy 'Chambaization' of matriclan peoples. Pere marriage prohibitions are very similar to those found under the Chamba matriclan regime: it is not permitted to marry within the matriclan section, and remarriage cannot take place to a woman of a matriclan (in practice, probably, matriclan section) into which marriage had occurred previously. There is additionally a prohibition on marriage with a woman of the F matriclan who is of the same generation as a FZ (i.e. any woman called Z by F, irrespective of her age). Neither FZD nor MBD marriage is said to have been forbidden, and both might be convenient under different circumstances of residence. The marital residence was established virilocally, but a man might be living with his father or mother's brother, depending whether the mother's brother had exercised his right to have his sister's child come to live with him. Like the Chamba, the Pere remember that marriage within the matriclan might sometimes be contracted between a sister's son and a slave girl received by his maternal uncle as a pawn, or as vengeance compensation. The Pere recollection that monogamy was almost the rule amongst them before the recent adoption of Fulani customs of polygyny, especially by their chiefs, receives support from early French reports (cited by Lembezat 1961: 225). The major contrast between Pere and their Chamba northern neighbours seems to be the absence of patriclanship among the former, and this in turn may relate to the shifting patterns of Pere cultivation and settlement.

---

13. This is reported by Pere informants and corroborated by the local historian Garbosa's account of the history of Donga in which he independently claims the mothers of some early chiefs to have been Pere (see Fardon 1988a).

From the vantage point of clanship and marriage, there are striking similarities between the Pere and their western neighbours the Taram and Dirrim. These peoples speak dialects of Chamba Daka, the language of the majority of the Chamba of Chambaland; however, they do not appear to consider themselves Chamba, nor are they considered such by Chamba. Like the Pere, the Taram had a Crow system of terminology and were organized into matriclan categories. Meek records that matriclans were non-localized, but he also talks of matrilocal residence and claims that marriage might be favoured with a FBD or a father's paternal half-sister's daughter because the man could continue to live in his own home. This suggests that while some elements of matriclans were localized, other elements of the same clan might be found elsewhere. Matriclans were exogamous, and a man was forbidden to marry or have sexual relations with a woman of his wife's clan. The prohibition on marriage with the full FZD probably implies a general prohibition on repeating the marriage of the father. Meek goes on to tell us that a man should not marry a paternal half-sister if their respective mothers belonged to the same clan. Unfortunately, he does not remark that the possibility of a choice having to be made about such a marriage implies that Ego's grandfather had twice married into the same clan. Perhaps, the rules should not be interpreted genealogically but in terms of clanship: as prohibitions respectively on marriage into the wife's sub-clan and the father's mother's sub-clan. But just as likely. Meek has garbled his information. By analogy with other societies in this area, we might guess that rules about remarriage probably applied symmetrically to women. By virtue of their uxori-patri-local residence system both Daka Taram and Dirrim are said to have been virtually monogamous and to have enjoyed stable marriages (Meek 1931 1: 398-402). In this, they are unlike the Mapeo Chamba and the western Chamba (Daka-speaking) and the Chamba of Yeli amongst whom marriage was unstable, but may have resembled the south-eastern Chamba on Frobenius's not very reliable report (during the period when matriclans were exogamous) and, more reliably, the Pere and Potopo.

Information on the remainder of the peoples around the fringes of Chambaland is, at present, fragmented and confused. The eastern and northern neighbours of the Chamba are called Verre and Koma, but neither of these is an ethnic term used in self reference.[14] Rather than two distinct peoples, we may instead be faced with a couple (or even series) of dialect chains, which are endowed with ethnic pertinence only externally. Meek's notes on the Verre, to take these first, offer snippets of information on ten groups which he distinguishes (Meek 1931 chap. VII). With the exception of the Wom, who speak a dialect of Chamba Leko, all the people visited by Meek belong to the western or Momi group of speakers (Blench personal communication; Boyd 1989). The Momi seem to have only slight cultural affinities with Chamba. The easterly speakers of Mom Jango (a dialect which is closer to some of the Koma dialects than to Momi) are neighbours of the Mapeo Chamba. If Mapeo Chamba testimony is reliable, the Mom Jango and the Koma both have Chamba-type matriclans. Mapeo informants state this proposition in two ways: that their own matriclans exist amongst these neighbours, and that such matriclans were implanted, or have been augmented, by the gift of Chamba children who inauspiciously cut upper before lower teeth. Large numbers of Mom Jango seem to have been 'Chambaized' in Mapeo, and they are supposed to be especially prominent in two matriclans. Other Momi were picked up by the northern Chamba immigrants and became their close allies. These Momi formed distinct 'Chambaized' patriclans which retained the ethnonym as a patriclan name; this recalls the presence of Chambaized Pere amongst the emigrant Chamba, which I noted previously.

The situation amongst the 'Koma' is little clearer than amongst the 'Verre'. Three speech communities have been identified on the Cameroon side which may correspond to speech communities given different names on the Nigerian side of the border.[15] Two kinship terminologies I collected from informants of different groupings show very clear features of Crow-type skewing, although this formal feature is not

---

14. Chamba use the term Koma but they also do not use Verre or Koutine, who are respectively Momi and Pere to them.

15. For the three Koma speech communities identified on the Cameroon side of the border, see ALCAM; Boyd 1989; Mohammadou 1983: 221-2. They may correspond to groupings recognized in Nigeria: 1) Koma Ndera (Cameroon), the northern Koma, possibly the same as those called Vomni in Nigeria; 2) Gimnime, with dialects Ritibe and Gimbe (Cameroon), the central Koma, living on the eastern Alantika Mountains and the adjoining plains; 3) Gimme, also equivalent to Kompana (Cameroon), probably the Koma Mbeya of Nigeria and the same as the Koma around the Mission Station at Tantile.

achieved identically.[16] In both cases, informants were able to confirm the existence of matrilineal groupings but not of patrilineal groupings. As in the Chamba form of extended matriclanship, the categorical relation between matriclan members and the children of matriclan men is given recognition. Matrilineal groupings were said to be non-localized and exogamous. It was also prohibited for a man to marry into the matrilineal grouping of his father. Residence was uxorilocal for an initial period, but might subsequently become neolocal. Some Koma groups, especially those known to Cameroon Chamba as Kompana, are showing a tendency to 'Chambaization', speaking one of the Chamba languages and adopting Chamba cultural features. The existence of a large, internally differentiated, matriclan in Mapeo called the matriclan of the Koma suggests this process may be longstanding. Mapeo Chamba consider the neighbouring Koma (like neighbouring Momi) to have matriclans identical to their own and, again, explain this in terms of the gift of anomalous Chamba children to them. Overall, it seems likely that Chamba ethnicity was prestigious (relative especially to Koma, Momi and perhaps also Pere) before the Fulani jihad.

Such indications as we have imply that the constellation of features suggestive of this local system did not extend to the north of the Chamba (among the western Momi, Mumuye or even some of the

---

16. My two Koma schedules were collected from informants at the Dingtere Catholic Mission. I refer to them only because nothing better researched is yet published. The groups represented appear to be the dialects of Gimnime. The skewing in the Gimbe schedule gives us:

MB = MF = FF = FeB and MBW = MM = FM = FeBW.
F = FyB = MZH = FZS = FZDH and M = MZ = FyBW = FZD = FZSW
MBS = MBD = S = D and MBSW = SW and MBDH = DH

In this schedule there is no distinct term for MB or FZ. Both MB and FeB are raised a generation although attitudes are markedly different (MB is a joking relation, FeB is not). FZ is addressed by the same term as MZ. Skewing in Ego's own generation is straightforward.

The Ritibe schedule gives us:

MyB = eB; MBW = eBW and FZ = M
MBS = MBD = S = D and FZS = FZDH = F and FZD = FZSW = M

This is a different pattern of skewing in the adjacent senior generation since MeB is called by a sibling term with a suffix that does not appear elsewhere in the terminology, while MyB is addressed as eB. Matrilateral cross cousins are demoted a generation, while patrilateral cross cousins, indeed all members of the father's matriclan below the grandparental generation are assimilated to parents.

Both terminologies are clearly associated with matriclan organization.

more northerly Chamba groupings). While the situation to the east is not wholly clear, the same generalisation may apply.[17] The 'matriclan belt' with its typical Crow skewings, may have extended further to the west and south. The Kam, Wurbo, Jibu and even Jukun perhaps formed a western extension of these regional similarities.[18] To the south we are again handicapped by lack of information. A full analysis of Buti (Voute) kinship terminology by J.-L. Siran shows no Crow features, but his data are from groupings which migrated south, where he tells us that matriclanship died out (Siran 1981). It seems likely that the common regional features of the central Adamawan matriclan belt would have been found amongst the eighteenth century Buti. I have been unable to find relevant data about other peoples further to the south of the Pere.[19]

Conclusions

There is little point in continuing a line of thought which has run so far ahead of its ethnographic support. My suggestion is that the Chamba data are indicative of an earlier regional system of resemblances on the wane. The Mapeo Chamba variant could be the relatively incoherent result of a couple of centuries of change, it lacks consistency between marriage regulations and kinship terminology, and it suffers from such a high rate of divorce as to effectively sever the tie between marriage and alliance (indeed the relation is virtually rendered negative). Without questioning the means by which the class of Iroquois systems is constructed (like Barnes 1984), I have argued that the equation 'marriage is alliance' has to hold before the current theories of semi-complex marriage systems become applicable. I have further argued that historical

17. Dowayo do not seem to have matriclans, but Barley does not give us the cross cousin terms (Barley 1983: 6). The Kolbila, although speaking a Chamba language, also appear to lack matriclans. Here might be the place to remark that not all speakers of Chamba languages have a 'central Chamba' clanship system (e.g. Kolbila, Wom, Mumbake amongst Leko speakers, Dirrim, Taram, and possibly some of the northern groupings of Daka speakers), but wherever central Chamba speakers lacked Chamba clanship they do not seem to have developed Chamba ethnicity either. This suggests that ethnic identity and the double clanship system developed together.
18. This distribution may conceivably turn out to have implications for our conception of the types of similarities that went into the regional system that was Kororofa.
19. There may be data on Suga or Nyam Nyam but I have not found them. Presumably the Duru would be related typologically to the Gbaya-Mkako belt, but I cannot confirm this either.

circumstances, along with their politics and economics, are crucial factors. But I would acknowledge the productivity of the theoretical developments which have suggested ways to question ethnographic data: classes and theories entail one another; without theories we have no questions - not even questions about the inapplicability of theories. Furthermore, I have suggested that the theory may have offered more direct returns applied to stable Crow systems of the central Adamawan type. I simply lack data to make any judgement.

I conclude in regional terms. When I was in Mapeo, the misfit between terminology and marriage rules never excited my suspicions, I simply adopted my hosts' view that marriage was not politically significant. But put into historical and regional context, and given a theory of semi-complex marriage systems, it becomes legitimate to ask the extent to which Chamba marriage practices have to be seen as transformed versions of preexisting, more systematic systems of practice. I have arranged my materials in summary form to give a synoptic view of this process that can be related to the map of the region. The more I look at the regional materials, the more I am convinced that the patriclan features of Chamba society are more recent than its matriclan features and that there has been a consistent trend to processes of change over a longer period than that since the Fulani jihad. In the period before Chamba Leko diaspora, a correlation between the stability and size of settlements, the degree of centralization and the significance of patriclanship seems to suggest itself on the basis of comparison between the central Chamba and their immediate neighbours, both Chamba-speaking and speakers of other languages. To proceed any further, would require more data on two fronts: we need comparative surveys of the Adamawan region of a relatively superficial nature to give us an idea of the overall picture and, at least, one in depth study of a functioning Crow-type marriage system in this area so that we can begin to infer some of the features of a possible pre-jihadic regional system that crossed the present ethnic boundaries that usually, necessarily, but nonetheless misleadingly, tend to circumscribe our individual researches. The diversity of research underway or planned by a number of fieldworkers suggests that before long materials will be available to modify and refine or to reject the tentative reconstruction attempted here.

ACKNOWLEDGEMENTS

I am indebted to Françoise Héritier-Augé for her kind invitation to present this paper at her seminar which suggested to me that central Adamawan materials might be susceptible to analysis from the perspectives of alliance theory, as well as for her extensive comments on the analysis I have proposed. Elisabeth Copet-Rougier, while tactfully correcting the French version of the paper delivered at the Collège de France, also refined my argument. I have incorporated revisions and new perspectives suggested by questions posed at the seminar. I am particularly grateful to researchers who have worked, or are proposing to work, in the area for their generous assistance, especially: Alfred Adler (Moundang), Françoise Dumas-Champion (Koma), Charles-Henry Pradelles de la Tour (Pere), Jean-Louis Siran (Vouté) and Claude Tardits (Bamum). Pierre Bonte posed a crucial question about the organization of slavery in emigrant Chamba chiefdoms to which my response both in the seminar and here is inadequate. Intensive anthropological research in these communities (especially in Nigeria) would be needed before a detailed answer could be given.

Chapter 3

'AFRICAN ETHNOGENESIS'
Limits to the comparability of ethnic phenomena

Ethnicity and comparative anthropology

Recently there has been a profusion of books and articles concerned with ethnicity; exercises in global comparative anthropology also continue to make their appearance, although these seem less numerous than once they did. But the twain meet rarely: few anthropologists have explicitly addressed the relationship that should obtain between ethnicity and comparison.[1] At first sight the omission appears puzzling. Ethnic terms furnish the benchmarks for comparative anthropology – the appendices to any book in the *Human Relations Area Files* tradition of comparison contain long lists of ethnic labels which refer the presence or absence of particular cultural traits to human societies as they presently exist or once existed. The ethnic labels stand as guarantors of the relation between the characteristics isolated and people to whom the characteristics can be attributed. These names are tokens of reality which we assume can be redeemed. Take away the ethnic labels, and you also remove the link between the culture and its carriers. The rhetorical role of naming seems obvious in the case of the American exemplars of comparative method, but it must be true of all comparisons which employ ethnic tags. Comparison depends upon ethnic tags having a constant 'reality value'.

---

1. Galton's problem presupposes the identification of units in a region and so begs the question with which I am concerned.

Recent approaches to ethnicity, on the other hand, tell us that ethnic labelling is a complex process. Questions about the status and fixity of ethnic boundaries and the internal homogeneity of ethnic cultures cannot be answered *a priori*. In this light, the anthropologists' practical approach to comparing institutions (kinship systems, marriage rules, productive units or whatever) seems to rely upon a startling, even wilful, naïvety about the ethnic units compared. Explicit approaches to ethnicity and implicit uses of ethnicity as a benchmark for comparison hardly seem to belong to the same 'episteme'. Troubling questions arise: 'Does the viability of comparative anthropology rest upon the comparability of ethnic identities?'. Or, to put it differently: 'If there is not a unitary ethnic phenomenon, how are units for comparison to be isolated?' To respond to these questions it is necessary to recall some elements of the career that ethnicity has enjoyed in anthropology and to draw attention to three related assumptions which inform much contemporary anthropology. I regard all three with deep suspicion.

1. The 'ethnic phenomenon' describes a relatively distinct and universal circumstance which can be abstracted from the welter of appearances for comparative purposes.
2. Ethnicity also furnishes the basis for isolating units to be compared in other terms.
3. Ethnicity has subsumed a collection of earlier distinctions which had different labels (race, tribe, culture, nation etc.). For a variety of reasons this is a good thing.

I shall discuss these assumptions in the abstract, then in relation to a specific (ethnically-defined) ethnographic context and, finally, with respect to African ethnicities in general. I begin with the existence of an 'ethnic phenomenon' (van den Berghe 1981).

Why ethnicity is difficult to define

To start with the obvious – ethnic terms are elements in the practical philosophy and sociology of the peoples studied by anthropologists. Anthropologists press such distinctions into comparative service at second hand; like Lévi-Strauss's mythical *bricoleur,* they find themselves doomed to construct from the debris of other people's previous creations. Thus, a practical difference may be invoked in a context which calls for objective collation and comparison – a task for which it was never designed. Long before current preoccupations with *la différence*, Georg Simmel had neatly summed up the issue:

> It is above all the practical significance of men for one another that is determined by both the similarities and differences among them. Similarity, as fact or tendency, is no less important than difference. In the most varied forms, both are the great principles of all external and internal development. In fact, the cultural history of mankind can be conceived as the history of the struggles and conciliatory attempts between the two. (Simmel 1950: 30)

When anthropologists appropriate indigenous terms for the business of comparison, they implicitly alter the practical significance of those terms. This is to ignore what I shall call Nietzsche's pocket problem: 'As if every word were not a pocket into which now this, now that, now several things at once have been put!' (Nietzsche 1977: 153).

Precisely because ethnic terms serve and inform practical significances, which are liable to change, they share with Nietzsche's pocket the characteristic of sometimes containing this, sometimes that, and sometimes several things at once. Contents tend to reflect the habits of the user, subject only to the broad constraint of the design of the pocket. Like pockets, ethnic terms have complex histories of use.

Such complex use histories mean that ethnicity shares with a kindred concept, nationalism, the property of being virtually impossible to define in a way that is not either ambiguous or tautologous (Seton-Watson 1977: 5; Anderson 1983: 9). Nonetheless, anthropologists appear to experience little difficulty in deciding that certain types of distinction constitute ethnic discriminations. Perhaps here, as elsewhere, we may suppose that anthropologists implicitly draw on a polythetically constructed category. The clustering of a goodly number of the characteristics we hold typical of the set labelled ethnicity suffices for us to recognize another member of the set (Needham 1975; Southwold 1978). Most of the generalizations we are able to make about ethnicity might be properties of a polythetic definition we implicitly use. The polythetic definition would be something like this:

> Ethnic categories are broad classifications of people; they are frequently mapped according to a series of binary discriminations which oppose an 'us' to a 'them' (R. Cohen 1978).

> Although ethnic discriminations appeal to shared characteristics of the inclusive category, we have no way in advance of the facts, to specify what these characteristics will be in particular cases. (Experience of comparative cases leads us to anticipate

that language, common history, descent, race, or some aspects of culture or religion will be used to 'naturalize' the commonality of the inclusive category (Isajiw 1974).)

The characteristics of the exclusive categories are also stereotyped, frequently in a pejorative manner. In extreme cases, we find the demonization or animalization of out-categories (Kuper 1977). In less extreme cases, we may find that the social and cultural habits, sexual morals and so forth of exclusive categories have been found wanting under the lens of the inclusive category's perception of its own life habits. Ethnic stereotypes are usually based in the self-regard of the classifiers.

However, the sum of these characteristics is not sufficient to account for our ability to discriminate a class of ethnic distinctions; most of the criteria could apply equally to race, class, or gender classifications. Implicitly, our definition must contain a clause which removes from the ethnic set any types of distinction which can be attributed to other sets. Ethnicity may be a residual polythetic category. But even if this is dismissed as fanciful, ethnicity is clearly not amenable to essential definition. We could also look at the arbitrariness of ethnicity from the perspective of the broader contexts in which terms of distinction are employed. Ethnic discriminations are elements of more general classifications which identify relations of similarity and difference within social universes. As such they are always 'adjacent' to other elements of these classifications which we choose to treat as non-ethnic. Ethnic idioms draw sustenance from and plagiarize these other idioms (all our neighbours are witches; our neighbours are effeminate …), while themselves serving as metaphors for internal classification (witches are like our neighbours rather than ourselves; women are strangers amongst us …). Both in practice and in principle, the cut-off point for the application of the term ethnic to bodies of social classification can be decided only on the merits of individual cases and in the light of the proclivities of particular analyses. Somehow, the ethnic has to be wrenched from its adjacent idioms if it is to label a people and a potential comparative instance.

Despite, or perhaps because of, its inchoate senses, ethnicity has become a vogue term.

How ethnicity just grew and grew
Once there was a large vocabulary to describe types of differences (of race, of language, of nation [in its old sense][2] and so on). These

---

2. The history of the term is reviewed by Kedourie who writes that, '*Natio* in ordinary

categories were often ill-defined and sometimes pejorative, but they did preserve the important, and I think justifiable, sense that not all of these differences were of the same type. Since ethnicity gobbled up these distinctions and regurgitated them as variants of a single type of 'ethnic' difference, it seems that many notes on the scale of difference have become muted if not lost. The contemporary coherence of the ethnic phenomenon in anthropology stems from the rejection of earlier distinctions and, in particular, the term 'tribe'. 'Tribe' used to connote a particular type of ethnicity characteristic of the people whom anthropologists traditionally studied and of a dim and distant period in their own national histories. It has virtually disappeared from professional usage under a barrage of criticisms, at the same time as 'tribalism' has become a politically loaded term purporting to describe and explain the chronic dissensus supposed to exist in many new states. The developments are not independent, and anthropologists have been justified in distancing themselves from appearing to endorse a popular prejudice. Nonetheless, I shall argue that acceptance of some of the reasons anthropologists have given for abandoning the term 'tribe' does not necessarily imply endorsement of a universal ethnic phenomenon. I shall review anthropological discontent with 'tribe' under four headings.

The nominal objection

One of the arguments of a series of important papers which Aidan Southall wrote on African ethnicity during the 1970s was that many of the terms which found their way into the literature as tribal epithets were not genuine ethnic terms (Southall 1970, 1976; for reception of the point see for example Young 1976). Some of these terms were bestowed by neighbours or by colonial authorities; others designated language groups without ethnic salience; others simply meant something like 'the people'. In the broadest sense, this objection is empirical. Ethnographic techniques have failed to represent indigenous societies by their own

---

speech originally meant a group of men belonging together by similarity of birth, larger than a family, but smaller than a clan or people. Thus, one spoke of the *Populus Romanus* and not of the *natio romanorum* (1960: 13).

The term has a further complex history of use before its emergence in modern guise around the beginning of the nineteenth century. The sense of race also appears to crystallize at this period, so we might be able to argue that a set of discriminations in terms of birth concurrently assumed something like their contemporary pattern.

ethnic terms; although it could also be argued that the abusive usages of neighbours, or the misunderstandings of colonial authorities, become instrumental terms in their own right and equally subject to analysis. Southall, but not all those who repeated his criticism, recognized this.

The reificatory objection

A second charge against 'tribe' was part of the more general attempt anthropologists made to recognize and expunge the unacceptable elements of their structural-functional heritage. Earlier anthropologists, so the argument goes, had naïvely supposed a concordance of boundary phenomena, and so implicitly introduced the coincidence of tribal identity, culture, social and political organization. The reified tribal units could be directly compared with other units isolated in the same way. Charitable observers noted that influences ran the other way also, and the current understanding of comparison had probably led to the reification of tribes (Cohen and Middleton 1971: 4-5). Writers like Fortes (1945) and Nadel (1935) had paid explicit attention to the non-coincidence of boundary phenomena in classic structural-functional works, and Leach's influential critique of tribal reifications was published by 1954. However, in 1978 Ronald Cohen was able to see the replacement of tribe by ethnicity as indicative of a paradigm shift. If the reification of tribes had resulted from the older understandings of comparison it remained unclear how comparison was to take place under the new ethnic paradigm. As well as to the comparative method, the blind spot in structural-functional analyses could also be attributed to the neglect of history, which would have revealed changing tribal terms and referents, to the tendency of colonial administrative methods to create tribes in the process of administering them and, perhaps, also to an implicit export of some of the tacit assumptions underlying European notions of nationality. Like the nominal objection, the reificatory objection supposes a failure of ethnographic technique. Once identified, such a failure is remediable. It has no bearing on the existence of a universal ethnic phenomenon.

The derogatory objection

A further set of objections is directly critical of 'tribe' as a term which is held to be imbued with derogatory and evolutionary implications.

Glazer and Moynihan, in the preface to a collection of essays that was itself a symbolic landmark in the legitimation of ethnic rights, attribute the first use of the term to David Riesman in 1953 (Glazer and Moynihan 1975: 1). The 'ethnic revival' describes a process by which more and more categories of people have been persuaded to see ethnic identity as an argument about which to mobilize claims to specific types of entitlement (A. Smith 1981, 1983). Anthropologists found themselves compromised as the proponents of a distinction within what was generally supposed, especially in the nationalists' and ethnic revivalists' own rhetoric of 'primordial sentiment', to be a universal phenomenon. Ethnicity could be construed as an element of 'personhood', and ethnic groups could appear as the natural carriers of rights (see, for instance, *'les droits des ethnies'* in Breton 1981: 122-4). It seemed as if everyone had ethnic groups unless they were studied by anthropologists, in which case they had tribes. Since no-one was willing to say what distinguished an ethnic group, or strictly ethnic category, from a tribe (other than the dubious privilege of attracting the attention of an anthropologist rather than a political scientist or sociologist) it seemed right that the distinction be dropped and everyone admitted to a world order of ethnic categories. 'Tribe' appeared as another of the devices which, Fabian has more recently claimed, tend to deny coevalness in time between societies (Fabian 1983). In a surprisingly short time, ethnicity cornered the market in forms of social distinction that were argued from a backward glance.

Apart from a populist use associated with anthropology via the exotic, 'tribe' also suffered from implication in more academic theories of evolution. In terms of a broad theory of evolution, tribes were supposed to intervene between bands and states. Conceived residually in this fashion (more than a band, less than a state), the category of tribe necessarily lacked coherence (Godelier 1977). The tribal stage may have encompassed more organizational forms than the rest put together, and it became difficult to understand how such an assortment could constitute a step on the way anywhere.

'Tribe' may be compromised irrevocably as a term both inside and outside anthropology, but this is not tantamount to an argument that there are no distinctions to be drawn between modern and pre-modern ethnicity, only that 'tribe' cannot draw these distinctions with appropriate connotations.

The situational objection

A fourth set of objections relates closely to the charge of reification levelled against writers in the structural-functional tradition described above. Analyses by members of what we now recognize as the Manchester School, to a large extent in the Copper-belt and southern Africa, stressed the situational character of ethnicity.[3] According to this view, ethnic identity is a claim negotiated in the course of events that occur in determinate settings. The settings, the types of identity to which a claim is made, the referents of the ethnic terms, the symbols representative of ethnic identity and the contribution which these make to the construction of personal identities, are all subject to variation. The thrust of the Manchester critique is against the essentialist reading of tribal entities and towards the circumstances in which claims to a category membership can be envisaged as a useful, pointed, persuasive and coherent argument about something. This train of thought can be pursued more or less far. It would be possible to argue that ethnicity has no existence other than in the rhetorical claims made upon it during events; Manchester writers, on my reading of them, stop short of this conclusion and prefer to look upon ethnicity as situational to a degree rather than absolutely. Most typically, the situations have been defined by polarities of rural and urban location, often in a context of labour migration.

The realization that ethnicity is 'situational' cogently supplements the reification objection described above, but it is mute about the possibility of difference between types of ethnicity.

Subjective and objective ethnicity

Anthropologists drew two main conclusions from objections made to the use of the term 'tribe'. First, that the term 'tribe' and category of societies it was supposed to designate were both indefensible, and that tribal discriminations should be shifted into an undifferentiated class of ethnicity. Second, they decided that the debate had been dealing with two senses of ethnicity which needed to be distinguished: these came to be labelled subjective and objective ethnicity. Subjective ethnicity was

3. I have in mind the early classics on situational analysis by Gluckman (1940) and Mitchell (1956). The Manchester tradition is maintained in later works such as Abner Cohen (1969, 1981) and Epstein (1978). For a review of the work of the school in Africa, see Werbner (1984).

'subjective' because it was defined in terms of meanings and intentions attributed to social actors by anthropologists. Objective definitions of ethnicity, on the other hand, were solely to be defined in terms of the agency of analysts, consisting of sober judgements about the distribution of features of culture, language and dialect, historical processes, institutionalized forms of organization and so forth. Objective analyses might accord with subjective judgements, which would thereby be validated, or they might alternatively denounce subjective judgements, or propose ethnic distinctions which were subjectively unrecognized.[4] Since ethnic discriminations were held to constitute a universal phenomenon, it followed that the subjective/objective distinction could be used globally and that comparisons could be joined on the basis of the distinction. It was then open to different commentators to declare themselves either as purists or as being in favour of varied mixes of the subjective and objective approaches.[5] I shall argue that this whole train of reasoning is flawed and, worse, that its conclusions are ideological.

The objections made to earlier uses of the term 'tribe' certainly told against a western tradition of representation of other peoples crucially predicated upon key associations of tribalism, in particular atemporality, atavism and isolation. This tradition was, and continues to be, a legitimate target. But, and this also is typical of criticisms of representative styles, the critique was hijacked by interests which found any representation of difference suspect.[6] Earlier anthropologists may often have reified tribes, ignored the situational nature of ethnic loyalties, used names

4. See, for instance, van den Berghe's attempt to adjudicate genuine ethnicity in the case of American Blacks, and genuine nationhood in the case of new nations (1981). I prefer to align with Gellner, who sees the attempt to withhold national status from new states as a naturalization of the nationhood of old states (1983).

5. Ardener (1974) and Ronald Cohen (1978), who form the distinction with particular clarity, are basically subjectivists; proponents of the *Human Relations Area Files* style of comparison are necessarily objectivists (e.g. Naroll 1964, 1970). Barth, as Okamura (1981: 459) has observed, is inconsistent. In theory, Barth is a subjectivist; his practice is objectivist (Barth 1969a and b). Van den Berghe holds ethnicity to be subjective and objective (1981). The aims of theories of pluralism, which lie outside the scope of this paper, mean they tend to objectivism (e.g. M. G. Smith 1971).

6. M. G. Smith has voiced objections to the assimilation of racial difference to a form of ethnic difference (1982). In a related vein, James Clifford, in a largely sympathetic review of Edward Said's *Orientalism,* points to the difficulties which the representation of difference poses to analyses sensitive to the political implications of admitting difference at all (1980).

other than those used self-referentially by the people about whom they wrote, and some of them may have subscribed to evolutionary presuppositions, explicitly or implicitly, but the acceptance of these points singly or together does not logically imply the existence of a universal ethnic phenomenon. Without such a phenomenon, it is not possible to argue that the subjective/objective distinction can be applied in all cases. To this extent the propositions are interrelated. But I shall argue that, anyway, the propositions are flawed both individually and collectively:

1. The subjective/objective distinction cannot be maintained on the grounds proposed.
2. Not all distinctions with 'ethnic intention' have the same significance and, therefore, there is no universal ethnic phenomenon.
3. The application of a concept of universal ethnicity is ahistorical and so obfuscates the course of historical change.

I call the sum of these errors ideological, rather than simply wrong, because it has the effect of distorting our perceptions by including the pernicious and non-pernicious in a single category. Even if the logic were unassailable (which it is not), the result would not assist us to act in terms consistent with common humanity. By creating a universal ethnic phenomenon we falsely naturalize ethnicity and may even put ourselves in the absurd position of seeking a literally natural solution to this falsely naturalized entity (van den Berghe 1981). Here, I would want to make a distinction between objectifying the common position of a group of people and reifying or naturalizing that common position. However, I think my argument about the error of some implications of the conventional anthropological approach to ethnicity might find support even where my opinion about the ideological nature of this error would not.

To start with the subjectivist position: this position seems to have much in its favour. Since ethnic boundaries do not necessarily coincide with cultural distributions, and since these boundaries are situational, when looked at in contemporary terms, and unstable, if looked at historically, then it follows that it is counterproductive for anthropologists to try to legislate regarding their locations. Ethnic boundaries are between whoever people think they are between. I have no quibble with this, but to call the phenomenon subjective is suspect. Ethnic ideas are, presumably, no easier to attribute than any other kinds of ideas, and conventional anthropological caution warns that it is not possible to move from what people may 'do' or 'say' to what they 'think' without an interpretative leap. Quite how this is to be made continues to be contested. Because 'subjective' ethnicity is attributed to social actors on the basis of our theories about their speech and activity, I would prefer to relabel it 'performative ethnicity', recognizing that it is deduced from a performative basis. But 'objective' ethnicity is also deduced from performative evidence. The difference between the two concepts lies not in the type of evidence upon which they draw, but in the assumption that the status of an actor's conceptual category can be attributed to 'subjective' ethnicity. However, such a reattribution of concepts would have to be justified and faces a significant hurdle.

People whom anthropologists study do not necessarily distinguish a category of differences akin to our ethnic differences. When we attribute 'ethnic ideas' to subjects we do more than simply translate, we also attribute a technique of social distinction, and one that we have only managed to define in our own culture as a polythetically constructed residual class (and then by dint of charitable interpretation). To argue that subjective ethnicity is universal is covertly to globalize the category of ethnicity, and I am not aware of the research base which permits us to do this. Our own societies did not discover the general form of a universal difference, rather they invented this form of difference. Once ethnicity was objectified and given autonomy as a form, to borrow terms from Simmel in translation (Simmel 1980), actors were able to pursue ethnic goals or adopt ethnic stratagems. Such goals and stratagems are a part of what ethnicity now means as a practical relationship of similarity and difference. But the presupposition of a universal class of ethnic difference attributes the same potential for action to those who do not read their differences in terms of ethnicity. This error is only compounded by calling the upshot 'subjective ethnicity'.

Nationalism and the autonomization of ethnicity

The great, but valid, paradox is this: nations can be defined only in terms of the age of nationalism, rather than, as you might expect, the other way around. (Gellner 1983: 55)

It is always possible to argue developmental (archaeological) views of history against disjunctive (epistemological) views. After all, the identification of change takes place from an interested point of view. My interest here is to extend Gellner's view of nationalism to ethnicity in general and to argue that the growth of nationalism, the 'ethnic revival' and the acceptance of the national state as an international norm, have created forms of national and sub-national ethnicity differing significantly from the styles of distinction current in earlier periods.

Contemporary nationalism is generally held to be the legacy of the Enlightenment and the European 'Age of Revolution' abetted by the development of industrial society (Hobsbawm 1962: chapter 7). The diffusion of nationalist sentiments in European societies has been related to the development of literacy and the circulation of ideas through print in several ways: through the creation of a common literate culture, the wider dissemination of ideas and the development of the capacity to imagine identity in terms of a community larger than that of the immediate circle of fellows (Gellner 1983; Anderson 1983). Imperialism and colonialism were responsible for delineating Third World states and encouraged nationalist sentiment within them, both by intention and despite it. Decolonization, often attended by struggles for a 'national' liberation, tended to encourage the growth of these sentiments, and state systems of education, national armies and bureaucracies have continued this process as much through their manifest purposes as by offering advancement to new elites through state-sponsored channels. Internal mechanisms have been consistently reinforced by the exigencies of international and regional realpolitik, as well as by the presupposition of the national state as an international norm (polycentric nationalism in A. Smith's 1971 terms). It is from this political, economic and cultural background that the 'ethnic revival' derives its sense of unity. The failure of nationhood to be realized and the rhetoric of more successful nationalists equally draw upon and endorse the idea that ethnic identity furnishes an argument for rights which the ideal of nationhood guarantees: of which equal rights, cultural autonomy, personal dignity and political self-determination are felt to be amongst the more important (Kedourie 1960).

I have emphasised the political conditions under which ethnicity crystallized as an autonomous form, and most especially the role of the State in this; some other writers have given prominence to the economic conditions associated with the spread of capitalist organization of production and marketing (van Binsbergen 1985; Ranger 1982). The difference may result from regional focus, since my immediate problems have come from an economically underdeveloped area of West Africa, whereas emphasis upon economic factors occurs in analyses of southern

Africa. (However, others have seen limitations in Marxist approaches to nationalism in Europe: Nairn 1977: chapter 9; Anderson 1983.) In either case, the emergence of modern ethnicity seems to occur with other changes of perspective; the past has to be read as history, and to it must be attributed the force of an argument with respect to the evaluation of present conditions and the possibility and desirability of changing them. Nationalisms may be construed as 'old' by association with idealized notions of tradition and the collective destinies of 'peoples' and their culture presented as actors on a historical stage. Alternatively, 'newer' nationalisms may be construed as projects the inception of which is to be invoked in events more immediate than 'primordial' (a common heritage of oppression or struggle for liberation). The rhetoric of contemporary nationalism and ethnicity is inherently limited in its dependence upon a stream of exclusive first person plural possessives. It has to precipitate a new high age of the 'invention of tradition' (Ranger 1983). As the statuses of nations are defined in relation to a world order of United Nations, so are the saliences of ethnic groups homologized with reference to the State. National states exhaustively and exclusively partition the world, and there is an expectation that ethnic groups should be capable of doing the same in a national territory.[7]

Pre-colonial notions of distinction were rarely party to the same kinds of argument. Their practical significances and adjacencies were defined differently. We read ethnic intention into them with the benefit of hindsight, but in themselves these distinctions were not part of a unitary ethnic phenomenon. By ignoring the essentially local conditions of emergence and persistence of pre-colonial idioms of difference, we manage to fit them into a crudely tailored Nietzschean ethnic pocket. But with the help of an example, I want to show that the pocket in which they properly belong is part of a garment of an altogether different cut.

Chamba ethnogenesis

Today the name Chamba is used in self-identification by perhaps a quarter of a million people living in Nigeria and Cameroon. The term presupposes for its users and listeners an entity on a logical, if not

---

7. For an instructive attempt to establish precise mapped boundaries for Nigerian ethnic groups (a national version of the international division of territories), see Gandonu (1978).

numerical, par with Yoruba, Ibo, Bamileke or Fulani: a recognized identity within one of two West African republics. Used of relations outside the Chamba people, but inside Nigeria or Cameroon, it is scarcely subject to situational variation. Individuals belong to a people, to a state or region very weakly, and then to a nation. Matters were not always so clearcut, and Chamba was not traditionally a term of practical salience. Several writers have demonstrated how, in different parts of Africa, new ethnic terms and identities emerged during the colonial period and have persisted into the present (for example, Lancaster 1974). Like most such terms, Chamba has a historical genealogy but, in the senses in which it is currently employed, it also is a recent invention. Presently, it refers to people whose cultures, traditional political institutions, dialects and even languages varied widely. It is worth reiterating that current ethnic identities often emerged from the colonial process, but I pursue the argument further. I think that the ethnic modern term Chamba refers to an isolable type of difference which was not distinguished in a pre-colonial context.

Limitation of space forces me to supply background in very broad strokes (for detail see Fardon 1983; 1988a). Most Chamba live in an area of almost exclusive Chamba settlement which straddles the Nigeria/ Cameroon border. By far the larger part of this area is in Nigeria. In the west, these Chamba speak a language which has come to be known as Chamba Daka, in the east, Chamba speak Chamba Leko (Meek 1931). Recent linguistic research suggests that the two languages may not belong to the same class (Bennett 1983). The, apparently correct, implication to be drawn is that the central Chamba were formed by the fusion of speakers of the two languages. Other Chamba live to the south and southwest of the main area of settlement, below the River Benue in Nigeria and in the Bamenda Grassfields of Northwest Cameroon. Chamba presence was introduced to these areas by mounted raiders during the nineteenth century. Where a Chamba language has been preserved amongst these people this has been the easterly, Chamba Leko speech. On the face of it, we have evidence for a pre-nineteenth-century convergence, followed by nineteenth-century migrations, which together account for the present distribution of a recognized Chamba ethnic identity. Chamba oral traditions tend to support such a view. The intermingling of Leko and Daka speakers is accounted for by the migration of a Daka-speaking chiefly family into a Leko area, where they founded a chiefdom (Yeli) and adopted Leko speech before becoming the source of other western chiefdoms. The impact of Leko upon Daka was reinforced during the early part of the nineteenth century when the Fulani *jihad* waged in Adamawa forced the easterly Leko speakers to abandon their homelands: taking refuge in the hills, joining the Daka speakers to the west, or else taking part in one of the migrations which led to the implantation of a Chamba presence outside the older homelands. The upshot of these movements was the socially and culturally varied patchwork of peoples who now call themselves Chamba.

Chamba possess an extensive set of terms with which to discuss differences amongst themselves. Two of them have furnished the terms by which the languages are conventionally distinguished in published works:

1. Following Meek, I use Daka to refer to the language of the western central Chamba; this usage reflects that of the Leko speakers towards their western neighbours, speakers of the other Chamba language, whom they call Daka (or some variant or synonym of this term). However, this term is not accepted by members of the Daka-speaking chiefdoms which trace an origin from Yeli or some other Leko source. These groups call themselves Nnakenyare or, more simply, Sama (Chamba); they would claim the Daka to be the people living to their west. Daka, which is without etymology, connotes for them hill-dwelling backwardness, and they find the term insulting when applied to themselves. Only amongst the most westerly of the Chamba does Daka appear to be accepted as a term of self-identification.

2. The popular etymology of the term Leko derives it from a way of introducing a statement in that language: *mə baa le ko*, 'I say that'. If there are no indications to the contrary (home of) Daka and Leko can mean west and east. Like Daka, Leko can refer to speech, culture, or people; unlike Daka, Leko does not have pejorative implications, but synonyms, like *Jangbu* used of Leko by the Nnakenyare (and also by southerly Leko of northerly Leko) has similar connotations to the pejorative sense of Daka. Like the Nnakenyare, the Leko preferentially call themselves Chamba (Samba in Leko).

3. Nnakenyare is simply the normal greeting in Chamba Daka; its sense is close to the English 'How are you doing?'. The term is also used to refer to the dominant dialect of Chamba Daka

in the central Chamba homelands, to the culture of the people speaking this dialect, or to the people themselves. As a term of self-identification, Nnakenyare tends to be assimilated to Leko when contrasted to Daka. Leko and Nnakenyare may, in some contexts, consider themselves collectively Chamba in distinction to Daka.

4. Sama (in Chamba Daka) or Samba (in Chamba Leko) is the term from which Chamba appears to have derived, initially through corruption by Hausa sources, and then by adoption in different spellings into German, French and English. With the possible exception of the westernmost Daka and very minor groupings, all speakers of a Chamba language preferentially lay claim to a Sama or Samba identity. Only this identity is prestigious regardless of context, and a sense of 'More Chamba than thou' pervades the Chamba area. Each Chamba group interprets its own culture, language and history as uniquely and estimably Sama or Samba and classifies other communities according to their divergence from this self-centred ideal.

The four terms can be accounted for historically according to the series of migrations I mentioned above: a convergence, followed by the foundation of chiefdoms from Yeli and the establishment of the Nnakenyare identity mediating the Leko/Daka distinction, in turn followed by a second set of migrations. These historical circumstances furnished the broad parameters of present relativistic usages. Some early writers attempted to withhold the status of Chamba from one of the language groupings (usually the Daka, for example Frobenius 1913), but in order to reflect Chamba's own usage we have to recognize explicitly that Sama and Samba were members of a relativistic set which became more absolute only after the establishment of the colonial and then national state. But I want to say more than this, and pursuing the example a little further is a way of illustrating the point.

The four relativistic terms are also found in contexts from which we might choose to withhold the term ethnic. In accordance with standard Africanist practice, it is not difficult to distinguish levels of differentiation amongst Chamba which we can call patriclans and patriclan clusters. Chamba also recognized levels of distinction, but they assessed them in terms of the relativistic ethnic terms analysed above. Some of the patriclans had no names other than Leko (Jangbu), Daka (Daka-bu,

Doobu) or Chamba (Samabu). In terms of anthropological categories, the ethnic terms were sometimes also patriclan names and often ways of grouping or evaluating patriclans. If we look at the usages amongst the nineteenth-century migrants now settled outside Chambaland, the variety is yet wider. Amongst the Bali Chamba, Sama and Ndagana have become terms in a dualistic organization which essentially contrasts chiefly and priestly sections of the community (Chilver and Kaberry 1968; Fardon 1988). Terms like Kaga and Pere (which operate as 'ethnic' terms for Bata and Koutine in Chambaland) have become terms for patriclans of people considering themselves Chamba. In the Donga chiefdom of the Benue Chamba, Sama occurs as the name of the royal patriclan, and, in reports of a reconvergence between the Benue and Bali streams of migration in the 1830s around a place called Takum, we find the Benue Chamba referring to the Bali Chamba as Daka, although the groups spoke the same Chamba language (Garbosa c. 1956: 16-17; Fremantle 1922: 29-40). These usages, like the emergence of Chamba as a modern ethnic term, can be elucidated historically, although it would not be to the point to do so here. In terms of my present argument, the variations illustrate the extreme heterogeneity of purposes for which a few terms can be worked. The Chamba uses share little more than the assertion of a kind of difference which, in a given context, is irreducible. Had I space to expand the argument, I could show that other Chamba idioms of difference, especially those traced through women or more broadly through matriclanship, are interpreted to be far more biddable, and that within Chambaland the Chamba work with a notion of matriclanship which encompasses not only the maximal identity of Chamba but several of the Chamba's neighbours in a single grid of differences. This would be to labour the point that Chamba speech and practice suggest that they had no informing presupposition equivalent to our notion of ethnic difference. Rather, they recognized more and less irreducible forms of difference which were qualities of all types of relationship. Translating only one part of this complex usage as ethnic simply rends the fabric of Chamba notions of distinction in the interests of finding a chunk which fits the Nietzschean pocket of ethnicity. The plausibility of this translation effort is enhanced because the circumstances of incorporation into nation states, partly through the use of European languages, have caused the Chamba to do something similar themselves.

African ethnogenesis

My argument has been that the Chamba did not exist in the nineteenth century, not just because Chamba describes people whose origins, languages and cultures are diverse (the Chamba are an extreme rather than abnormal or atypical case in this sense), but because ethnic entities which have the form of the modern Chamba ethnicity are modern inventions. This invention did not take place in a vacuum – invention never does, and the term Chamba has historical precedents – but it resulted in a form different from those before it, one which was predicated upon the existence of unitary, essentially ethnic, boundaries. The effect of this invention was to curtail, perhaps even end, the processes of 'African ethnogenesis' which had been a pervasive feature of political change prior to the imposition of the nation state.

I am not alone in arguing along these lines; a number of writers on Africa have recently stressed similar points, although not all have been concerned with the dynamic implications of idioms of difference.[8] They agree that traditional terms of distinction seem to have applied pervasively to the differences between individuals, groups of people and localities; they were relatively reactive to events, where modern ethnicity is relatively unreactive to events which it tends to inform. In all probability, the way in which anthropologists define units of study for research, pursue their investigations in practice and write about their results tends to conspire in the reification of ethnic entities (van Binsbergen 1985). The exigencies of comparison work towards the same outcome: if the 'so and so' exist they must have a kinship system, political system and other institutions which can be compared with those of another 'so and

---

8. In a West African context, Brain and Kopytoff have emphasised the mutability of ethnic boundaries (both in Tardits 1981: Vol. II); the summaries of discussion amongst participants in that conference, as well as a recent review (Pontié 1984), point out the degree of ethnic diversity amongst the constituent clans of local Cameroonian communities. R. Cohen has related the emergent Pabir and Bura identities to growing political differentiation (1980); Tonkin has discussed the creation of Kroomen within a network of changing economic relations (1985). For East Africa, Southall has called attention to the shifting boundary between peoples we know as Nuer and Dinka (1976), and Ranger has drawn from many sources to document the manufacture of 'tribal' groups by colonial administration (1983: especially 247-52). Coquery-Vidrovitch has argued forcefully for a political contextualization of ethnicity and the recognition of a disjunction in the practical significances of ethnic difference, but at the cost of invoking a rather idealized notion of pre-colonial ethnic sentiment (1983: 57-8).

so'. But how would the logic of this position stand up to a recognition that identities crystallize transiently and in terms of different registers of difference? That only our reading in of ethnic intention to elements of these classifications taken out of context reinforces the starting assumption of a unitary ethnic phenomenon? Surely, comparative method on the grand scale draws implicitly upon the most naïve version of the invention and reification of ethnic units? Is the comparative method so vital to anthropology that gross reification can be accepted as a necessary cost? This would appear to be a dangerous argument. Should we limit comparisons to regions to draw upon a network of interrelated emergences of difference? This would seem to be a more controllable and nuanced procedure. Perhaps globalist aspirations to comparison can be preserved only by recognizing that comparison intrinsically defines units. Kinship systems, for instance, are contrasted analytically, and comparison between them implicates people to whose practices the analytic categories can be attributed. There is no necessity for the group of people implied to be an ethnic group, or for people to fall into the same groups for the purposes of different comparisons. On this argument it could be claimed that our comparisons only ever seemed to be based upon the contrasts between tribes, when they truly emerged in terms of analytic contrasts which were attributed to named units of people.[9]

The rejection of 'tribe' in 'favour' ethnicity seemed to be a liberal step which emphasised a subjective viewpoint and a situational grasp of context. But the gain was achieved at a cost. Reading ethnicity in textual terms diverted attention from its practical informing of activity, while the liberal generalizing of ethnicity was achieved on the fragile basis of assuming that differences can only be of a single type. Although many factors played their part, the major reason for these shortcomings may have been the failure sufficiently to take to heart the probability that, 'Europe's most enduring legacy to Africa is the nation state' (Mazrui and Tidy 1984: 373).

---

9. Naroll's development of his notion of culture-bearing unit appears to sever the ethnic knot by recognizing various criteria for the definition of units. But the results of the exercise tend to read as a justification for going on as before (Naroll 1970). Köbben's notion of a unit appropriate to the level of comparison may correspond to my contention that the definition of units is intrinsic to the analytic content of the comparison, but I am unclear how he would put the idea of appropriateness into practice (Köbben 1967, and especially 1970).

ACKNOWLEDGEMENTS

An early version of this paper was read at the University of Kent in autumn 1980 when I benefited from the comments of a seminar group led by Roy Ellen. Final revision of the version given to the St Andrews conference in December 1983 is indebted to participants' comments, notably Bob Barnes for a reference and Mark Hobart and David Parkin for points in the argument. I especially recall conversations with Barrie Sharpe when we were both writing up middle-belt materials a few years ago; his recent article is an important contribution to understanding the colonial manufacture of ethnicity. Marilyn Strathern kindly read and commented on the paper.

Research amongst different Chamba and neighbouring people was carried out in 1976-8, 1984, 1985 with financial assistance at various times from the Social Science Research Council, Economic and Social Research Council, Central Research Fund of the University of London, Hayter Fund of the University of St Andrews, and Carnegie Trust for the Universities of Scotland. I am also grateful for official affiliations and support in Cameroon and Nigeria.

Chapter 4

THE PERSON, ETHNICITY AND THE PROBLEM OF 'IDENTITY' IN WEST AFRICA

Argument

The similarities between people with common attributes of 'ethnic' and 'personal' identity can be recognized only once such attributes are conceded as essential features of the way 'people are made up'. When these features are anticipated to constitute 'human kinds', novel inductive arguments may arise (arguments unthinkable were such features not conceded). However, following Goodman,[1] similarity is never given; resemblance is institutionalized and enjoys a virtuous relationship with rules of induction that demonstrate how similarity becomes operative. As such rules are mute about the grounds for sameness, the success of induction merely demonstrates the workability of grounds for sameness – not how well found those grounds are – or, indeed, how they are found at all. 'Ethnic' and 'personal' identities are productive, allowing novel kinds of inductive argument to be made, thus confirming by their very productivity the well-found, or argument-rich, status of the categories. This is evidently circular. Instead, 'whenever we reach any general conclusion on the basis of evidence about its instances, we could by the same rules of inference, but with different preferences in classification, reach an opposite conclusion' (Hacking 1992: 181). In making new attributes of human kinds, as it were, speak to one another, a redefinition of the past is effected. Rather than pursuing these propositions abstractly, I want to explore two related instances that are, again to borrow Hacking's terms, 'lively and complex' (1992: 192).

---

1. See Douglas and Hull, 1992 for reprints of Goodman's 'Seven strictures on similarity' and 'The new riddle of induction', and especially the emendation of Goodman's argument to apply to 'human kinds' by Ian Hacking in that volume.

The first example involves a sketch of a pair of polarized 'conceptual clusters' (Bloch 1990) concerning interrelationships between person, ethnicity and identity in 'traditional' and 'modern' types of West African society. I argue that this contrast is attributable to the way in which social anthropological method has found novel human attributes problematic in West African societies. The second part of the chapter develops an example, largely derived from Sally Chilver's meticulous historical work on the chiefdom of Bali-Nyonga in the Northwest Province [now Region] of Cameroon, of the way in which novel human attributes have been handled in the societies there. I am not concerned here to argue the rightness or wrongness either of the categories themselves or of the arguments they make thinkable. My target is the discreteness, or incommensurability, of anthropological and 'local' models. I suggest instead that these models are historically connected in numerous ways, and that contrasts between them derive largely from what seems 'not to fit' in the two cases. As the boundedness of personal identity and 'collective belongings' (such as ethnicity and nation) were not novel to European and Euro-American anthropologists, they were struck by the degree to which the bounded entities failed to fit West African materials and interpreted this 'resistance' in terms of earlier (traditional) and complex states of affairs. West African accounts focus instead upon the work involved in attaining a modernity conceived in terms of bounded identities. It might seem that I am suggesting only that anthropologists tended to over-traditionalize the West African societies they studied. I believe that this argument has some truth, but that it involves claims more complex than its current status as conventional wisdom implies. The hinge between my two examples is supplied by a brief discussion of the idea of identity in which I note the slippage of that term's range of connotations from sameness to unique difference. I argue that it is this slippage (though not necessarily around the English-language term) that fundamentally connects my two examples. If this is so, no case can be made for an argument that would oppose, in simple-minded terms, the European imagination to African realities.

The 'traditional' West African model: a synthesis

I follow well-known sources in seeking a 'traditional' model in southerly West African societies, described in an 'ethnographic present' that precludes the influence of major world religions (both Islam and

Christianity). My use of 'traditional' is twofold: applying both to the pre-modern African situation which the models describe and to the 'traditional' status the model has achieved in West African ethnography. Relatively low population and high land availability; relatively invariant agricultural technology in terms of tools but not technique; political relationships made problematic by the scarcity of supporters; relationships between people differentiated by status categories; and a capacity for societies to be made anew at the frontier – these form a scenario[2] to which to relate the attributes of the person in West Africa. Each generalized feature is produced by contrast to a European, or modern, counter-instance which causes it to become discernible (as the use of 'relatively' suggests). Although the contrasts are diverse[3] their net effect is to produce an ideal-typical West African scenario at variance with both 'traditional' Europe and 'modern' West Africa.

If control over people, as this background scenario argues, was the foundation of West African political systems, how were these people spoken about? The main generalizations on this subject aver to a composite, unsynthesised nature of the person ('human being' might be a closer translation of most West African concepts). If we ask: in relation to what was the West African person composite as opposed to unitary (or unsynthesised as opposed to synthesised), the obvious answer is in relation to one particularly influential European idea of the person as unitary and internally consistent. The West African person was an internally organized composition, but each element of the composition was unlike any of the others and derived from a source initially external to the person. The elements could not be conflated with one another and, by virtue of the original externality of elements, the person embodied numerous relations of derivation. These derivations were both the antecedent condition of the individual's conception, formation, birth and development, and the intrinsic form taken by continuing relationships with those who shared or transmitted the same qualities. The widely reported instance of the donation of bodily substance by the mother,

2. This owes much to Goody (1971) (as developed by e.g. Terray 1972, Meillassoux 1981) and the related arguments of Kopytoff (1987). Counterexamples have been produced (e.g. Hopkins 1973; Law 1976, 1978), but the generalizations hold over a remarkably wide range of societies.
3. See Fardon and Furniss, 1994a for discussion of the tropes of 'dearth' and 'plenty', and Palmié (1995) for other instantiations of the idea of frontier.

by virtue of her retention of blood after conception and subsequent suckling of an infant with milk, was both the antecedent condition for individual corporeal existence and the continuing basis for recognizing identity, in terms of this component, with the mother, with her matri-siblings and, more distantly, with matrikin. The living individual was a cathexis where numerous connections were made, some transiently and others more permanently, in ways that might outlive the individual. The person was thus a field of tension between elements (Horton 1961). From the viewpoint of European conceptions of a unitary self, the West African person plausibly resembled the jural concept of the cor-poration (Strathern 1985). Formalized behaviours related the person to others in terms of the rights and obligations anticipated between par-ticular categories of people. Positions might be heritable: for instance, a son could succeed to features of his father's being (most evidently under systems of positional succession). Similar features are described throughout West Africa.

Françoise Héritier (1977) has presented what may be a limiting case of complexity in the Samo distinctions between nine elements of the person. Each element: blood, bone, shadow, etc. led diversely away from the individual and, correlatively, each element in the world of agencies (gods, other people, animals, etc.) led back to the person. The person was not simply an analogical model of the social and cosmological world but an instantiation or actualization of it. Regionally widespread features of this actualization include:

1. Parentage: a person has different relationships to each parent. Frequently, bodily relationship (often literal consanguinity or con-substantiality) is stressed in relation to maternity ('one mother', 'one womb', 'one blood', 'one breast suckled us' and such-like idi-oms are widely reported). Maternal kinship comes closest to what Europeans often mean by kinship, i.e. consanguinity. Paternity is envisaged as contrasting with maternity (sperm, bone, skull, name, incarnation, potential ancestrality, etc.). Quite *how* paternity and ma-ternity are defined matters less to the present argument than *that* they are defined differently.

2. The living and the dead: this distinction is not defined in quite the same way as in European systems of thought (a conclusion follow-ing the debate initiated by Kopytoff 1971). Elders and the dead converge, partly because the dead continue to play a role similar to

that of the elders. How this happens is quite variable: in particular, the degree of individual 'ancestrality' accorded the dead, either individually or collectively, varies with the conventions for tracing descent, and the significance attributed to doing so at all (McKnight 1967). However, the continuing influence, in some form, of individual or collective dead upon the living is typical of West Africa, as is some degree of identification between the dead and elders in particular, and between the dead and the living more generally.

3. Forces emanating from 'society' are typically counterposed to forces from the 'wild' (Horton 1983). This is not a singular distinction, but has complex interrelationships with other distinctions to which it can be likened with varying degrees of flexibility (Jackson 1989, chaps 5-7). However, there is typically a distinction between village and surrounding bush. Relative wildness is also a characteristic of forces which play upon the individual (in the form of spirits) and of elements internal to the composition of the person (sometimes associated with maternity, animality or both).

4. Gender polarities are complexly articulated with attributes of parentage, relationships between the living and the dead, and the contrast between village and bush. Components of the individual are gendered by association with their derivation. This means that men and women are both masculine and feminine in certain respects (Amadiume 1987b). Particular attention to the complex gendering of sexual subjects is marked at turning points of a sexual subject's gender career: defeminization for boys at initiation, correlative demasculinization for girls, and remasculinization for women at menopause are common. Particular gendered attributes, otherwise treated as non-dominant in sexual subjects, are foregrounded under particular circumstances: in relation to some rituals, offices, inheritance procedures and so on. This is feasible because the sexuality of subjects is treated apart from the gendering of their personal components; there is near-universal local opinion (whether presumptive or factual) that homosexuality was not thinkable in the types of society I am discussing. By contrast with, for instance, documented Melanesian examples (Strathern 1988), the sexuality of a person seems to follow unproblematically from human sexual dimorphism. However, gender discriminations, distinguishable here from sexuality, are highly complex, far from dimorphous, and

relate to the gendering of the component elements of the person. In contrast to Melanesia, the relationship between sexual partners was less important for the definition of the person than the relationships between generations involving parentage. Parentage was predominantly defined in terms of gender (elaborated symbolically) rather than sexuality (relatively unelaborated, but of no less concern for that). Elaborated parental relationships and sibling seniority – rather than conjugal relationships and egalitarian siblingship – make West African kinship systems appear hierarchical relative to Melanesian examples.

5. Some forms of personal anomaly were regularly explained by slippage of the normal relationships between categorizations: shape-changing, witchcraft, twins, breech births, anomalous dentition, fear of particular diseases (notably leprosy, smallpox, epilepsy and madness), returnee children who refused to remain among the living and so on.

Idioms of relationship, and possibilities for changing them, are prefigured by these suppositions about the person. Two frequently noted features of West African societies follow from this. The second, derivative, feature illuminates the first. The composite nature of the person allows the detachment and reallocation of certain personal elements: the best known feature of this is the partibility of rights in women which could be transferred between kin groups (e.g. the Bohannans' [1953] distinction between rights *in uxorem* and *in genetricem*). Different marriage regimes transferred different types of rights in women; for instance, rights to filiate children could be withheld and the mother treated as a male link in the continuation of agnatically defined descent (e.g. Amadiume 1987a, 1987b). The co-occurrence of different marriage regimes was almost a West African norm (e.g. Fardon on Tiv and middle-belt societies of similar type [1984/5] Chapter 1 in this volume; Muller on secondary and other marriage systems [1982]). The partibility of rights to be transferred was prefigured according to the definition of the components of the person (their detachability or permanence). Thus, the cumbersome terms patriliny and matriliny, or worse patriarchy and matriarchy, were led into paradox when attempting to track more subtle West African thinking on the subject (Amadiume 1987a). Does relatively high transference of rights in a woman indicate the strength of patriliny (relative to her husband's group) or its weakness (relative to her father's group)? As the nature of the operation of transference had been misconstrued, the question could not be resolved; it required acceptance of presuppositions about the unitary nature of the person. West Africans operated with a more flexible concept allowing greater complexity of personal allegiance.

The routine transference of rights in components of women's personhood was only one of a number of such operations: transference of people to settle blood debts, pawning, adoption and so forth. West African systems were notably inventive in these respects. The prevalence and general form of these institutions concern us here; local instances can often be interrelated with other features of the bricolaging of sociality by the application of transformational analysis at a regional level.

Kopytoff and Miers (1977) have noted, controversially, that West African slavery can be fitted into this series of rights and obligations vested in corporate, composite persons as an extreme of kinlessness – an extreme detachment from their usual moorings of aspects of full personhood. Significantly, where slaves were not commodities such detachment could be reversed by a process of reattaching components of the person over two to three generations. Kinlessness was a transitory, not a permanent condition; and it was a relative rather than absolute condition: most people were more or less securely moored to most sources of their personhood.

From what were components of personhood detached? This goes back to the relational idioms of personhood. The components of the person were related in different appropriate ways to the domains from which they derived. To each component of the person corresponded a network of socialities: matrikin to maternal derivation, patrikin to paternal derivation, relationships to singular and plural divinities to a 'divine' component, relationships to the wild to a wild, animal side and so forth. Very often, the closest kinship was defined in terms of maternal commonalities, and paternal commonalities were envisaged in terms of place. These qualities might bifurcate not just in terms of matrikin *versus* patrikin, but on a repeated internal basis: for instance in a 'patrilineal' system where special recognition was accorded to mutuality with a mother's patrikin. Patrilineal and matrilineal are potentially misrecognizing terms, since they fail to address the constant feature, the recognition accorded to complementary and different features of paternal and maternal parentage. These fields were complexly articulated with one another and with features of the dead, anthropomorphized agencies and so forth. At more abstract levels, human proclivities corresponded to relationships of sociality: humour to the relationships defined by privileged abuse, respect to those defined by degrees of avoidance or highly circumscribed behaviour.

What follows from this model of the person as a corporate personality, made up of juxtaposed elements, derived from outside the individual and instantiated in a particular human existence? First, I would suggest, a situational sensitivity to similarity and difference. In the African languages of which I have knowledge, similarity and difference between people are most commonly spoken about in terms of 'one' and 'different' – discussions of West African kinship in close translation suggest this to be a common feature ('we have one father and one mother', 'one father and different mothers', 'one mother but the father divides us', and so forth). It is as if identities and differences are established starkly, but only for very particular situations. Those who are completely 'one' in a particular context are different in another. It would be difficult to know how to clinch this impressionistic point but, if it is conceded momentarily, it could be argued that this relatively definite way of characterizing difference and identity might correlate with the diversity of personal components to which judgements of similarity and difference can be applied. Ally this to typical West African village settings (in which everyone seems to be related to everyone else in several ways), and to a diversity of situations (which call for the same people to do all sorts of different things with one another – what used, following Gluckman, to be called multiplex social relationships) and it may be reasonable to suppose that such complexity of sociality needs to be handled without undue recourse to the grey areas between identity and difference.

Identity between two people, therefore, would derive from a particular component of personhood that became relevant because of a certain situation in which (minimally) two people (or perhaps not only the living but also the dead, gods and animals) discovered an identity. Identity was called forth transiently in the course of activity. From this perspective certain things are not possible: difference and identity cannot be fixed apart from the situations under which criteria of identity are relevant. This may be a truism, but in the context of the composite and corporate design of the person I have been discussing, it means that the whole person is not subjected to identity claims by another. It appears that only twins are potentially identical in terms of their componential make-up, and it may be significant that twins are always differentiated in West African societies.

Several other features of reported West African sociality are reconcilable with an account of the person in composite terms. Seen processually, the composite-ness of the person invites particular kinds of attempts at human regulation of its internal relationships: by assembly, mutual adjustment and dispersal or reallocation. Numerous accounts seem to attest to attempts, often by means of 'ritual', to modify internal personal relationships and, especially, to deal with the dissolution of the corporate person by the inheritance, special emplacement (in ancestral reliquaries and shrines) or expulsion from the space of the living of differentiated components of the dead. The changing composition of the person is attested not only in periodic rituals of passage or of curing, but also in the externality of naming (by reference to times, places, group membership and so on) and in the multiplicity and changeability of personal names during a lifetime.

At this point, I conclude briefly before leaving my epitomization of a 'traditional' West African person, and the reports of sociality consistent with it, in order to ask: what was incompatible with this 'natural kind' of person? My summary and elaboration of West Africanist ethnography started from a material contrast between Europe and West Africa that suggested a crucial role for relationships between people unmediated by land; it continued deductively to examine the elaboration of this concern with relationships between people. Although the material contrast clearly involves conceiving Africa as some kind of contrasted counterpart to Europe, it would be difficult to reconcile the specific features of West African personhood as the merely negative products of European positive self-knowledge. This is not to say that features of West African personhood did not forcibly, and selectively, impress themselves upon researchers because they differed from what Europeans normally understood to be, say, slavery, conception or kinship. These features clearly challenged the observers' suppositions familiar from everyday or specialized anthropological parlance; therefore, they had to be described in vocabulary that expressed divergence from conventional expectations or by a modified descriptive lexicon. The consistency between the propositions I have synthesised is attributable neither to the unfettered operation of the European imagination nor to reported West African realities, but to a historical dialectic between the two that calls attention to itself by inviting the discovery and modification of the suppositions with which it starts out, and thereby changing the terms of European imagination and reported West African realities themselves. However, European ethnographers did consistently construe their counter-imaginings as evidence for a precedent state of affairs that was disappearing in the face of global religions, politics and economics – in short as a traditional West African condition. Furthermore, this precedent condition became the key focus of anthropological scholarship.

Identity, ethnicity and the person

I have been, very literally, using the term identity in a way which is presumably not what is usually meant by someone's identity – who they, or some defining other, think they are. That is part of my point. At least in Chamba, I cannot think of a term that translates with our sense of identity. However, there are numerous other terms, crucial to the style of construction I am calling 'modern', which also do not translate easily into Chamba nor, I imagine, into hundreds of other West African languages. Prominent among these are ethnicity and nation. These terms form a second 'conceptual cluster', definable in their current usage only in terms of one another. Their current prominence derives from situations in which their relationships may become mutually charged in an irreversible fashion. Ethnicities, it seems, can more readily be made than unmade under present circumstances. Chamba have been called into being by a set of circumstances such that, whatever the vagaries surrounding exact criteria of inclusion in Chamba-ness, it is difficult to envisage a near future in which this label will become a less salient category of identity.

Current ethnic identities were not called into being from nothing. Great, historically specific labour went into the outcome, and that outcome could have been different (some people could have been left out, others included; the ethnic crystallization might conceivably have occurred around a different term ...) Nonetheless, Chamba became the ethnic term (especially in Nigeria) and, once established, plenty of historical justification – that is to say antecedent usage – can be found for it. It could hardly be otherwise; a set of salient differences cannot plausibly be conjured from thin air, especially when they involve a collective construct (tribe or ethnicity) that by definition has historical moorings.

That there is a redefinition of history around this ethnic term, involving the elaboration of a collective memory, needs no amplification. No ethnic or national identity is impugned by noting that it arises historically and is represented as the culmination of a historical process – none is impugned because none is exceptional – notwithstanding that some got there sooner, some have made greater investment in the outcome, and some have gained more unchallenged purchase upon people's loyalties.

To return to identity. Its current usage is recent, although it is an old word apparently derived from Indo-Germanic pronominal bases I and DE (*Oxford Etymological Dictionary of the English Language*). Originally, identity meant simply sameness, the nominal form of *identitatis,* from the roots *id* and *dem* – a present state of enduring sameness (a sort of this-that-ness between things). In relation to the person, we may ask: the same as what? Presumably, the same as the person previously. For institutional purposes, individual identity is proved by an identity card, identity disc, fingerprints or voice patterns, social security number or whatever.

Personal identity involves an integration of memory which allows people to demonstrate that they are the continuation of a previously existing state of awareness. The philosophical controversy over relationships between memory and identity draws attention to the commotion always found around the weaker points of a way of world-making. Such unresolvable activity is manifest around cognate elements of the terms ethnicity, nation, and indeed race. A variant of the same problem is involved in each case: whether memory is evidence for the existence of an entity, or whether its existence is the precondition of its memory. The queries chase one another in circles: I am an individual by virtue of my memories; but only by having been an individual (of the sort my memories are supposed to demonstrate) can I lay claim to continuity of existence, which is the condition of these memories in fact being mine (see Warnock 1987). To the extent that ethnicity, tribe, nation and race are narrated in similarly bounded terms, the same conundrum must apply.

This movement in focus along the semantic range of the meaning of 'identity', from sameness to a unique difference, demonstrable by something being essentially the same only as itself at a previous moment, is symptomatic of the presuppositions shared by terms such as identity, ethnicity, tribe, nation and race. Stretching an analogy, we might say that the West African notion of the person – under the description offered here – is reminiscent of the identikit photograph, which allows the resemblance of a unique individual to be constructed from a set of parts which could be recombined to make up someone else. At least in English, one may ask whether the semantic history of identity has been motivated by its resemblance to other terms with connotations of uniqueness, ideation or boundedness, although these are of Greek derivation (idiom and idiosyncracy; idea; ideology). Whatever the case, a word that once stressed the 'very same' (as something else) has come to be synonymous with 'unique' (identical only to itself). A conundrum of defending bounded sameness over time comes to apply to personal identity, Chamba identity, or Nigerian identity – to which correspond modes of recollection of a past to which a present has become identical – at least under some privileged descriptions. I am not suggesting that this was a mode of recollection unknown in West Africa. I noted earlier how, under systems of positional succession, the present incumbent of an office becomes identical to his predecessor, so that, for instance, the foundational history of a chiefdom may be told by the present chief in the first person, albeit that the history refers to events a century earlier. Generally, however, the older sense of identity seems to fit the traditional West African notion of 'oneness' between personal elements better than the newer sense of identity as 'uniqueness'.

Modernity and identity

My typification of a modern style of identity is largely implicit in the foregoing. I shall treat modernity as the problem that results from the insertion of post-colonial states into a system of global internationality put in place after the Second World War. The experience of colonialism was the condition for this insertion, just as the supersession of the colonial powers was the condition for the international norm of the nation state to become globalized. The post-colonial state was bequeathed various devices of government from the colonial period, varying from very general techniques to highly specific institutions: maps, lists, censuses, judiciary and legislative arrangements, military and police forces, the commodification of land and so on. In relation to legal and economic systems of the state, the individual was called to respond in terms of an understanding of identity as something bounded and unique, especially in so far as it determined rights and, in practice more importantly, defined obligations.

The post-colonial West African state thus created a political space into which were interpellated subject citizens. Creating bounded nations of bounded personal identities simultaneously realised a third ideally bounded subject, the tribe or ethnic group, within this political space. Identity, ethnicity and nation crystallized as a cluster in West Africa, drawing on such similar presuppositions that the self-evidence of each was underlined by its analogy to the other two. Language difference, in particular, was politicized in this matrix because of the indissociable relationship it could seem to enjoy with the essences of personal identity, ethnicity and nationality.

Much has been and remains to be written about issues over which I am skimming rapidly. My present interest concerns the four basic entities involved in textual accounts of the movement from tradition to modernity; entities commonly 'structured like': an individual self, an ethnicity, a nation state and a global system. To each corresponds a position of privilege within types of account: (auto-)biographical, tribal historical, national historiographical and the various accounts of the broadest context of these three. Although the transition between tradition and modernity, and the problem of relating the entities structured as I have suggested, are very common features of the textualization of West African societies, quite how such accounts work in detail cannot be known in advance of the facts. Particular identities entrain specific problems of narrative to which solutions must be essayed.

Bali-Nyonga identity: whence Chamba-ness?

Bali-Nyonga is the most populous of five chiefdoms in the Bamenda Grassfields of the Northwest Province [now Region] of Cameroon which, by dint of their assertion that their founders were of Chamba origin, have come to be known as Bali-Chamba chiefdoms.[4] The mounted

---

4. Between 1976 and 1990 I spent roughly three years researching among Chamba, but my experience of Bamenda occupied only ten weeks – in 1984, during research funded by the Economic and Social Research Council. Even then, I was not based in Bali-Nyonga, and I do not have a command of Chamba Leko (the minority language of Chambaland). While passing acquaintance with the local scene in Bamenda, as well as a more thorough-going immersion in the history and culture of Chambaland, have been helpful to writing this paper, my discussion is historiographic: reliant upon previous writings and devoid of further ethnographic specification. My argument would be greatly enhanced were I able to go beyond the texts at my disposal, for instance to know how written opinions relate to local oral debates. As in every previous foray into Bali-Chamba affairs, I am indebted to Sally Chilver for her advice, encouragement and guidance both personally and through her publications.

Bali-Chamba raiders reached the Grassfields towards the end of the first quarter of the nineteenth century as part of a diaspora of Chamba-Leko (the eastern Chamba language) speakers from their homelands around the current Nigeria-Cameroon border, some five hundred kilometres to the north (Fardon 1988a). Events in Chambaland prior to the final exodus of the raiders have been the subject of competing interpretations, encouraged by the scant evidence available. The definitive departure of most Chamba raiders coincided with intensification of Fulani *jihad* in Adamawa (the eastern extension of the Sokoto Caliphate) involving the establishment of Fulani lamidates within and around Chambaland, one of which took the name Tchamba. The ancestors of the Bali-Chamba were not the only raiders active in the early nineteenth century. Those whom we know to have been operating in Chambaland and in the plains below the River Benue entertained fluctuating and tactical relationships of alliance with the Fulani jihadists. One of these Benue Chamba chiefdoms, Donga, briefly concerns us later. It is likely that the future Bali-Chamba, who are recalled as being united under a leader called Gawolbe, also entertained relationships of periodic cooperation with the Fulani, although their expansion took them ahead, and eventually beyond the range, of Fulani state-building prior to the imposition of colonial rule. In very general terms, local freebooters, like Chamba and their allies, were probably useful to competing Fulani factions during the early nineteenth century when the impact of *jihad* was first felt. However, as raiding consolidated into a movement of conquest, the support of erstwhile allies became dispensable, and many of them came under pressure themselves to submit to Fulani overlordship. By the time colonization of Chambaland occurred, the interests of Chamba and Fulani as categories (though not necessarily as individuals) were defined by antipathy – and in general terms have so remained.

Grassfields traditions recall two waves of raids by Chamba and their allies. These intrusions were eventually halted at a battle near Bafu Fundong, called Kolm (in variant spellings). The defeated Chamba, whose hero leader Gawolbe was killed, then split into several factions. The faction that eventually founded Bali-Nyonga seems to have contained a minority of the core Chamba and their close allies recruited before the sweep across the Grassfields. Apparently, the succession was contested, and the ancestors of Bali-Nyonga may have set off under a female leader to settle on the borders of Bamum. Here they incorporated a large group of people called Bati, whose numerical preponderance may have caused the group to abandon the Chamba Leko language in favour of a Bantoid language called Mungakka, related to the language of Bamum. Settling near its present site, Bali-Nyonga engaged in a number of – what are now seen as – internecine wars during the 1860s with another of the Chamba states, Bali-Kumbat which (like three other smaller kingdoms) retained Chamba Leko as its language. By force of arms, a position of influence was established in the Grassfields by Bali-Nyonga before it became the focus of German interest after 1889 with the arrival of the German explorer Eugen Zintgraff. Bali-Nyonga briefly became the brokers of German interests in the Grassfields, and Mungakka expanded in importance.

I want to register some problems that were to face later historians of Bali-Nyonga by virtue of events prior to the end of German colonialism, as well as some telling anachronisms, in my brief account. The chiefdom of Bali-Nyonga was to take a leading role in the definition of Chamba-ness in the Grassfields, yet most Bali-Nyonga did not speak a Chamba language, although Chamba Leko survived as a court language. The composition of the chiefdom had become extremely mixed, so that a minority could argue descent either from Chamba or from their adherents picked up outside the Grassfields. In terms of language, descent, culture and organization, Bali-Nyonga was a Grassfields chiefdom and might well have established an historical account of itself as a Grassfields successor state, albeit one that had frequently been the scourge of its neighbours. However, this did not happen. Even precolonially, the leaders of Bali-Nyonga seem to have been concerned to retain their 'Chamba' status, for instance by petitioning help from other Bali to reconstitute 'Chamba' cults.

Why then did they make such efforts? Moreover, and here is the anachronism: what identity were they claiming when they stressed their northern, immigrant 'origins'? Despite the terms I have used above, it clearly could not have been a Chamba identity in any simple sense. Although the origins of the term Chamba are not beyond dispute, we do know that 'Chamba' is not a Chamba term. Neither Chamba language has a {ch}; the cognates of Chamba are *Sama* or *Samba*. Since Chamba is not of Fulani origin either (their term for Chamba retains an initial {s}), it seems most likely to have been a Hausa traders' term, adopted and textualized by Europeans via their translators. Given the complexities of interpretation – often via intermediary languages – and given also that we have to work from published reminiscences with unknown relationships to any utterances which they purport to record, quite what particular Bali were saying to particular Germans is difficult to guess. In any case, the term Chamba is notably *not* prominent in early German sources.

What Bali were calling *one another* around the turn of the last century is yet more difficult to guess. Given their rather frantic history of relocation, splitting, recruitment and dispute during the nineteenth century, it is readily understandable that collectivizing terms would be in a fluid state. *Ba'ni* (singular *Ya'ni*) might refer to all the inhabitants of the five Bali states, or it might distinguish the longer-term adherents of these polities and their predecessors.[5] *Ndagan* could be used to designate elements whose origins lay outside the Grassfields; this term is probably cognate with Daka (a term which contrasts situationally with *Sama* in Chambaland). Nowadays, *Ndagan* is sometimes taken to be synonymous with Chamba; however, the remaining clan names in Bali-Nyonga suggest that *Ndagan* included peoples who, were they in the north, would now belong to ethnic groups distinct from Chamba (e.g. Pere, Bata). *Sama* (the likely cognate of Chamba) was used as a royal clan name and as the term for a class of royal appointees (encharged with the *lela* martial ritual) who contrasted loosely with *Ndagana* (the custodians of *voma* harvest ritual). Between themselves, and when it suited them, the five Bali chiefdoms could refer to one another by locational terms (each of which had a composite form, Bali-something, as well as a non-composite form without the common term).

---

5. The derivation of this term is problematic. Raiders from the north, of whatever ethnicity, were called Bale, Tibale, Tibar, Tipala or Tibana in the Grassfields. Chilver and Kaberry (1965, 1968) examined the records of recaptives (collected in Sierra Leone by Koelle) in which cognate terms appear as names for their original captors, and have noted that this name was known to a British parliamentary commission by the mid-nineteenth century. Whether this term derives from, or is the source of, Bali cannot be decided as things stand. Although some commentators claim Bali to be a European misrendering of Bare, {r} or {l} are substitutable in Chamba Leko dialects, and Mubako favours {l} (for instance what Bali call *lela* would be *lera* in most Chamba Leko chiefdoms). Moreover, the singular of *Ba'ni* is reported to be *Ya'ni*, whereas Chamba Leko generally form plurals through the addition of suffixes. One of Chilver's sources (Fokunggan Sambum, recorded in 1963) claims *Ba'ni* to be a Bati word (personal communication).

Early German sources tended to use the term Bali and to note that the Bali came from the north, or southern Adamawa, but located this place more precisely by reference to known extant Fulani chiefdoms.[6] Nonetheless, the pieces of a jigsaw of Chamba diaspora had begun to be put together. For instance, Zintgraff's first voyage took him from Bali-Nyonga to Takum (now in Nigeria) where he assured himself that the rulers of the two chiefdoms shared descent from the movement under Gawolbe, as well as a common language. However, Benue Chamba were generally known as Dinyi (or some variant), so the relationship was based on common origin from a raiding movement rather than on the common ethnic term Chamba.

There were moments in its history when Bali-Nyonga could have equally, or probably more plausibly set in train arguments for an ethnic identity other than it did. So why, and when – eventually – Chamba? Minimally, Bali seem to have been telling Zintgraff and subsequent German interlocutors that they were from the north, and therefore distinct from the Grassfielders among whom they dwelt. In a variety of ways, northern origins may have been prestigious. In Bamenda we find the odd spectacle (from a Chambaland perspective) of 'Chamba' claiming kinship with Fulani (the 1961 *Chamba National Almanac* has a caption to a photograph of a Fulani and a Bali observing that they are of 'common stock'). However, Fulani and *Ba'ni* were both northern raiders, and to liken *Ba'ni* to Fulani might suggest their special suitability as intermediaries in the regulation of their northern Kamerun colony – for whom the Germans, at least in the person of Zintgraff, were looking

---

6. The cartographer Moisel, basing his report on information derived from Ernst and Dorsch of the Basel Mission in 1907, claimed that the original Chamba, homeland was unknown but they were once settled around Koncha (a Fulani lamidate). Keller's 1919 account brings the Bali from Garoua, another lamidate, and suggests a Mubako derivation for the name. The ethnographer, Frobenius published two accounts of his 1911 researches in Chambaland. The first, in 1913, remarks the relationship between Chamba and the chiefdoms below the Benue (notably Donga), while the second (1925) stresses the relationship between Chamba and Bali to the exclusion of the Benue connection. Strümpell's wordlists show clear appreciation of the linguistic relation between Chamba Leko and Mubako. Although Ankermann's account of the *lela* ceremony is based on observations in 1907-8, he does not explore the historical precedents of Bali; neither does the missionary Vielhauer in his account of the *voma* festivals in 1910 (Baumann and Vajda 1959). For general discussion of early German sources, see Kaberry and Chilver 1968: 355-8.

at that time. Prominent among the Fulani lamidates to the north of the Grassfields, which the Germans were yet to conquer, was one called Tibati, which in turn had been founded from Tchamba (the lamidate founded in Chambaland) by Hamman Sambo.[7] The term Chamba linked connotations of northern power and Fulani-ness, while simultaneously differentiating the Bali from their neighbours in a fashion which may have corresponded to German perceptions (or Bali perceptions of German perceptions) of the exceptional character of the Bali.

The precise period at which the Bali chiefdoms became definitively 'Chamba' in their own accounts is unclear. My sense from readily accessible documentation is that, once the term became available, there was a two-stage crystallization of a sense of collective Chamba-ness, involving all five of the Bali chiefdoms, around the earliest and latest years of the British administration. One thread running through the period (see Chilver 1963, 1967) concerned Bali-Nyonga local hegemony, and what a contemporary local writer dubs 'Baliphobia' (Nyamndi 1988). Military exploits both before and after the arrival of the Germans, and various German and British ratifications of its position, had enabled Bali-Nyonga to assume formal administrative control over a relatively widespread population. By virtue of active resistance, both on the ground and in the courts, this position was gradually eroded from the later German period onwards. Numerous enquiries were pursued and reports written[8] with a view to clarifying the situation. Bali-Nyonga

---

7. This resemblance of terms, especially once Barth's early reference was taken up, seems to have caused confusion between Chamba, Tchamba and Hamman Sambo (for instance Jeffreys 1962a represents Hamman Sambo's exploits as evidence of Chamba expansion).

8. Chilver (1967) provides a vivid account of the establishment of the Zintgraff-Galega axis. Despite the relative decline of Bali fortunes under later German rule, 1905 is the date crucial to later disputes, since it was then that Fonyonga II's control over thirty-one villages, predominantly south of Bali, was promulgated (Ibid. 499). Further groups were added in 1906 and 1907 but not retained when reversal of this policy ensued by the end of the German period. Rumblings of discontent continued, beginning when land claims against Bali-Nyonga were refused by Hunt in 1921, a position that was ratified by Goodliffe's enquiry and report in 1949. Further unsuccessful legal action ensued in 1952, followed closely by rioting (the 'Widekum Riots') which claimed fifteen lives and caused considerable damage. The Manson Report of 1953 (reproduced in Nyamndi 1988, Appendix Four) ratified the existing position and awarded compensation to Bali. However, the issue did not go away. Copies of Goodliffe's report, appended to letters to the State Governor and Head of State from the Bali Fon

became adept at handling the succession of consultations which required them to account for themselves historically. The more general efflorescence of Grassfields historical studies[9] argues against over-emphasising the point, but the embattled position of privilege that Bali-Nyonga had attained must have added immediate point to their historicizing efforts.

Early British reports show that the Chamba connexion had become conventional wisdom for District Officers – and presumably for Bali also.[10] The majority Chamba populations of the north were either in Nigeria or the northern Cameroons Mandate (a very small minority was in French Cameroon). Ethnographic developments in these British-administered territories were to have an impact on 'Chambaization' in ways that could hardly have been foreseen. The Government Anthropologist C.K. Meek spent six weeks of 1927 in Donga (the most significant of the Chamba chiefdoms below the Benue in Nigeria). His published account (1931) makes evident the skein of resemblances among the dispersed and varied Chamba in Nigeria. As an assistant, Meek employed the services of a young man who went on to become Gara of Donga in 1931. Mallam Bitemya Sambo Garbosa II's own book on Chamba history and the Donga chiefs (privately published in Hausa) was the fruit of a long process of research. Garbosa tells us that he wrote a first draft of his book in 1923, renewing his efforts after working with Meek to complete a further draft in 1932-3. The private publication of the two volumes, which include details of his visit to Bamenda in 1954, probably occurred in 1956. How widely earlier versions of the book circulated I do not know, but it was available to Bali commentators on publication if not earlier.[11]

in October 1977, were circulating in bound form when I visited in 1984, as the Fon attempted to repudiate another land demand. By 1977 the Fon had conceded that the Bali had conquered land in Bamenda but argued, via the by-then established Chamba connexion, that the Bali had themselves been dispossessed in Northern Cameroon and were not, for that reason, either inciting their Chamba 'kith and kin' to join them in Northwest Province, or themselves intending to launch land claims in the North. Extensive Chamba ethnicity, at least rhetorically, had become a serviceable device in argument.

9. Njoya's historical work on Bamum is an obvious early instance (see Tardits 1980).

10. Hunt, in 1925, notes 'The Bali clan belong to the Chamba-Leko tribe and originally came from Tschamba' (para. 7). Hawkesworth's 1926 Assessment has the Chamba divide in Ngaoundere to form the Bali tribe 'via the Tikar route' or to follow the 'Jukun route' to Donga (para. 16).

11. M.D.W. Jeffreys (1962a: 172) notes that he had a translation of Garbosa's work made by a member of the Veterinary Department in Bamenda; its date is not given.

The scholar/administrator M.D.W. Jeffreys[12] not only published materials on Bali history collected by himself (e.g. on Bali-Kumbat in 1957) but in a 1962 article synthesised previous sources. Prominent among these sources is a text transcribed by Isaac Fielding Pefok in 1933 (see Jeffreys 1962b) from the testimony of Tita Nji ('son' of Galega I, d. 1901) at the instigation of Fonyonga II in 'the vernacular' (i.e. Mungakka).[13] Among the many interests of this text is the addition of five chiefs to the Bali regnal list prior to the generally accepted hero-leader Gawolbe (Jeffreys 1962a: 185). Jeffreys (who accepts the integrity of the additional five chiefs whom he incorporates into his own dating) reports (1962a: 192-3) that a meeting of the Fon's council was specially convened in November 1960 to discuss the discovery of the chiefs, about whom they previously had known nothing. The oldest men were 'intransigent in their refusal to accept Tita Nji's account as Bali tradition'. Tita Nji not only added five unknown fons but supplied them with a history. A first Gawolbe settled in Tchad from Syria and conquered the Fulani; four generations later a second Gawolbe, who had quarrelled with and killed Sama (a half-brother by their common father Gangsin and a Fulani woman), led the incursions into Bamenda. Gawolbe II died at the battle of Kolm and transformed into a bull elephant; following this the confederation dispersed to form the present Bali chiefdoms.

Jeffreys (1962a, Appendix C) notes the formation in 1960 of a Bali Historical Society, while deploring some of the more speculative attempts to reconstruct Bali origins. Renewed interest in history had immediate local antecedents in conflagration over land issues (the 'Widekum Riots' of 1952, see note 8), and the visit of Garbosa II of Donga to Bali in 1954 as well as the broader implications of impending reunification with Cameroon. The Bali Historical Society became the focus of Phyllis Kaberry and Sally Chilver's initial investigations of Bali-Nyonga history. As they tell us in their published account of the political system of Bali-Nyonga (1961), their visit in the previous year was only of twenty days but:

---

12. Jeffreys was in charge of Bamenda Division between 1936 and 1945.

13. Sally Chilver, who has also translated this text, suggests it may have circulated in several versions as a manuscript copied by school teachers from the original in 'Church Bali' (i.e. the Mungakka of the Basel Mission orthography) dictated to Pefok by Tita Nji II, the grandson of Galega I, in the mid-1930s. Jeffreys appears to have confused Tita Nji II with his eponymous father, who was son of Galega I and known to Zintgraff.

occurred during a period when the new intelligentsia and the traditional office-holders were seriously discussing the traditional system of government and its significance for local and national elective party government. We had the collaboration of the History Committee of Bali-Nyonga under the presidence of Mfon Galega II. Regular meetings were held in which important men, conversant with the history and government of Bali-Nyonga, thrashed out the questions we put to them and arrived at agreed answers which were translated to us by Councillor Alfred W. Daiga (the Mfon's secretary). (Kaberry and Chilver 1961: 355)

Sally Chilver's two-part report (1964) – unpublished but greatly cited in regional literature – was submitted to the Bali Historical Society after her second period of research in 1963. A pan-Chamba Union was formed but seems to have come to little, beyond a well-produced 1961 Almanac. However, Bali-Chamba history came on apace. Part of the impetus derived from publications edited by the anthropologist Edwin Ardener and published in Buea by the Government Printer, making them readily available to local schools. Two volumes in the series consisted of a resume of Bamenda history and tradition based on Kaberry and Chilver's researches (Chilver 1966; Chilver and Kaberry 1968). The success of this venture[14] was noted by the Secretary of State for Primary Education and Social Welfare in his Foreword to a shorter volume – Sally Chilver's translation and synopsis (1966) of the parts of Zintgraff's writings (Zintgraff 1895) relevant to Bamenda history. Roughly between 1960 and 1968, the readily accessible material at the disposal of local historians increased exponentially[15] and school history projects flourished (Chilver personal communication). Published accounts for the early 1970s are less numerous but this may represent only the result of the vagaries of my access to sources. From the later 1970s fresh initiatives are evident in the publication by 'a group of Bali-Nyonga youths' of a series of historically oriented brochures.[16]

---

14. More recently, Paul Nkwi and Jean-Pierre Warnier have written an account explicitly designed to succeed Kaberry and Chilver's volume (1982: 4).

15. Phyllis Kaberry and Sally Chilver produced numerous publications around this time and both took pains to assure their published and unpublished accounts were available locally (e.g. Fohtung 1992 [1962]).

16. The first of these, 'The *lela* festival' (16 pp. locally cyclostyled and bound) appeared in 1978. In the following year a record of *lela* music was issued in France on the Arion label, recorded by Dr Errol Leighton. The third 'attempt', as the series is described, largely consisted of a collection of personal names. Apparently distinct from this series is a 'Portrait of Their Royal Highnesses' (i.e., the fons of Bali-Nyonga) compiled by Augustine F. Ndangam and Dr Elias Nwana, who together motivated

Perhaps little of practical significance can be claimed for a Chamba identity that crossed national, provincial and state boundaries.[17] But the sense of a Chamba-ness that included peoples in North Cameroon, Northern Nigeria, Nigeria below the Benue, and the Northwest Province of Cameroon had clearly become an established fact – at least in the imagination – by this time (see note 9). Chamba identity fits the overall scheme of larger-scale ethnic identities emerging in West Africa during the twentieth century. It had, though, been a work of great effort – and of no great likelihood from a late-nineteenth-century commentator's point of view. Had colonization not occurred when it did, there is little reason to suppose that Bali-Nyonga would have 'become' Chamba. Given another century, the claim to common origin with the other four Bali chiefdoms (had Mubako survived in all of them) might have been dropped, or retained in a fashion as perplexing to putative ethnographer/ historians of the early twenty-first century as the common claim to Tikar origins (on the part of many other Grassfields chiefdoms) has been to ethnographers of the twentieth century. Of course, the Chamba-ness of Bali-Nyonga is a very selective appropriation of the past. Descendants of some of the raiders from outside the Grassfields would probably – had they stayed where they were – have become elements of the Chamba of the homelands (themselves defined through an historical process). It is difficult both to put the case more strongly and to decide whose representation of whom the 'Chamba-ness' of Bali-Nyonga is. My earlier question about African realities and European representations ceases to make sense. At best we can describe the work as comprising interrelating historically-situated suppositions, and the tendencies towards a particular outcome. The retrojection of entities (here, the Chamba) into the narrative of a period (the nineteenth century and earlier) when they clearly did not exist is virtually impossible to resist given the conventions for putting collective 'actors' into a comprehensible history.

---

much of the effort of the overall historical initiative. (Dr Nwana kindly put me abreast of this research as it stood in 1984.)

17. The Chamba National Union in Cameroon, formed in 1958, apparently 'died a natural death' because the five chiefs could not agree about 'precedence, always reading into it a retrospective legitimization of power that went back as far as Gawolbe's succession' (Nyamndi 1988: 156). Over the years the Nigerian Chamba Union has sporadically issued calendars, and relationships have been maintained between the more important chiefs.

Bali-Nyonga: narrating modernity

To pursue the question of identity further, I shall refer in greater detail to two locally produced volumes of Bali history. Both were published in 1988: Ndifontah B. Nyamndi's *The Bali-Chamba of Cameroon: a Political History* and the collectively authored account *An Introduction to the Study of Bali-Nyonga: a Tribute to His Royal Highness Galega II, Traditional Ruler of Bali-Nyonga from 1940-85* (Titanji et al. 1988). The death of Galega II prompted both publications, since the first is apparently a history that outgrew the possibility of placing it in the second. This skewing in my sources may fit all too easily with the argument I want to make.

The insertion of Bali-Chamba identity into modernity, by which I mean strictly a narrative task of writing history evaluatively, is achieved in particular via the representation of the individuality of Grassfields rulers. This is striking to an observer more familiar with Chambaland, where this is rarely the case. Reasons for the emphasis are all too obvious: Grassfields chiefdoms in general attribute great centrality to their fons, and Bali-Nyonga has been portrayed as an extreme of this tendency; German accounts, particularly Zintgraff's travelogue (locally accessible as Chilver 1966), tend to stress the personal relationships between the German explorer and the African king. The variant of indirect rule practised by the British consolidated the political functions of chiefship; many of the writers of Bali history presumably absorbed a 'Kings and Queens' account of British history as part of their education. Finally, as we have seen, the occasions for the production of the literature are themselves likely to skew representations in favour of chiefly centrality.

The Bali-Chamba story recounted in these books concerns origins, dispersal and reunification. Northern, Chamba origins are conflated with stereotyped Fulani characteristics. Bali-Chamba are portrayed as the racial inheritors of the martial virtues of the Chamba, 'a tall, negroid people with a distinctly imperious bearing' and an 'inherent love for independence' (Nyamndi 1988: 1, 4-5). Defeated at Bafu Fundong, the united Bali-Chamba dispersed to engage in local conflicts until the meeting between Zintgraff and Galega. Both sources note that Bali-Chamba people looked Zintgraff straight in the eye, something he had not met elsewhere in Africa, and that the two leaders subsequently made a blood pact.[18] Zintgraff brought Bali into the wider world, a clear theme, dated exactly to 16 January 1889 (Gwanfogbe in Titanji et al. 1988: 23) and recognized in the Bali the martial virtues they now feel in themselves – as it were externally and objectively.

Most of the German colonial period, the transition between British administration, and reunification with Cameroon, occurred within the reigns of two Bali-Nyonga fons: Fonyonga II (1901-40), son of Galega I (mid-1850s to 1901) and his son Galega II (1940-85). Their descent line is traced from the leader of the Chamba alliance, Gawolbe. In the accounts, the rulers make the transition to modernity. I present Galega II, the 'Fon of a new age' (Nyamndi 1988: 139), through a brief collage of our sources. He was sent to school because his father had enthusiastically supported education since the earliest establishment of a German missionary school. Fonyonga II had learned to read and write at the age of forty-five (Ibid. 115). The future Galega II eventually became a pharmacy dispenser. Although he never attended secondary school he left a son with a PhD to succeed him (Ndangam in Titanji et al. 1988: 63).

> The idea of development appears to have been uppermost in the new Fon's mind as seen by the fact that a few months after his accession to the throne he organized the Bali Development Committee in 1941 to plan streets for Bali town and to open up roads in the area.[19] Two years later in 1943 he founded the Bali Improvement Union (BIU) to foster the education of capable young men. The organisation launched a scholarship scheme from which a good number of young people were able to do higher education abroad in Europe and the U.S. (Nwana in Titanji et al. 1988: 72)

> In the mid 40's V.S. Galega II became the Chairman of Bali Area Rural Council. When later on the Gah of Bali Gham assisted him as Vice-Chairman of Bali Council the idea of an association for the Chamba family occurred to him. He contacted the other Chamba Fons in the North West Province and the *Chamba Wat-Coon* (Pan Chamba Association) was formed to preserve the rich cultural heritage of Bali Chamba. The five Fons of the Chamba group met frequently

---

18. Zintgraff seems to have been rather profligate in making blood pacts, as the excerpts in Chilver 1966 attest. Ian Fowler and David Zeitlyn comment on an irony, that from Zintgraff's account and also from Sally Chilver's researches (personal communication) it appears that it was the envoy of the Bali Fon, sent out to welcome the explorer, who looked directly into Zintgraff's eyes. This envoy was of Bati (i.e. Bamileke) origin.
19. For an analysis of town planning as a ritual of competitive modernization, see Richards 1992.

and exchanged visits especially during the *Lela* festival. (Ndangam in Titanji et al. 1988: 47)

He was born in a grass-roofed palace. He died in a modern one that contrasts sharply with the old one in magnificence. The painful etiquette by which people entered the palace bare-footed got discarded in one stroke of reform. (Ndangam in Titanji et al. 1988: 62)

His *private world* [he had 35 wives and over 200 children] ... reveals an ordinary human being with extraordinary responsibilities and obligations (Ibid. 61, my emphasis)

To his wives he insisted on three things: The first, based on economic consideration was that they should learn a traditional craft appropriate to women and keep themselves busy. Most of his wives learnt how to weave grass-trays *(Kukad)*. Secondly he insisted on their keeping themselves and their premises clean, an idea, no doubt ingrained in his life-style from his medical profession. Thirdly he got all his wives actively engaged in the learning of Bali culture. He organised cultural classes for his wives and children and got experts ... to teach them the *Mubako*, the original language of the Balis as well as the *Lela* songs and dance. These private classes clearly yielded positive fruits as could be seen by the role played by the Fon's wives at the *Lela* dances especially in the production of *Lela* music. (Ibid.)

Galega II was the first Fon to clothe his wives in North West Province and went around to encourage his colleagues to do the same. It is said that Galega II, a close friend to the Fon of Bafut, Achirimbi II, forced the latter's wives to be clothed by providing the first dresses to them. (Nwana in Titanji et al. 1988: 73)

Galega II seems to have recognized in himself the qualities his obituarists also note. When British settlement of the 'Widekum Riots' (see note 8) awarded Bali compensation of £9,000, the sum was astutely transvalued through investment in a modern, pipe-borne water supply for Bali town (Gwanfogbe in Titanji et al. 1988: 38). Galega II was a British-nominated representative to the Regional House of Assembly for Eastern Nigeria, a proponent of unification with Cameroon rather than Nigeria, and actively involved in the leadership of the single Cameroonian political party in his region following Independence.

I leave the final word on Bali-Chamba ethnicity in the modern world to one of our authors:

ideally [a] consolidated kingdom remained the dream of many Bali. But practically it seemed so unfeasible in geographical terms as to be completely out of this world. Yet on closer examination the prospect is not all that farfetched either. After all there are many components of that unity, and common territory is only one of them. (Nyamndi 1988: 154-5)

Conclusion

Basil Davidson (1992) has recently argued that Africans have been alienated from their own history by Europeans. Evidently he intends a greater theme than my narrow example can contest. In Bali-Nyonga the seizure of history as argument has been part of the sense of transition to modernity (measured also in airstrips, cash crops, doctorates and priesthoods, involvement in national affairs, town planning, educational institutions, church buildings and so on). If the history has not been entirely of their own making, then it has not obviously been entirely of European making either. The opposition simply fails to capture even such subtleties as I have been able to glean from extant records. Entities structured as individuals, ethnicities, nations and a wider context, perhaps a global one, may be a common terminus but this is hardly to suggest that other entities (Africa or Europe) can be portrayed in any simple way as the agencies responsible for this outcome. One is struck rather by the way in which professional anthropologists and local historians, both accepting bounded identities as a norm, find different problems. To oversimplify: while the anthropologist tends to construe what fails to fit as indicative of a preceding situation, the local historian has to interpret it as precursive of modernity, and a possible future. As remarkable, though, are the complex connexions between these projects.

A note of reflexivity (historical rather than personal) may be an appropriate way to end. As a postgraduate student, looking to do fieldwork in Nigeria or Cameroon – the specializations of my anthropology department – I read C.K. Meek's chapter on the Chamba and chose fieldwork in Chambaland on account of the extraordinarily varied forms of social organization he described. Meek had collaborated with Garbosa, and I was given a copy of Garbosa's book by the Chamba Chief of Ganye on my arrival in Nigeria. Earlier Garbosa took some responsibility for galvanizing interest in history among Bali chiefs, and it was from the meetings of the Bali Historical Committee that Phyllis Kaberry and Sally Chilver composed their early accounts of Bali-Nyonga history. Phyllis, one of my teachers, arranged for me to have access to Sally's handwritten reports to the Bali Historical Society and then to meet her. Putting together a synthesising account of different Chamba communities seemed an 'obvious' task, the step that had to be taken before anything else could be done. Chamba intelligentsia in the homelands consistently reinforced my sense of purpose by defining what they thought I was doing in pan-Chamba terms. Looking back it is far from clear whether I decided to write a pan-Chamba account or whether the feasibility of that account was lying in wait to kidnap a likely passing author. Skipping ahead almost twenty years, I find myself reading Nyamndi's account of Bali history, which draws upon my own doctorate and many of the resources for writing Grassfields history that are locally available in the Phyllis Kaberry Resource Centre founded in memory of her pioneering work.

Event rich in fact and recollection, to borrow Edwin Ardener's phrase, Bali-Nyonga history has involved a skein of collaborative moves, themselves compounded of academic careers, political trajectories and theoretical proclivities – both Cameroonian and European. Quite who is writing whom, and in terms of what, becomes increasingly difficult to decide, quite apart from the steps (some of them now lost) by which we got 'here'. In retracing these steps I have tried to offer one interpretation of the sense of modernity, and some sense of the context in which a historiographic tradition has revolved around the intellectual and practical formulation and insertion of identity.

ACKNOWLEDGEMENTS

The two halves of this paper were written with a single argument in mind but originally delivered to different audiences. The first was presented to the 'Identity in Africa' seminar at the University of Bayreuth in February 1993. An earlier version of the second half made up the bulk of a paper for a seminar on 'Modernity and Communication' at the University of Manchester the following month. The stimulation of these invitations is traced in the themes I try to articulate here. Thanks are due to Janos Reisz for his invitation to Bayreuth, and for the focus on identity; commentators at Manchester provided numerous suggestions of which I have availed myself.

Chapter 5

'CROSSED DESTINIES'
The entangled histories of West African ethnic and national identities

Complex resemblances

This essay primarily concerns the senses in which terms popularized in writings on ethnic and national identities over the last decade and a half can be applied to recent West African history. As well as invention, the terms I have in mind include also narration and imagination (often cited as 'what Hobsbawm (1983) calls invention', 'what Bhabha (1990) calls narration', and 'what Anderson (1991, originally 1983) calls imagination'). Part of the purpose of introducing these terms was to rebutt primordialism and the related, but not identical, realist assumption that ethnic groups existed unproblematically in some 'out there' (wherever 'there' might be). Invention, narration and imagination had the virtue of foregrounding the fact that identities have to be 'made up'; but how noteworthy this 'made-up' quality was depended upon the thorough-goingness of the constructivist paradigm invoked. To claim that ethnic identities were rather more 'made up' than most of their context (as Hobsbawm seems to) is quite different from the claim that national identities were just as – and as just as problematically – 'made up' as any others (a position closer to Bhabha's[1]). If analysis of identity in constructivist terms is to involve more than rejoinder to primordialism or realism, how much theoretical baggage should it carry – and what ought to be in it?

---

1. 'If the problematic "closure" of textuality questions the "totalization" of national culture, then its positive value lies in the wide dissemination through which we construct the field of meanings and symbols associated with the national life' (Bhabha 1990:3).

A general theoretical answer is beyond the ambition of this essay, but in asking how these terms may be applied best to West Africa I shall also attempt some observations about the look of the terms themselves from a West Africanist perspective. It may assist the reader if some prejudices are confessed at the outset (they are largely unreconstructed since Fardon 1987a, Chapter 2 in this volume). I have an anthropological suspicion (not shared by all anthropologists, by the way) of the universality of ethnicity. The kinds of human differences considered ethnic strike me as so diverse that they can be classed together only if ethnicity is construed broadly under a multi-stranded, or polythetic, definition. When this is done, however, we find that the definitional net woven for ethnicity has also captured kinds of human difference that our intuition tells us can more plausibly be put under headings such as class or, in other instances, race, region or religion. These kinds of differences need to be removed to temper an idea of ethnicity that would otherwise tend to absorb a widening scope of differences. More technically put: our concept of ethnicity is both polythetic and residual. If it is the case that ethnicity has to be defined by reference to a list of characteristics present in only some its instance – and even then must be narrowed down to a residual category (after some non-ethnic differences have been weeded out) – I would suggest that the likelihood of it corresponding to a human universal in realist terms can be discounted. It would, of course, be foolish to suggest that because a concept in ordinary usage lacks tight logical coherence it is therefore incredible or has no effects (one could convincingly argue the opposite – often, unhappily so as in this case). But given that ethnicity is so evidently jerry-built as an idea its spread becomes the more interesting. Part of the attraction (and problem) of ethnicity is that it offers a kind of democratization of differences. The varied sorts of differences that once seemed to exist (to take only Eurocentric examples – between races, tribes, peoples and so forth) can now be revealed to belong to a single register of difference. Contemporary ideas of ethnicity, I would suggest, tend to hegemonize other kinds of difference. A more extensive account of the conditions for the growing pervasiveness of ethnicity would need (*inter alia*) to stress 'internationality' as its englobing context (Rée 1992) and the hegemonic standing of the USA in the post-war period among its causes. Given the close relation between ethnicity and multiculturalism in the USA, we may find that the concept has already passed its apogee there. In Africa, differences have not yet all been translated into ethnic difference, and may never be.[2]

If ethnicity is, as I am claiming, a polythetic and residual classificatory category, then ethnicities may have only complex resemblances with one another (such that ethnicities A, B and C have common characteristics but these are not of necessity the same for A/B, B/C, C/A). In set theory terms, the characteristics of ethnicities may overlap one another. A loosely articulated category of this sort is highly amenable to translation, because there are so many potential grounds for membership in it. And each translation makes the category more complex. Ethnicity is therefore, and additionally, a historically changing category.

What I believe to be significant about this will, I hope, become clear as we go on, but it is worth spelling out at the outset some questions which are simply not worth asking if it is accepted that: ethnicity is a polythetic and residual category, that ethnicities have complex resemblances, and that translation of ethnicity and recognition of new ethnicities have tended to make that already broad category ever broader. The questions not worth asking are those with binary answers: ethnic groups or tribes were/were not invented, ethnic groups or tribes do/do not have histories, ethnic groups are/are not real, and so forth. These questions are not worth addressing because they presume that ethnicity, or ethnicities, or both, are or were the kinds of stable entities about which such questions could be answered definitively. On the contrary, I want to argue that ethnicity and ethnicities interrelate in ways far too complex for this to be possible. Whatever their problems, it is a virtue of a curiosity pricked by terms like invention, narration and imagination that this point becomes evident.

Crossed destinies

Appropriately, given my concern with narratives, their circulation and their *dramatis personae,* I begin with a story – and, even more

---

2. From my patchy knowledge of the literature, the study of idioms of difference in African languages – and in African pidgins and creoles – seems underdeveloped. For instance, 'tribe' as used in contemporary Nigerian English seems to me to have resonances not wholly identical to its sense in British English. A comparative study of such idioms would contribute to understanding the historicity of such categories as 'ethnicity', 'tribe', and their African language counterparts which I discuss later.

appropriately for my theme, the story is someone else's – Italo Calvino's from *The Castle of Crossed Destinies*.[3]

A collection of travellers converges on a castle in the midst of a dense forest where they will spend the night. It is unclear to the narrator whether the castle is really an aristocratic dwelling – which time has turned into a tavern with a faded courtly past – or whether, being established close-by an abandoned castle, the inn has been given aristocratic pretensions by its host as a way to conceive of the constant flow of guests passing through his halls.[4] Other than bidding the narrator to be seated with a nod, the host, or perhaps the lord, hardly features until the end of the tales, and then he gets only to half-tell his own tale before being interrupted by his wife.

The travellers, seated at a common meal table where they have supped, discover that they have lost the power of speech in their passage through the forest.

Their host offers them a deck of tarot cards.[5] Each traveller narrates his tale by, literally, putting his cards on the table. The cards already have general meanings but the teller of the tale tries to augment or alter these by a gestural language through which – Calvino's narrator believes – a structure of feeling is invested in the relations between the cards used. Because each story is constrained to use cards that have been set in a pattern to tell previous stories, the tellers become increasingly cramped by the resources already on the table or the cards remaining in the deck. The resources for story telling should become governed increasingly by tales told earlier. But this does not appear to hinder the raconteurs, for the stories they tell seem familiar to us anyway. Eventually, our narrator has to construe his own tale from a pattern almost entirely established. But he is no longer able to distinguish his from the tales already told, which run in rows and columns through the arrangement of the deck of cards on the table.

Before presuming too far on your patience I should explain – if it is not already obvious – why I draw upon the ingenuity of an Italian author

---

3. The story is drawn from Italo Calvino's two novellas translated into English and published together as *The Castle of Crossed Destinies,* which is the title of the first novella – the second being 'The tavern of crossed destinies'. The first story was originally published as *Tarots: the Visconti Pack in Bergamo and New York* in 1969.

4. The tale of the traveller unable to tell an inn from a castle is itself recycled from Don Quixote of course.

5. It is important for my argument that the pack itself has a history. The tarot deck has come to consist of seventy-eight cards consisting of ten numeral cards in each of four suits – Cups, Coins, Clubs (or Rods) and Swords – four court cards for each suit – King, Queen, Knight and Page – the twenty-one *Major Arcana* or Tarots proper, and *The Fool.* The pack used in Calvino's first novella consists of miniatures handmade by Donifacio Dembo and Antonio Cicognara between 1441-47 to satisfy the desire of Filippo Maria Visconti, Duke of Milan, for a pack with a gold background. In his second novella, Calvino illustrates the Marseilles pack, so-called because it was mass-produced by printing there in the eighteenth century.

to broach some questions about West African ethnicity and ethnicities. Calvino's works, about which I claim no expertise, mix playfulness with serious concern for the way stories are told. Indeed, whatever else they are about, such works of his as I have read are also about invention, narration, and imagination: *If on a Winter's Night a Traveller,* in which the central character fails to locate subsequent chapters of the book he is trying to read (a fate we – as readers of his saga of reading frustrated – share); *Invisible Cities* in which Marco Polo tells Kublai Kahn of the great cities of his Empire that he may have visited or imagined; and *The Castle of Crossed Destinies,* the gist of which I have just summarized. These stories about telling stories are artful enough to make one wonder whether by shifting their terms of reference for understanding ethnicity and nationalism into the register of cultural creativity, historians and social scientists have not exchanged something they might hope to understand for something which only the greatest of imaginative authors can address, and then indirectly. Surely it is right to insist that tribes, ethnicities, and nations need to be 'made up', but how to think about cultural creation without a lapse into voluntarism? A first reading of Calvino's travellers' tales in counterpoint with the narratives of tribalism, ethnicity and nationalism suggests some of the problems.

1. In their narrations, the travellers are caught up in both constraint and empowerment; I shall call the principled difficulty of deciding which of the two the Foucault effect for short.[6] There is the occasion itself; would the travellers have told their stories but for the accident of finding themselves together in the castle? Given that they are struck mute, they are also constrained to construct their stories from the material of the tarot pack. As it happens this material is extremely rich, but suffers from the problems of frequent use and accreted meanings that must be exploited or forestalled gesturally. In this respect, the travellers seem, like the *bricoleurs* of the younger Lévi-Strauss's writings, to be constructing their own myths from

6. The unsettling flip between seeing constraint as empowerment, and empowerment as constraint, strikes me as a movement quintessential of the middle-Foucault of power/knowledge: what looks at first like the exercise of individual agency is revealed to be described better as the productivity of power at the unwitting site of an individual (the revelations of the psychoanalyst's couch are an obvious example). This suggests the unreliability of people's sense of 'doing what they want to'; in terms of the Foucault effect, desire is always open to construal as subjection.

the mythemes of myths told before. We are left with the sense that they could have told their stories more exactly had they been able to use their 'own' words to do so. But then there is doubt it could have been otherwise; what if they shared no other language? In that case the cards and non-verbal gestures would have been the only resources they could command to communicate with one another without the mediation of formal translation. Anyway, what might their 'own' words be? Would they feel the lack of them but for telling their stories? And why should they tell the story of coming to be in the castle, tavern or inn if not for their being there?

2. The sequence in which the travellers tell their stories seems to constrain those whose accounts come later. Again, is this really the case or is it only apparently so? The later story-tellers have had the advantage of witnessing how stories are told in this manner and, joining their own stories to those enunciated before, can draw upon a narrative resource to construct or contrast their own tale. Quite how the stories are constructed seems relatively open: the travellers in the castle use rows and columns to do so, the travellers in the tavern – the setting of the second novella – use more disorderly clumps of adjacent materials, one story growing almost organically through the material of the others.

3. Calvino's narrator makes it clear that the tellers of tales are not coerced into explaining the circumstances that brought them to the castle. As each traveller tells his or her story, the others seem increasingly to feel the inner necessity to add their own to the collective story. In the tavern we find the travellers scrambling to collect the material from which stories can be told. And, in both settings, the story-tellers find that they have to incorporate some element (that is to say a card) used in a previous story in a determinate position within their own story but with quite different meaning. As Calvino has his narrator remark,

> ... the task of deciphering the stories one by one has made me neglect until now the most salient peculiarity of our way of narrating, which is that each story runs into another story, and as one guest is advancing his strip, another, from the other end, advances in the opposite direction, because the stories told from left to right or from bottom to top can also be read from right to left or from top to bottom, and vice versa, bearing in mind that the same cards, presented in different order, often change their meaning, and the same tarot is used at the same time by narrators who set forth from the four cardinal points. (1978:39)

4. Finally, what are we to make of the reliability of Calvino's narrator? Are we to trust someone who cannot find his own story to be able to decode for us the nuances of others' gestural language? Moreover, his status is uncertain to the point of undecidability: we might consider him the creation of the author Italo Calvino had Calvino, ever helpful, not thought to add an Appendix purporting to detail how Italo Calvino, author of the book and begetter of its narrator, was himself caught up by the attraction of the narrative machine he hoped to tame. In this note, Calvino assures us that while Tarots have been read previously through formulae 'symbolic, astrological, cabilistic [and] alchemistic' in his own book 'the cards are "read" in the most simple and direct fashion' (1978:116). But we have heard authors appeal to naturalism sufficiently often to harbour suspicion of a claim to writing-degree-zero – especially when enunciated under the name of one of the twentieth century's least realist of story tellers.

In summary, questions can be posed in terms of Calvino's conceit – questions about constraint and empowerment, sequentiality, inter-textuality, and authorship – which make answers like 'tribes/ethnic groups are imagined, narrated, invented ...' seem to beg more issues than they resolve.

Making the analogy even more direct, if we decided to allow the castle/tavern to be the nation-state, and the lord/host its somewhat unlikely *laissez-faire* liberal government, then the story tellers might be ethnic groups. The compulsion to tell their stories is the operation of power in narrative: the upshot their crossed destinies (part being together where they are and part the compulsion to narrate that event). The resources at their disposal are formally limited (the well-used cards of the tarot pack), but so productive that this constraint can almost be ignored. And the most important story concerns how they came to be, where indeed they are, at the point of beginning to need to recollect themselves and tell their entangled stories.

Invention – narration – imagination: how sameness inhabits the world

If ethnicities or nationalisms[7] were felt by intellectuals to be unreservedly good things, then redescribing them in the 'constructivist' language of

_____

7. For the purposes of this paper only, I have allowed myself to use ethnicity loosely in

'invention – narration – imagination' would have thoroughly positive connotations. Of course, intellectuals – especially contemporary western intellectuals (with no exemption claimed for the author) – by and large prefer to think of themselves in cosmopolitan or universalist terms.[8] Their attitude to nationalism and ethnicity tends to stretch from downright negative only so far as half-hearted endorsement when an identity of this exclusive sort can be argued to be working as resistance to something bigger and nastier (and preferably doing so in the short term). Something like 'culture', for instance, can be said to be 'invented' with rather more positive connotations.[9] The almost-aestheticizing terms (invention – narration – imagination) that were introduced to discussions of tribe and nation as ripostes to readings of ethnicity that were realist and/or primordialist also beg questions. Above, I showed how this was so of narration; invention is similar.

Following the philosophers of science we might note that the idea of invention itself belongs to a heroic account of innovation. Seldom are things unproblematically new, which is also to say that novelty is difficult to locate temporally. I do not want to follow this train of thought in detail (interesting though it might be), but taking general inspiration from it, we could ask of the idea of tribe: quite what is being invented, by whom and when? I want to make my argument via a digression related to the last: this time on the history of the tarot pack.[10]

> Although there are many tarot packs around not all of them seem to have developed from a single tradition, and no-one knows quite where or when the first pack appeared. The cards of the four suits may have come to Europe with the 'Saracens'

two senses: as the term that historically 'replaces' tribe, and as a term of a higher order than either tribe or nation (in which sense tribe and nation are both ethnic identities). Notwithstanding this looseness, the distinction between the singular and plural of these terms (particularly ethnicity/ ethnicities) is important to my argument because 1 use the singular to refer to the general phenomenon and the plural for instances of it.

8. If they can get away with it without being accused of what Michael Howard (at the annual conference of the *Association for the Study of Ethnicity and Nationalism* at the London School of Economics, March 1995) dubbed 'Enlightenment imperialism'.

9. Although the argument that the relations between culture and ethnicity (or even race) may be too close to be dispensable has become sufficiently widespread for the benignity of culture (even in its 'anthropological' or 'small c' version) to become questionable.

10. These brief notes on Tarot are taken from a single popularizing account (Mandel 1994). I cannot vouch for its historical well-foundedness, but that hardly matters for my analogy.

as gaming cards. While the twenty-two trumps (strictly twenty-one plus 'the Fool') or Greater Arcana are reminiscent of the avatars of Vishnu, they actually seem to date from the Renaissance. The trumps, or triumphs, may derive from the pageants of the Renaissance Italian city states – themselves based on Roman and Medieval precedents. Particular cards may even have specific historical referents – as for instance in the otherwise inexplicable card called 'the Female Pope' which may refer back either to the actuality of a female pope in the Visconti family (see note 5) or to the Wilhemite heresy. The individual Trumps have diverse yet interrelated meanings: for instance 'the World' indicates reward in general and: achievement, completeness, success, ecstasy, triumph, success at work and absolute knowledge. Thanks to the efforts of eighteenth century scholars, in addition to their relation to an astrological symbol, the Trumps also correspond to numbers and to the letters of the Hebrew alphabet (and thence to the Cabbala). To these meanings is added, in Calvino's use of the cards, a series of – in strict terms – misreadings, those that Calvino argues are the 'simple and direct' meanings of the cards (see above).

Because tarot cards were originally hand-painted, their use was restricted to the wealthy and nobility. When cards were mass-produced using later technologies the centres of manufacture and export changed according to fashion, and fashion also dictated changes in the identities of the suits, the numbers of cards per suit and so forth. Cards produced in Germany had, what now seem, rather odd suits for a while: unicorns, deer, monkeys, rabbits, parrots, lions, swordsmen, books and castles. Although, when you think about it, the present set of hearts, diamonds, clubs and spades is just as much of a Borgesian encyclopaedia, except that we are used to them.

The best known use of Tarot is in foretelling the future. There are numerous techniques to do this, but the 'Ancient method' involves different cards being assigned value in relation to the past, present, immediate and more distant future as factors influencing a situation and its eventual outcome. However, in France Tarot is a relatively innocent card game, somewhere between twist and bridge, and the trumps of the tarot pack are simply numbered from one to twenty-one.

While the history of the Tarot is quite thinkable and writable, it does not seem to offer either a definite starting point, or a teleology. Quite what Tarot might become or be used for remains very open. The relation between, say, the Cabbala, Roman triumphal processions, French diversions, the avatars of Vishnu and so forth would submit with difficulty to most conventional accounts of similarity. Instead, the best that can be said is that Tarot – as a kind of project which we survey from a moment in its trajectory (the present) – has wrought relationships that are now apparent retrospectively.[11] The difficulty of deciding who invented

11. The idea of ethnicity as 'project' is indebted to Nicholas Thomas's general use of this term (Thomas 1994).

Tarot is not factual but principled; we would need to decide what aspect of Tarot interested us before we could begin to trace its history let alone its inception. Depending what we recognize as Tarot, a genealogy is precipitated which in retrospect can be seen to have exercised greater or lesser influence on Tarot's historical development. The project of Tarot precipitates complex resemblances in the world by virtue of the ways in which human efforts have been called forth and governed.

The problems of conceptualizing the inception (or even invention) of ethnicity are rather similar to those involved in the historicity of the Tarot. When ethnicity (in the form of nationalism or tribalism) got started very much depends on how the historical cake is sliced. Looking at any one ethnic identity developmentally (or, in presentist Foucauldian terms, 'genealogically') there can seem with hindsight to have been a logic and even inevitability about the particular ethnic identity which people came to assume. Thus, ethnic groups have history (Chrétien and Prunier 1989); how could they not? But looked at 'archaeologically', identities which have the characteristics of contemporary ethnicities and nations seem different from preceding identities (and to the extent that they share their difference from precedent forms they appear relatively alike) (Fardon 1987b). Sometimes it is possible to see the genealogical and archaeological aspects of ethnicity clearly articulated. To give a minor example: the Pere of Cameroon have for some time been engaged in an attempt to be recognized under this name rather than as Koutine, a name attributed to them by Fulbe which they believe means 'dogs' in Fulfulde. During the nineteenth century, Fulbe conquered what we now need to call Pere-land and reduced people there to virtual slavery. Fulbe ascendancy – and naming practices – were ratified by early colonial practice. Nowadays, Pere is to substitute for Koutine (i.e. to signify with dignity what Koutine signified pejoratively). However, it seems likely that during an earlier period Pere – rather like Sama which is the source of the current term Chamba about which I have written elsewhere – was a much more fluid term in its reference. In resisting Koutine and desiring dignity, Pere find themselves caught in the logic and presuppositions of ethnic difference. The agency involved in this outcome is highly diffuse, but genealogically Pere has an 'authentic' and continuous relationship to a prior 'Pere' term, while archaeologically it belongs to the set of (some two hundred or so) Cameroonian ethnic identities. Verily, which the singer and which the song?

This remote example (Pere are off the beaten track by Cameroonian standards) is intended as an example of how the global and local become articulated. Aside from cruder material McDonaldization (the litany of burgers, cokes, Michael Jackson and video-nasties – none of which are available in Pere-land so far as I know) that has attracted so much attention, the articulation of global and local goes on more subtly and yet unavoidably (operating here on the level of presuppositions and implications; most pervasive and coercive when people seem most to be 'doing their own thing' – the Foucault effect I noted earlier, footnote 6). Similarity, in this case in the form of ethnicity or tribalism, comes to inhabit the world in roundabout ways, which is why I asserted earlier that we had to be prepared to address historical processes of complex resemblance.

Entanglement: the contrapuntal characteristics of ethnic narratives

The pattern of story-telling in Calvino's first narration could be called recursive turn-taking.[12] It is a rather genteel version of a game one might imagine having any number of forms. In Calvino's second narrative, the scramble for cards on the part of the narrators suggests a more agonistic attitude to the implications of one person's story for another's. Pere and Fulbe identities are in a third relation: one of unequal 'contrapuntal' development (to borrow a term recently adapted by Edward Said, 1993). Most, but not quite all, of the cards have been taken by Fulbe who have used them to lay out a spinal narrative to which others are compelled, at least initially, to join their story.

In all three cases, the cards are less like a particular language game (à la Wittgenstein) than they are a language in which so many games can be played that, for the analyst, the implications of the deck being finite can be deferred indefinitely. However, the infinite possibilities of the pack are not apparent to players who, at different times and holding different resources to play with, join a game which has already begun to develop its conventions. If the history of the game accounts for the generic quality of ethnicity, then the manner of joining it contributes to the uniqueness of ethnicities. Ethnicities are not the vestments of interests

---

12. Following David Parkin's suggestion (personal communication).

that would palpably be political or economic if seen in their native buff, nor are they so much in the nature of things as to have become a natural (for which read atemporal) feature of African society that has survived into an (elsewhere) cultural twentieth century. These two approaches to ethnicity (the 'cultural clothing of secular interest' as much as the 'pre-modern promontory in the twentieth century') are as crude as one another;[13] they refuse to recognize either the complexity of resemblance or the narrative entanglements between ethnicities. Rather than being inert identities that contributors bring to the fray, ethnicities – and changes in ethnicities – are what they learn about themselves.

Africanist concern with understanding how, in my terms, ethnicity and ethnicities became related locally has largely focused on the significance of the colonial period. Because the 'invention of tribes', the subject of this section [of the collection in which this essay was published originally], is a narrower aspect of this same problem, I want to look at the arguments of a couple of recent authors in the light of the points I have already made.

Peter Ekeh's ambitious recent article sets out both to critique a current fashion in anthropological analysis that has too readily abandoned the term 'tribalism' and to annotate the transformations of the colonial period (Ekeh 1990). He argues that pre-colonial African societies were dominated by kinship because the state was too weak to provide personal security. In particular, the state was unable to provide security from slavery, and to that degree the prominence of kinship is related to the history of slavery. British anthropologists were right, in this sense, to latch onto the importance of kinship and to see African societies as different from their European counterparts – to represent them in this sense as 'tribal' societies – however they failed to realize the historical nature of what they studied. Since African states, both colonial and post-colonial, have remained weak and largely extraverted, kinship has continued to play a major role in their organization. Ethnicity thus

---

13. Surprisingly, J.-F. Bayart's analysis seems to develop in just these terms: discovering that 'ethnicity cannot provide a basic reference point for postcolonial political areas' (1993:49), and does not 'provide [the] basic fabric' of politics (1993:55), Bayart concludes that we 'cannot seek *the* key to contemporary politics in ethnicity' (1993:59, emphasis added). But his attack is on the straw man of primordialism; revealing that as an imposter does not permit the conclusion that ethnicity is therefore a mere 'shadow theatre' of 'consciousness without structure' (main and sub-headings of the chapter).

arose during the colonial period as an expanded form of kinship. The counter-ideology to this kind of favouritism is 'tribalism'; a term largely used in a critical sense within Africa.

This is one of those curious articles for which one feels sympathy – so far as its central thrust (to do with historicity) is concerned – allied to disagreement on almost every particular point it makes. The list of these would be long, but among the most damaging for the historicity that the argument addresses is the notion that kinship afforded individuals security, and that its relation to slavery was predicated on this, as it were, oppositional character (also oppositional to the predatory state in its involvement in slave trade, see Ekeh 1990: 676 fn 11). I would rather suppose that kinship (depending quite what one is including of course) pointed both ways on the issue. Kinship devices were used to commit people to slavery, and some kinship devices can be seen as the outgrowth of slavery (for instance in the societies, like many of those of western Cameroon, where matrilineal stems develop apparently in order to trace rights of lordly wardship in the descendants of slave women). So the relationship between kinship and slavery is close but not simple. Colonialism offered 'opportunities' for ethnic groups, or for their 'crystallization' (1990: 684). Quite what to make of this depends on what one means by several of the terms. Centralized or not, pre-colonial political systems in Africa were internally articulated on the bases of differences between the categories that composed them. Differences between clans were explained in terms of their of different origins, a distinction that might be developed into one between indigenes or first-comers and later-comers, or between chiefs and chief appointers, or guardians of the earth and guardians of the ancestors and so forth. Forms of association cut across one another both within local communities (as matrilateral and patrilateral kinship and affinity did with greater or lesser formalization) and between communities (in the form of ideas of common descent, ritual interdependence, relationships of privileged abuse and so forth). Some of these differences we might, with the benefit of hindsight, wish to call ethnic (or, with necessary teleology: proto-ethnic).

For Ekeh, post-colonial Africa suffers from the confrontation between

> ... rampant kinship ideology inherited from colonialism and the efforts of a fraction of the new rulers to destroy what they saw as a divisive instinct standing in

the way of the evolution of a united and composite political organization in the fashion of the European state. (1990: 685-86)

Ekeh's subscription to the view that tribes were invented during the colonial period depends upon his sense that as means of mutual and self-help, pre-colonial kinship and colonial tribalism are similar. In his view, ethnicity is locally produced from the bottom up. Jean-Loup Amselle and his associates reach a similar conclusion concerning the colonial invention of tribalism for different reasons.

Amselle's views have already been critiqued in ways that are justifiable in terms of passages he has written but may take a less than comprehensive view of his arguments. Consider, for instance, this hostage to fortune on which Kees Schilder and Wim van Binsbergen justly seize,

> Nothing like an *ethnie* existed in the pre-colonial period. *Ethnies* derive from the actions of the colonizer who, in his desire to territorialize the African continent, carved out the ethnic entities which were themselves taken over later by the people. From this perspective the *'ethnie'*, like numerous institutions supposed to be primitive, would be no more than a false archaism (Amselle 1985: 23).[14]

Of this approach (under which they subsume that of Vail and his collaborators on Southern Africa) Schilder and van Binsbergen not unjustly note that it attributes seeming passivity to African people and denies the historicity of some elements of ethnic identity that have pre-colonial precursors. In the passage preceding the one quoted, Amselle has introduced his argument by reference to his colleague, Dozon's, demonstration (in the same 1985 volume) that there had existed no entity called Bete pre-colonially and that Bete was a colonial creation. To this denial of the salience of pre-colonial history, Schilders and van Binsbergen respond that the influence of the state (whether colonial or post-colonial) has been overemphasised in studies of the 'dynamics of ethnicity' to the detriment of continuities with 'pre-colonial processes of group formation' (1993: 8).

---

14. My translation is of the full passage which Schilder and van Binsbergen (1993:7) quote in part.

> … il n'existait rien qui ressemblât a une ethnie pendant la période précoloniale. Les ethnies ne procèdent que de l'action du colonisateur qui, dans sa volonté de territorialiser le continent africain, a découpé des entités ethniques qui ont été elles-mêmes ensuites réappropriées par les populations. Dans cette perspective, l'« ethnie », commes de nombreuses institutions pretendues primitives, ne serait qu'un faux archaïsme de plus. (Amselle 1985: 23)

Since the sense of the French *ethnie* is not part of my topic here I leave it untranslated.

Ralph Austen, addressing himself to Amselle's later work (*Logiques métisses,* 1990) in general, and additionally including Hobsbawm and Ranger's (1983) work which gave the idea of 'invention' its current currency, complains that such approaches are, first, difficult for Africans to accept and, second, that by publishing conclusions of this sort expatriate researchers may feel they are undermining local tradition. There may be good reason not to wish to do either of these things, but that reason is not strictly academic (home or away, our decision to suppress a sincerely held suspicion of the historicity of some 'traditions' demands a more cogent argument about non-intervention).

Reading Amselle's contributions belatedly, and after those of his critics, has at least afforded me the surprise of discovering him not to have said *only* what his critics had led me to expect. Among Amselle's other observations I would note:

1. That anthropologists had rather uncritically (he is writing in the first half of the 1980s) accepted the *ethnie* as a unit of analysis and comparison (1985:11). As Jean Bazin notes in the same volume, the most elementary procedures of ethnographic representation conspire in this, since it is difficult to avoid use of an ethnic term even in order to deny the homogeneity of those covered by that term (1985: 90).

2. The ethnic terms used by anthropologists were, for the most part, also those used by colonial administrators and suited administrative needs for defining units, censusing languages, appointing officials from the 'natives' and so on.

3. For various reasons, the relation between this ethnic grid imposed by the colonial powers in terms of colonial knowledge and anything that preceded colonialism is debatable.

   a. Historically there was an absence of clear-cut, cultural blocs.

   b. Ethnic processes were flexible such that identities were the outcome of political, economic, cultural, religious, linguistic and so forth processes which operated inter-societally (1985: 23). In this sense, pre-colonial ethnicity operated similarly to today.

   Explicitly, in this sense, 'it seems that there is *no* radical break between "modern tribalism" and its ancient counterpart' (1985: 41, emphasis added). Qualifying his assertion quoted by Schilders and van Dinsbergen, Amselle seems to suggest that *ethnies* remain ideational constructs.

> From this point of view, *ethnies* no more existed in the pre-colonial period than at present, at least not in the sense of entities that are racially, culturally or linguistically homogeneous; what always prevailed, on the contrary, were social units of unequal and heterogeneous composition (1985:37).[15]

c. pre-colonial societies need to be envisaged spatially other than as a patchwork quilt; they should be seen as 'chains' or in terms of 'englobed' and 'englobing' societies.

d. Colonialism disarticulated the relations which previously defined peoples, cutting them into distinct units which were: created from nothing, or named in new contexts, or named according to toponyms and so forth. And these names were often taken up by the colonized.

Contrary to Austen's accusation (1992: 286) that Amselle's approach 'can lead to the nihilistic position of reducing all historical claims about cultural identity to the more easily documented dialectics of colonial and post-colonial struggles' – a position he then attempts, for unstated reasons, to identify with darkly unspecified 'post-modernist theory' – I would rather note how Amselle's attempt to produce a generalizing account of the historical development of ethnicity in Africa develops contradictory features as he faces the complexity of his subject. I have quoted his arguments above to the effect that ethnicities are in some respects colonial creations yet in others unchanged from their pre-colonial antecedents. In both cases I suggest he is mistaken. To return to my earlier analogy, tracking the history of ethnicity is similar to tracking that of the Tarots: the cards change their design and suits, the deck changes its composition, packs become mass-produced, new ways of telling the future or simply playing games evolve, and the players are not the same – but the sense of tracking something remains.

Ethnicity, of course, is a tougher nut since we don't have even the physical existence of cards to help us. Instead, we have to track the uses of human differences and similarities, themselves changing and man-made, within changing historical contexts – what I have called

---

15. De ce point de vue, il n'existe pas plus d'« ethnie » à l'époque précoloniale qu'à l'époque actuelle, au sens où l'on se trouverait devant des entités homogènes, racial-lement, culturellement et linguistiquement; ce qui a toujours prévalu, au contraire, ce sont des unités sociales inégales et hétérogènes quant à leur composition.

complex resemblances. Clearly colonialism is crucial, but how crucial? The colonial experience itself was highly variable in time and space south of the Sahara, and ethnic identities developed in Africa regardless of colonial history. Nonetheless, the idea that ethnic differences are special kinds of difference – traces of the past unlike other such traces – does seem to derive plausibly from interplay with European ideas. The vernacular idioms of ethnicity are usually (roughly) translatable into 'European'[16] with a sense somewhere between [transmitted] culture and [inherited] race – moreover these ideas can be translated from 'European' into the vernacular idea and inflect it. Ethnicities also develop 'contrapuntally', however, and this contrapuntal activity is an important means by which ethnicity becomes globalized. It is by virtue of this local contrapuntal development that ethnicities cannot be purely formal. Ostensible, though not unchanging, contents are necessarily involved in the definition of ethnicities (contrary to a view Eriksen 1993: 92 attributes to me). As de Saussure long ago argued, it may be true that 'twenty' is an unmotivated sound for '20' at the outset, and 'four' for '4', but this is why 'twenty-four' is already motivated. By analogy, given that social analysts can never get back to the unarguable and pristine moment of 'invention' of something (here, ethnicities) then our cases always have more of the nature of 'twenty-four' than '24' about them.[17]

Entangled identities and crossed destinies

I want briefly to recount some entangled tales from Nigeria and Cameroon to illustrate these points. These intersecting stories have been played out in what was Adamawa, the easternmost emirate of the Sokoto Caliphate, and is now a large region of northern Cameroon and Nigeria.

The first story to be told, at least on this occasion, involves the extension of the Sokoto Caliphate in carving out the Adamawa Emirate. These conquests had a different character from those at the cultural epicentre

---

16. 1 am risking that ethnic terms in the major European languages of colonization and Africanist writing (English, French, German, Spanish, Portuguese) are sufficiently similar *with respect to African languages* to lump them together. It may be a bad risk. Attention to pidgin and Creole languages, as well as indigenized use of more standard 'European', would provide an interesting middle-ground to this argument (see also note 2).

17. For a vigorous reminder of this element of de Saussure, see Ellis 1989: Chapter 2.

of the Caliphate among, predominantly, Hausa speakers. Because the Adamawa jihad could not credibly be presented as a reforming movement against lapsed muslim believers, it took on much more of the character of a Fulbe movement (Burnham and Last 1994). Numerous accounts have suggested how Fulbe identity (the identity of those dominant with the Adamawa Emirate) was particularly articulated around a few essential values which have themselves become sources of fascination for their 'carriers' (e.g. Burnham 1991 for discussion). Fulbe identity was based on highly self-conscious appreciation of a cultural essence, termed *pulaaku* in Fulfulde, which enshrined values of excellence (in understanding, comportment, mastery of Fulfulde, physical appearance etc.) and also came to include affiliation to a world religion and, at least nominally, a literate tradition (Burnham and Last 1994). These qualities were thrown into relief by the assumption of their absence among people who could be described indiscriminately as 'servile' *(haabe)* or 'pagans' *(kirdi)* (or even 'dogs' as we have already seen for Pere). Burnham and Last show how the social and demographic condition of the relatively small numbers of Fulbe in Adamawa, unlike their counterparts in Hausaland who rapidly Hausa-ized, led to a situation in which 'the Fulbe versus *haabe* distinction remained the dominant social cleavage' (1994: 342). Non-Fulbe who achieved economic or political position therefore attempted to Fulbe-ize their identities, that is to pass as Fulbe, and this was possible to some degree. However, judgements of subtle gradations in refinement of *pulaaku* remained available to differentiate between degrees of Fulbe-ness. This capacity to differentiate shades of correct comportment on the part of those 'passing' as, or into, Fulbe demonstrates the motivation of the cultural content of the named identify (that we are dealing with 'twenty-four' and not '24', as I put it above following de Saussure).

If, like one of Calvino's narrators, one had to tell the Adamawa story with tarot cards, then the series of cards describing the Fulbe story would need to occupy the position of a spinal cord, through which every other local story had to pass. The overlay of Fulbe identity must have affected the way in which non-Fulbe identities were conceptualized prior to European colonization. In previous publications I have suggested that Chamba reacted to changing circumstances in terms of an increasing importance attributed to relatively divisive idioms of patriclan organization to the detriment of alternative idioms vested in matriclanship. Several Chamba-led but 'multi-ethnic' raiding confederacies left Chambaland eventually to found chiefdoms at a distance of several hundred miles and, in many cases, beyond the immediate reach of the Adamawa Fulbe (Fardon 1988a).[18]

Colonization, whether by British, Germans or French, was initially experienced by non-Fulbe as a reinforcement of Fulbe domination. Ato Quayson has recently reemphasised that one of the problems involved in a policy of indirect rule which treated 'tribal entities as homogeneous and stable' was that 'their contradictory relationships with other ethnic groupings were entirely ignored' (1994: 113). One sees his point for many areas, but in Adamawa the argument needs reversing entirely. Because the spinal story established by the Fulbe, which included their own exceptionalism, became an anchoring narrative of indirect rule, resistance to it had to be articulated around non-Fulbe ethnic identities. Far from ignoring the contradictory relations among 'tribal' entities and the Fulbe, colonial administrators – especially those in the British-administered Northern Cameroons – were obsessively concerned with them. Local government was the favoured arena, and during the 1950s spokesmen of non-Fulbe were most often young Christians, especially Protestants, who had relations with emergent middle-belt political parties attempting to articulate a regional interest for those sandwiched between the south and north of Nigeria (see Kastfelt 1994). The numerous named ethnic groups that crystallized under early colonial rule: Chamba, Bachama, Bata, Koma, Vere and so forth, were forced to argue their identities contrapuntally with that of the Fulbe – more often than not denying the fact of Fulbe conquest and emphasising their Christianity in the face of Islam having become virtually an ethnic characteristic of Fulbe-ness.

Independence in Cameroon and Nigeria (with the Southern Cameroons Trusteeship joining Cameroon and its Northern counterpart joining

---

18. This last sentence is full of the anachronisms that brevity compels. Those who left were not yet Chamba, and their allies not yet members of non-Chamba ethnic categories. In all probability, relations between them were expressed in terms of clan names. However, some of those who were going to become Chamba during the twentieth century bear clan names which show that, had they stayed where they were in the nineteenth century, they would have become something else. Demonstration enough, I should think, of Bazin's point about the difficulty of avoiding use with reference to the past of a vocabulary naturalized this century.

Nigeria) led to early northern domination in both cases. While Northern Cameroon moved towards domination by its Fulbe bloc (which, with their national allies, also dominated nationally under the presidency of Ahmadu Ahidjo (Bayart 1979)), Northern Nigeria moved towards domination by its Hausa bloc. Fulbe-ization in Northern Cameroon (but not apparently among more southerly and stronger ethnicities like Chamba) was matched by Islamization campaigns in northern Nigeria. The Northern Cameroons Trust Territory had refused to join Cameroon – still called *Faransa* (France) in the local languages I have knowledge of – on the argument that do so was to embrace Fulbe hegemony.

Mundang in Northern Cameroon, as described by Kees Schilder, needed to find a way of being Muslim without Fulbe-izing (Schilder 1993). Initially, as it were, for Mundang as well as for Chamba there seemed to be difficulty in articulating a story line that allowed one to be Muslim without either Fulbe-izing or else clearly signalling political allegiances in that quarter. The identity of 'Muslim opposed to Fulbe hegemony' has been an achievement of the post-colonial period.

Some of the Chamba emigrants who – by virtue of getting ahead of the jihadists (to whom they probably owed their impetus) – actually escaped what were to be the limits of the Adamawa Emirate[19] found themselves in the Southern Cameroons Trusteeship which, unlike the Northern Cameroons, voted for reunification with Cameroon at Independence and became the 'anglophone' region of Cameroon.

This situation was to give rise to another play of identity: between anglophone and francophones in Cameroon (for a wry look at Francophonie, Cruise O'Brien 1991). Quite who could be said to have invented this one is equally difficult to decide. But the stereotypes traded certainly owe a great deal to the historically contrary images purveyed of one another by French and 'Anglo-Saxons'. Moreover, the arguments would leave us hard-pressed to distinguish between these, if not invented then, certainly introduced distinctions and 'authentic' ethnic prejudice. For instance,

---

19. Fulbe expansion had been halted at Bamum beyond which the Bali Chamba raiders had passed en route to being themselves arrested by defeat at the hands of Bamileke. Having acted as indirect rulers for German colonialists, Chamba in Bali Nyonga found themselves forced to defend a position in relation to the administration in Bamenda somewhat analogous to that of the Fulbe in the administration of Adamawa. Fardon 1996c (Chapter 4 in this volume) uses this example as the basis for a discussion of the notion of identity.

Anglophones see francophones as fundamentally fraudulent, superficial and given to bending rules: cheating at exams, jumping queues, rigging elections and so on […] The francophones are irked by what they see as the anglophone air of self-righteousness and intellectual superiority […] while cultural diversity is wealth, the two cultures and sets of values are not compatible […] however francophone intellectuals have also been heard to lament the failure of the anglophones to 're-deem this country with their Anglo-Saxon values'. (Ngome 1993:28-29)

For their part, the anglophones[20] obsessively revisit the grounds of the original unification, the arguments proposed in favour of it, and the dire warnings about its outcome issued by Dr E.M.L. Endeley, and finally endorsed even by the elderly John Ngu Foncha, the anglophone architect of unification.[21] However, during the disputed reelection of Paul Biya in 1992 the anglophone candidate, John Fru Ndi was able to make so strong a showing because he mobilized not just the anglophone vote but also that of the Bamileke by virtue of their opposition to the President Biya's Beti (Azonga 1993a/b; Gaillard 1992; Takougang 1993). And the language of his campaign was neither English nor French but pidgin.

Taking the foundation of Adamawa as a spinal story, I have tried to show briefly how much the other stories have had to be articulated around it. In the relation between ethnicity and ethnicities, I think it is fair to say that the Fulbe have had a head start in beginning from a conscious and dominant self-image before the colonial period. Other ethnicities crystallized – contrapuntally and without such clear-cut precedents – by disengaging a term from some of its previous relations and mobilizing it, in some degree, in opposition to the Fulbe. I am not suggesting that this case is typical – or indeed that any case is typical – my point is that rather than being invented (for administrative convenience for instance) by colonial powers and then reappropriated in a second moment by those to whom they referred, ethnicities developed through particular conjunctures of

---

20. They also seem to have accepted the label 'Anglo-Saxons' for themselves (and their new anglophone university), apparently not realizing that this is a French term for the English (who consider it to be a defunct language ancestral to their own). One of the advantages of the Anglo-Saxon legacy may be to permit the 'rigour' of the German colonial experience to be invoked at the same moment as 'uprightness' of its British successor regime (with the quotes signifying local representation as such). Regardless of this, the anglo/franco divide is remarkably and thoroughly moralized.
21. The most significant document in this vein remains 'The Buea Declaration' issued by the *All Anglophone Conference* after its meeting in April 1993. For the Cameroonian diaspora there is now the electronic billboard *Camnet* on which such issues are debated.

local circumstances in the course of the globalization of ethnicity. But ethnicity as a phenomenon is not unitary, was only ever partly achieved in Africa (contrary to the image of Africa as a land of 'tribes') and my own hunch would be that in Africa, as elsewhere, it is actually in decline.

Conclusion

And what of nationalism? The usual argument is that the collective culture of the nation remains something, for the most part, that African states are in the process of building (or not). But almost all African states have survived for thirty years since independence and even that longevity must conspire to create some fellow feeling (if only at the level of organized sport). The entrenchment of anglophone and francophone Cameroonians suggests rather more, and that the annexation of any of the smaller states by a neighbour would quickly demonstrate the reality of 'national' identities.

I have argued in this essay that African ethnicity deserves to be treated as a phenomenon more complex than either primordial identity or the flamboyant garb of self-interest. Put like that no-one is going to disagree with me; but I have also tried to demonstrate how writers generalizing on the subject of ethnicity recurrently fall back on some variant of these simple positions. In an effort not to do this I have to outline a cluster of related concepts within which the constructivist terms with which I began – invention – narration – imagination – can be applied to West Africa. In short, I have suggested that ethnicity is a polythetic and residual category and that from this it follows that ethnicities share complex resemblances. Ethnicity can also be conceived as a project in its own right, which significantly complicates attribution of human agency. Globalization of ethnicity has occurred by virtue of the concept's underdefinition and over-determination. Thanks to the Foucault effect, those most responsible for promoting the globalization of ethnicity have usually done so under the impression that they were acting on their own desires. One of the most significant reasons for the spread of ethnicity as a form is the propensity of ethnicities to be defined contrapuntally in terms of their ostensible local cultural contents. I borrowed plots of 'crossed destiny' from Italo Calvino to suggest some of the ways in which narratives could articulate with one another to this end. Finally, I have suggested that it is easy to overrate the importance of colonialism (itself a highly varied phenomenon) and as a result to underrate the significance of pre-colonial and post-colonial histories, as well as of the fact that colonialism does not exhaust the processes by which Africans have come to the late twentieth century.

ACKNOWLEDGEMENTS

A short and slightly tailored version of this paper was given at the March 1995 conference of the *Association for the Study of Ethnicity and Nationalism*. Thanks are due to Dominique Jacquin for the invitation and members of the meeting for helpful comments. David Zeitlyn added to his kindnesses over the years by initiating me into *Camnet*. Thanks are additionally due to Catherine Davies and Richard Rathbone for their suggestions and encouragement.

Chapter 6

ETHNIC PERVASION
Covering ethnicity? Or, ethnicity as coverage?[1]

To give credit its due: as an academic anthropologist and specialist on West Africa, most of my working life is spent in the Bloomsbury area of central London immersed in teaching and administration. To follow day-to-day events in the West African countries I have known best (and others I have never visited) I rely upon African visitors and coverage provided by the media – especially print media: specialist journals, like *Africa Confidential* or *West Africa,* and the diminishing flow of African news to be found in the 'quality' daily newspapers. When organizing business or diplomatic briefings through the Centre of African Studies, I am as much reliant on journalists and consultants as academics for up-to-date reports. So I have more admiration than criticism for the efforts of journalists and more daily reasons to be grateful to them than most.[2] It is all too easy to generalize about the media or those who work in it but, if journalists spoke for themselves, I hope they would insist on differentiating between types of report: contrasting those of the

1. That this chapter retains the feel of its original, a personal, off-the-cuff, reflection on anthropologists' definitions of ethnicity offered as a discussant at the Forum Against Ethnic Violence (FAEV) meeting and written up briefly for the workshop proceedings (Fardon 1996a), goes some way, I hope, to excuse its remaining self-referential quality (drawing on Fardon 1996b, 1996c Chapters 5 and 4 in this volume).
2. At the time of the FAEV meeting, I was in mid-term as Chairman of the Centre of African Studies of the University of London, and especially grateful for the generous support of Centre activities by a number of London-based journalists whose long knowledge of, and commitment to, Africa I found, and still find, inspirational.

on-the-spot specialist – whether local stringer or regional specialist with long-term knowledge – with those of visiting 'crisis' reporters; and explaining the negotiation which has to take place over the report that reaches its final consumer (whether in print, sound or image). What might be construed as criticisms of journalists are meant as observations on the state of our times, and apply to anthropologists as much as they do to journalists.

Over the course of the twentieth century, but most startlingly since the end of Eric Hobsbawm's 'short twentieth century' (Hobsbawm 1994), it has become difficult to envisage acts of collective violence that may not, from some or other perspective, be deemed ethnic. Some violence is still described in class terms; gender and generation are more generally seen as axes of violence that have collective aspects. But the overwhelming tendency is for an ethnic account to be available for collective acts of violence. To be against ethnic violence goes a long way towards being against collective violence in short; often the adjective 'ethnic' adds little further specification to the adjective 'collective'. What kind of understanding do we really gain from ethnicity?

Ethnicity seems to be in the air we breathe so that it becomes increasingly difficult to decide whether news reports cover the global phenomenon of ethnicity or whether ethnicity is the covering in which events are globally wrapped. Do reports document ethnicity or produce it? Is ethnicity part of the medium in which information is communicated, or is it the message? Can we even make this distinction? I believe these undecidabilities are principled; from which it follows that what we need to begin to understand is a world in which such unresolvable questions arise constantly in the mind of every intelligent commentator but cannot in essence ever be resolved.

One of these undecidabilities is not particular to ethnicity but may be particularly perplexing in that case. Is ethnicity a term of translation or of explanation? When we are told that 'such and such' is an ethnic term, are we simply being told, 'You may understand this best by thinking of it as, in some respects, like something you already know about', or, are we being told, 'You've seen this before and so you know what follows'? In practice, the line between translation and explanation is always difficult, sometimes impossible, to draw, but with terms like ethnicity there is the additional problem that it is not only reporters who may want to make local identities globally comprehensible but local proponents may also see, or want to see, their own situation as a variant of a global condition from which certain things are generally conceded to follow. Most obviously, there is an argument which can be made to run directly from concession of a local collective identity to ceding that identity the right to equality with other such identities, which equality entails representation among other like collectivities and the right to complete or partial self-determination. While all translations are purposeful, translation of a local identity is motivated in particularly urgent fashions because so much can seem to be entailed by it. For instance, immediate translation of bloodshed in Rwanda as an ethnic conflict between Tutsi and Hutu subsequently transpired to have been a gross oversimplification of a complex set of circumstances. Subsequent reportage had to concentrate on redescribing the hasty short-circuit by virtue of which the international community seemed to know already what followed from 'Hutu' and 'Tutsi' being ethnic terms *(Article 19* 1996). There is a constant danger that too much becomes self-evident once an identity is construed as ethnic.

The self-evidence of ethnic terms

I ask the reader's forgiveness for an autobiographical aside which helps me explain how this argument might develop: about a decade ago, when in the throes of writing an ethnography of a people of Nigeria and Cameroon who – regardless of great differences in language and dialect, political organization, history, and much else – claimed a single ethnic identity for themselves in certain contexts, I was asked to reflect for a symposium upon the relation between ethnicity and comparative anthropology (Fardon1987 Chapter 3 in this volume). The problem then looked to me like this: comparative anthropology usually sought to compare some facets of the systematic relations between a situation among the X with facets of the same situation among the Y. So, for instance, comparative anthropologists might ask whether there was some consistent relation between, on the one hand, rules of residence and descent and, on the other, the frequency of divorce in different societies. The grandest examples of such a thought style relied upon coded, and now computerized, banks of such apparently comparable information.[3]

---

3. The phrase 'thought style', to mean 'a communicative genre for a social unit speaking to itself about itself, and so constituting itself' is borrowed from Mary Douglas (1996: xii). A more faithful borrowing would go on to distinguish a variety of such

No exercise of this kind would be writable, or presumably even think-able, without some shorthand way of establishing who were the X and Y. Moreover, the X and Y would need to be unproblematic, since the thrust of the argument was elsewhere (in the comparison of other sys-tematic features). Where did these X and Y terms come from and how were they able to do their job?

The answer to the question, 'Where do ethnic terms come from?' was practically simple but historically and epistemologically complex. Practically, the names were – more often than not – simply those used by ethnographers to title the descriptions from which the comparative anthropologist's information came. However, an answer to the question where the ethnographers got the name from was far from singular. Each ethnonym (ethnic name) had its own contexts of local use, local history, relations with other local terms (some of smaller scale which it encom-passed, some larger which englobed it, some of which constituted its 'others' in different respects), and the ethnographer had decided – un-der conditions, as they say, not entirely of his or her choosing – what term to adopt and what to mean by it. Comparative anthropology was necessarily naïve about the uses of ethnic terms reported in the very ethnographies it drew upon. Over a long period ethnographers had been developing a 'hermeneutics of suspicion' towards ethnic terms: people's use of them was highly situational, some African ethnic identities were demonstrably colonial or post-colonial inventions and so forth. In short, it became difficult to define briefly what all the X, Y, Zs of comparative anthropology had in common other than that they were unit markers that could be used to play the game of comparison. Here, I use 'game' not as an easy insult but to describe an intellectual exercise with its own starting conventions and ways of going on.

Adding together all these ethnic unit markers, the analyst could not help but be struck by how much they differed from one another. From a viewpoint of Olympian detachment, the analyst might then ask what sort of synthesising definition of 'ethnicity' – the general phenomenon – might allow all these identities, translated as 'ethnicities' – in the plu-ral – to be considered its instances. No simple definition would capture them all. Ethnicity would have to be described as both a polythetic and

styles, but I am predominantly interested here in tracing how far a single style has been adopted widely. But this does not preclude later attention to the differentiation of thought styles about ethnic difference.

a residual category. By borrowing the term polythetic,[4] I meant only that ethnic terms did not share a single essential trait; instead, a term was recognized as an 'ethnic term' by virtue of having some, enough but not necessarily all, of the characteristics of that class. As a theoretically limiting but unlikely case, if we decided ethnic terms had ten defining features, it could happen that ethnic term X had characteristics one to five while ethnic term Y had characteristics six to ten. In other words, both could be construed as ethnic terms without sharing any of the defining features. To complicate matters further, any polythetic class capable of capturing all the instances of differences that might be considered ethnic was likely to cast a large net so widely as to catch examples of difference that had to be taken out and put into another category where they seemed more at home (under race, nation or class, for instance). So the design of our definitional net devised to capture ethnic differences, but only ethnic differences, would need to be both polythetic and residual. Put another way, ethnicities are only partially connected to one another: their resemblances are complex rather than simple.

From the point of view of the ethnography of a very varied people I was trying to write up, this meant that the game of comparative anthropology worked only at the cost of impoverishing the differences between local ethnicities that my ethnography demonstrated. My point, to reiterate, was not to demean comparative anthropology but to point out the necessary cost of playing that game (a cost one had to bear if taking part in the project warranted it). The cost, in short, was that highly divergent local phenomena had to be objectivized and treated as if they were analogous with one another. We shouldn't allow ourselves to forget, just because we could play the comparative game, that the objectification of ethnicities was a convention of the game; our usage was not so much wrong as limited to the purpose of the game. The danger was that in forgetting the conventional grounds of our objectivization, we reified the identities and believed their existence to be independent both of the conventions that had made them comparable and of our reasons for having played the game.

Before this comes to seem hopelessly digressive and indulgent: isn't it the case that we are all comparative anthropologists? We all

---

4. From its anthropological popularization in Rodney Needham's important essay (1975).

make contrastive comments about different collectivities. And, if so, we share the problem of needing the 'human kinds' (to borrow Ian Hacking's fertile phrase) we compare to exist self-evidently and to be self-evidently comparable.[5]

Recently, I rediscovered a more elegant and general formulation of this problem that I had forgotten since student days. In opening a clever little book called *Taboo* (1956) – based on lectures given at the Oxford Institute of Anthropology and edited after his death – the Czech anthropologist Franz Steiner noted how ethnography and comparative anthropology had tended to grow apart. Ethnographers sought increasing specificity in translation. Thus 'taboo', the term in European languages, had expanded its sense since first being reported by observers of Polynesia – it had been taken up widely (not least by Freud) and its relation to *tabu*, its Polynesian original, had become so remote that it became possible to discover that *tabu* was hardly an example of 'taboo' at all. Anthropologists, Steiner said, like other bilinguals, found themselves speaking two different languages (those of comparative anthropology and ethnography) between which they had difficulty translating. What could one do? What one couldn't do was to redefine 'taboo' by reference to *tabu*: they operated in different discourses. But one could document the historical relation between the terms in order to understand better how the situation had transpired, and one could replace 'taboo' with the more general idea that human societies imbued boundaries with dangers in order to evaluate morally and control behaviour.

Steiner helps us understand the very general nature of the problem we face in our use of terms which have pretensions to global relevance. The analogy with *tabu*/taboo is also helpful to the degree that it concerns the relation between particular and general, or local and global, usages. More generally, taboo – like ethnicity – exists as a set of practices. But there are important differences: the work of translating from *tabu* to taboo, as Steiner described it, had been largely European; but the work of translating between ethnicity as global and local condition has taken place from many sides. Moreover, ethnicities as 'human kinds' are eminently what Ian Hacking further describes as 'interactive kinds' – people

---

5. See Hacking's incisive article (1992) and his account of the statistical normalization of human categories (1990).

are changed by their relation to such types.[6] For instance, a citizen of the USA who serially identifies as a 'colored person', Negro, Black and African-American is changed by interaction with these categories of 'human kind' as is the character of the broader society (sensitively documented in autobiography by Gates 1995).

The argument that ethnicity is a polythetic and residual category has, as noted, a somewhat Olympian logical standing; the general consideration of 'interactive kinds' makes the same terrain problematic from a different angle. Let me revert to Steiner for a second. There might be philosophical argument whether translation is problematic because there is no corresponding usage in the target language or because there are many usages and the choice between them is underdetermined. In practice, Steiner generalizes, the world accepts an extension in sense more readily than a loss. This is not least so because we translate when we have a reason for doing so; therefore, we have an interest in translation being possible. Thus, words usually extend their sense in translation. Changing philosophers in mid-stream, it could be said that, pragmatically, translation does not require us to be able to match senses or classes but only to have conventions that allow us to identify similarities between exemplars (Goodman 1992). It is not that Nigerians, having worked out general criteria for membership of the category 'tribe', 'people', 'ethnic group', or 'nation', then decided that Yoruba, Tiv, Nigerians or whoever were legitimate category members. Instead, what happened was that similarities could be noticed between some exemplar of what counted as a 'tribe' and 'one's own' such that 'one's own' also became an exemplar of a 'tribe'. And if 'tribe' became pejorative in some circles and for some purposes, then any 'tribe' that became an 'ethnic group' would itself become the exemplar for others to follow that route. Ethnicity and ethnicities are thus engaged in a cumulative interaction of polythetic definition, seen globally, and exemplification, seen locally. As ethnicities, as it were, join up to the general category so the polythetic definition of that category, ethnicity, has to be widened, if only implicitly, to keep pace. And. as it widens, so there are further exemplars which provide the grounds on which new human kinds can be recognized locally. Eventually, one

---

6. In an article that combines brevity and serviceability, Hacking (1997) has summarized his ideas and also registered disquiet with some of the purposes for which they have been borrowed. I hope he would agree to loan his argument in the case of ethnic identities, since these strike me as clear examples of his interactive kinds.

supposes, the category must collapse under the burden of its extraordinary success. In the meantime, the dynamic by which ethnicities are created-as-already-subsumed under the label of ethnicity gives institutional grounds for our recognition of the increasing homogenization of the terms of people's identities. We find a global homogenization not of differences (although that might follow) but of the grounds for recognizing differences as similar.

To reiterate, this is not simply analytic but intensely practical. Ethnicity thrives because ethnicities thrive: they are the grounds to discover and pursue political and economic interest, seek or offer patronage, revise collective world-making and so forth. Certain questions about ethnicities become entirely normal features of our ethnic way of world-making. Of course such questions as 'Are they really an ethnic group?', 'Do they have a history?', 'Have they constructed their identity?' must flourish: they are the arguments inherent in this articulation of more and less general considerations. To attempt to explain Africa's ills as the results of ethnicity is to treat a translation as if it were a sufficient explanation.

Admitting that all ethnic and national identities – in fact all identities – have to be constructed, imagined and narrated in particular ways, their differences become just as interesting as their similarities.[7] After three and a half decades of independence, and a century of encapsulation within – more or less – what were to be the twentieth-century nation states of Africa, can one begin to detect differences in the style of making human kinds ethnically between neighbouring countries such as Cameroon and Nigeria? I think one can. What are the differences between, say, western and southern Africa with their divergent histories? The answers to these questions may begin to disturb any easy sense that much is explained when we are able to apply the label ethnicity.

---

7. Terence Ranger has construed this as a generational emphasis: the very success of those who demonstrated the non-primordial and non-essential character of ethnic difference has led to their successor generation taking for granted their achievement and perhaps underestimating the lag in uptake among a wider public (discussion at a conference in the Institute of Historical Research 1997). The anti-primordialist and anti-essentialist arguments still require restatement until such time as they are wholly normalized. Accepting this caution, it may be that the exploration of the implications of the argument might in the longer term be the best way to normalize the suppositions on which it rests.

A many-sided project

Assumption, in the senses both of the taking-on and the taking-for-granted, of an ethnic identity is a work of discovery that has implications for many constituencies which become apparent only as the work goes on. Translation into ethnicity is an act of transvaluation of difference.[8] Differences that become 'ethnic' are radicalized in their salience, singularity and consequentiality. Anthropologists, journalists and ethnic subjects translate differences into an idiom of ethnicity in order to achieve comprehensibility (to themselves as silent audience as much as to their eventual audience one supposes). Ethnic terms designate collective agencies that are brief and (presumably) correspond to (at least some) local versions. Ethnic subjects have attributes in terms of which stakes may be claimed. No wonder, if translation into ethnicity proceeds from all sides in a globalizing world.

Ethnic terms are proper names: not only are they highly convenient for meeting word limits, predicating subjects and objects and so forth, but proper names also suggest analogy between ethnography and biography. On this occasion, I mean by ethnography *not* the sense normal to my discipline (extended, usually written, accounts of anthropologists' local research) but a form of writing in which what the French call *ethnies* are made the agents of action.[9] (In my abuse of the term then, contemporary anthropologists would need to write anti-ethnographically in order to avoid reification in what is conventionally called their ethnography. This would be analogous to biography without the unitary subject whose lifetime's development gives biographers their narrative thread, and it would be just as difficult to sustain comprehensibly.)

One of the advantages of translation into ethnographic – by analogy with biographic – conventions of reportage is that irrational behaviour is made, not understandable, but predictable. Put differently, the rational incomprehensibility of some of its actions is what gives an acting

---

8. Franz Steiner, who was particularly sensitive to issues of translation, pointedly chose to use the term, in an analysis of the circulation of economic values, for circumstances when items exchanged have values which are not fully commensurable (Steiner 1956).
9. *Ethnies* are usually translated as ethnic categories (having identity but little organization) or ethnic groups (having both identity and organizational capacity). English lacks a single term that reifies a range of disparate entities in quite the same way as *ethnie*, but I would argue that *ethnie* does exist as a covert category in English with implications virtually identical to its French counterpart.

subject depth and complexity. Otherwise we are simply dealing with a calculating cipher. Just as human individuals have been conceived as motivated by their interests and by their passions, so too for ethnographic subjects. Thus, for instance, 'belonging' for ethnographic subjects might be analogous to what 'family' is to biographic subjects; overreaction is intrinsic to an intensity of attachment and thus always a likelihood for both types of agent. More generally, the description of ethnographic subjects by adjectives denoting personality that are used of biographic subjects is far from accidental since it evokes their individuality (the proud X, wily Y, and loyal Z).

Such ethnographic accounts provoke a highly typical range of suspicions and distrusts; so typical, indeed, that these doubts also should be envisaged as part of the 'ethnic' (by now I have argued 'ethnographic') air we breathe – and therefore as normalizing features of current discourse.

Ethnic relations, it can be suggested, are *really* the ideological fancy dress of perfectly comprehensible self-interest. Ethnicity is a folkloristic garment claiming rustic authenticity but *actually* available locally in your branch of that global player Ethnic Identities plc. *In truth,* ethnic identities are made up, and their fast-and-loose attitude to history is not difficult to demonstrate.

Academic commentators have produced illuminating critiques of ethnicity as a symbolic disguise for other interests (economic, political or whatever), but these critiques have their own problems. If ethnicity really is disguised self-interest, then there must be a deal of bad faith abroad: either at work between manipulators and manipulated or in some psychic process of collective self-delusion. Ethnic identities may be something we can find globally; but is this because they are universal, because they are becoming globalized, or because our way of worldmaking characteristically organizes the reality of other people into ethnic classifications? Moreover, ethnic identities may be made up in some respects but – in an age bent on telling us that everything is more or less fictional or made up – is this particularly damaging? And if ethnicities are invented, and if there is any sense in recognizing cultural difference, can we argue that invention is an acultural feature of all culture? It doesn't sound a very consistent argument. This process of arguing about ethnicity does not have the effect of dispersing the phenomenon; on the contrary, the range of possible argument is itself the mechanism through which ethnicity is entrenched. For instance, in the history of

Northern Cameroon and Nigeria which I studied, it was possible to witness the ethnic identities of minority peoples crystallizing as counters, contrapuntally related, to the arguments by which dominant ethnic groups sought to entrench their position vis-à-vis the colonial powers. And one could witness colonial officers in their reports lining up behind either the intrinsic capacity of the dominant people's quasi-racial capacity to rule, or else the minority people's legitimate right to be allowed spheres of self-determination. It didn't have to be Africa for the choice of sides to be seen like this.

Such development occurred within institutional and personal contexts highly conducive to a conception of all collective issues in terms of identity. In an international context, only players credentialized as 'nation states' (however improbably) got to gamble at the top tables; in interpersonal terms, various rights to personal identity vested in understandings of history, representations of what language is, relations to place and locality and so forth became derivative of the inalienable personal right to ethnic identity. To lack ethnic identity is thus to be devoid of some degree of normal (late twentieth-century) humanity; and to deny the centrality of ethnic identity is symptomatic of an indefensibly low level of self-knowledge. Both personally and collectively, identity has become a master-trope. But what is identity, and how is it demonstrated? Presumably, a person or group has to be identical to something. But to what? By definition not to something other than itself, for that would undercut the sense of identity as particular. In short, I would think, identical to itself: itself elsewhere, or itself at an earlier time.[10]

Attempts to challenge unitary conceptions of personal and collective identity have employed a vocabulary of terms such as hybridity, creolization, mongrelism, and so forth. But these words describe a condition that can exist only subsequent to speciation; as such they share the presupposition that unitary and exclusive identities have a prior or pristine existence. Because their reaction occurs on the epistemological

---

10. I have argued elsewhere – by reference to West African ethnographies – that some alternative African notions of personal identity might be construed, at least in narrow contrast with identity to the self, as dispersed. That is to say that the person is a point of confluence in numerous webs of resemblance to others who are related in various ways (through one's mother's and father's marriages, through affinal relations, etc.) (Fardon 1996c Chapter 4 in this volume).

terrain of essentialized identities, for most readers terms denoting 'mixture' actually reinforce the normative status of the presuppositions they
are designed to challenge and reveal how thoroughly assumptions of
human speciation in terms of ethnicity have colonized notions of difference.[11] To this degree, ethnicity has become additionally coercive.

Superficially, normalization of the expectation that people have ethnicity and identity, and that the two should be related, has had an effect
similar to inviting everyone to express themselves individually: everyone
has 'done their own thing' – but rather similarly. At least this is the cyni-
cal impression produced by using general (or globally relevant) notions
of identity and ethnicity to make other people's events readily comprehensible. These events become directly comparable to those elsewhere
and simultaneous with some of them. In short, coevalness in time and
space is suggested.

Here we encounter another indication of the epistemological air we
breathe, and again it comes in the form of a characteristic dilemma. Not
to suggest that people(s) living in the same age are coevals can be a device to project the 'other' into a time different from oneself.[12] However,
to suggest too easily that peoples are entirely coeval is to risk imposing a
hegemonic and homogenizing account of time and space quite contrary
to an argument that the parameters of local life are – at least in some
degree – locally produced. Thus, we find mutually impugning arguments.

The types of questions that arise, to reiterate, strike me as being entirely normative: they are questions intrinsic to ethnic coverage and
circulate quite happily within the parameters of an ethnographic world-
view to produce a comforting sense that serious thought is being given
to pressing questions. Ethnicity is powerfully reinforced by its position
as a middle term between the nation and the individual, drawing upon
the institutional entrenchment and self-evidence of both.

Any suggestion that there are simple, quick fixes to our situation
would be wrong. Commentators, whether academics or journalists, have
no place into which to step wholly outside the terms of these argument
nor can they navigate around and thus ignore them. We need ways to live

---

11. Kwame Anthony Appiah's is a remarkable attempt in this direction (1992).
However, this tendency is presently less typical of accounts of African identities in
Africa than it is of, for instance, post-colonial South Asian accounts of identity.
12. With results explored in a celebrated anthropological critique by Johannes Fabian
(1983).

constructively with a current thought style shared, in many respects, by observer and observed.

In and out of the whale

This brings me back to the potential role of an academic anthropologist – typically stuck in his or her university office. I realize there are anthropologists outside the academy (probably as many as within), and there are anthropologists close to the epicentre of ethnic violence. I do not wish to appear to speak for anthropology or, indeed, for anthropologists, but only on behalf of whatever generalizable aspects there might be in my own situation.

Most illuminating in the long run, I suggest, will be attempts complementary to those of on-the-spot reporters which seek to contextualize both ethnicity (the role of the somewhat ill-defined but ambitious master idea in the world) and the relation to it of particular ethnicities (local identities) and ethnically based organizations in the world. And such accounts will need to analyse the complex relations between multifaceted projects of ethnicity, nationalism and individualism.

This project lays claim to a different sort of coevalness: through recognition of the senses of local time and local space simultaneously abroad in the world, and in the attempt to understand how these articulate contrapuntally with one another in the globalizing system of historical and spatial claims that are made in the name of collective actors.

This is not an immediately newsworthy proposition, but a sense of, if not this, then something such must be why anthropologists occasionally allow themselves the sense of reading through the surface of the news reports of some journalists. (And why more specialist journalists know how the depth – or depthlessness – of their own reportage is tailored to a particular communication slot.)

The challenge is not just to see *through* the shibboleths of the age: to argue that ethnicity is not universal, or to challenge specific ethnicities by showing them as self-interested or historically contrived. Such challenges, I have argued, actually have a normalizing effect; perversely, as a phenomenon anchored to accounts of the past, ethnicity thrives on a history of such challenges. The greater challenge is to explain how the shibboleths of the age are produced, why they convince (ethnic and outside commentators alike) and how the dynamic of increasing ethnic speciation is accelerated. The problem, precisely, is to understand the superficial: the style of thought, of which ethnicity is a characteristic 'groove' through which the currents of explanation are readily channelled.[13]

The achievement of a previous generation of Africanists was to demonstrate that African ethnic identities were not primordial, that they had histories of invention or construction that belonged, just as much as their counterparts elsewhere, to the conditions under which the contemporary world came to be what it is (Ranger 1993). Where this is not understood, it needs repeating, for only once this is conceded is it possible to address more nuanced problems. Apart from the design of ethnic argument, these are twofold: the realization of the diversity of ethnic situations across Africa and, related to this, the diversity of grounds, other than ethnic, for identities differing.

The study of ethnicity is part of the study of how and why people objectify, reify and fetishize human collectivities on the basis of their perceived differences, and of the conditions for and consequences of their doing so.[14] Objectification, reification and fetishization are no more than arbitrary points along a continuum stretching from – something like – the capacity to recognize an ethnic group as figure against a wider ground, through treating it as thing-like (and forgetting the objectification process), to attributing to it various characteristics in which we decide not to collude. I use this loaded continuum and relate it to a 'we', because I cannot conceive how a commentary on ethnicity could be written without the commentator – whether or not by intention – also being situated in terms of an evaluation of particular ethnic differences. An outside commentator's judgement is often swayed by a broader end (perhaps liberation from domination in whatever guise) towards which an ethnicity can be envisaged as purposed. But whether or not explicitly: the question of evaluating ethnicity cannot finally be bucked.

Several recent developments strike me as helpful. One is the move from intensive study of single ethnicities – typical of ethnographers' early fieldwork – to the study of contrapuntally related local ethnicities

---

13. The image – of thought styles having grooves, worn by persistent use and institutionally entrenched, which offer the line of least resistance to thinking as usual – is Mary Douglas's.

14. As noted earlier, Steiner's (1956) account of 'taboo' moved to subsume the 'problem' of taboo under a broader rubric. I am attempting to follow the example of his argument.

– which can be studied intensively only on the basis of longer-term, multi-site ethnographic research. Philip Burnham's long-term study of Northern Cameroon, including collaborative study with ethnographers of neighbouring peoples, is a signal achievement in this context (Burnham and Last 1994; Burnham 1996). Such studies reveal the differences between local circumstances that are obscured by too ready acceptance of the global homogenization of the grounds of ethnic difference.

Building from this basis, one would also welcome more intensive studies of the grounds of African national identities and public cultures. How variable are the local idioms of difference in African languages, pidgins and in languages of European origin spoken in Africa? How varied are the 'solutions' proposed in African countries to the management of these perceived internal differences? The differences between official language policies in African countries tell us a great deal about the political imaginary of these nations that differ widely in size and in their perception of, and attitude towards, the differences among the people that make them up (Fardon and Furniss 1994b). These attitudes are susceptible of further study in, for instance, policy towards the ongoing liberalization, or simply privatization, of the air waves. How many languages are chosen for broadcast? How is air-time apportioned? How is access arranged? (Panos Institute 1993; *Article 19 and Index on Censorship* 1995).

A second recent trend challenges the extent to which African identities are rooted in ethnicity. Paul Richards' study of war in Sierra Leone has highlighted the importance of youth as a category of identification (Richards 1996). Louis Brenner has devoted a volume of essays to Muslim identity in sub-Saharan Africa (Brenner 1993). Richard Werbner has drawn more general attention to the plurality of African postcolonial identities (Werbner 1996). Study of identities that are not, primarily, ethnically intended may help to allay any sense that sub-Saharan Africa, as a sub-continent, is more easily and thoroughly explicable in terms of ethnicity than elsewhere.

A third more general consideration refers to the re-embedding of African ethnicity in the recent political and economic context of the countries of the continent. It is now clearer than it was at the outset, how far the Rwandan experience resulted from the failed imposition of a programme of transition to democracy (Prunier 1995). Generalizing, the environment of scarcity resulting from structural adjustment, which has been the context for coerced 'democratization', has inevitably incited resort to identity politics as a means of rationing and distributing resources.

Ethnicity can all too easily become a way of laying not just entire blame, but responsibility for the entire circumstances at the door of the natives. If little can be done about other people's atavistic fantasies, it might be suggested, better to stand aside. But it is one thing to say that the people most immediately concerned must have final ownership of any solutions essayed to their dilemmas, and another to suggest that the circumstances of their choice cannot be ameliorated. To say we need to understand better is banal but true; to say that part of this understanding might require nothing more immediately costly than a robust resilience to ethnicity as coverage is something a little more. I have tried to suggest, in brief compass, why ethnic coverage can seem convincing and why it is often wrong to be convinced. But I am not suggesting ethnicity be ignored or wished away. The simplest reaction to arguments about ethnicity in Africa is to say, 'Ah, so it wasn't *really* ethnicity, it was *really* politics, economics, religion …'. The simple reaction is to believe if ethnicity is not explanatory, it is entirely derivative of whatever is explanatory. Rather, my point is that reportage has to recognize the complexity of ethnicity as a project in Africa – and elsewhere. It is not *that* ethnicity explains (or indeed doesn't explain) but *how, when, why and in what form* ethnicity helps us to explain.

Picking up a phrase of Henry Miller's, George Orwell regretted the decision of those who, like Jonah, preferred the womb-like security of the whale's stomach to the raw experience of life outside.[15] The Biblical whale, as he reminds us, was really a fish, so we might add that the resident of one fish, emerging in anticipation of being dazzled by the light, might enter only the dark stomach of the larger fish that had eaten it. Is there any illuminated place outside the whale of ethnic discourse? Not in a simple sense. Yet, it seems to me that trying to discover what it feels like inside and outside this whale is as close to a method as the beast permits.

---

15. 'Inside the whale', originally published in 1940, in *The Collected Essays, Journalism and Letters of George Orwell*, Vol. 1: *An Age Like This 1920-1940*, edited by Sonia Orwell and Ian Angus (1970), Harmondsworth: Penguin.

Chapter 7

TIGER IN AN AFRICAN PALACE

What looked like modernist social anthropology's theory of history was – so this essay will argue – nothing of the sort but instead a theory of identity in need of a historical dimension. With some help from a tiger in a Cameroonian palace, I shall argue that even in the hands of sophisticated mid-twentieth-century anthropological theorists – such as Franz Baermann Steiner – a 'charter' theory of history was incapable of explaining why certain mementoes of the past became treasures. Because the transvaluation of material traces of the past into present-day treasures offers a close analogy, or so I shall claim, to the translation of past events into charters for contemporary affairs, examining the historic labour invested in creating a treasure can highlight some of the problems we face when trying to track changes in identities and their charters. These problems congregate densely around the fundamental issue of historic continuity: what remains the same when ground and figure may both change? I shall argue that no convincing sociological answer to this question can ignore the historic engagement of human labour in the project of creating historic continuity and, furthermore, that the most powerful of these connections are usually not established propositionally.

Present problems

As a modernist movement the social anthropology of Bronislaw Malinowski and the (more or less) two intellectual generations of anthropologists who succeeded him, set both itself and its theories firmly in the present. *Itself,* partly because modern simply means 'of the now', and *partly,* because functional anthropology made much of its displacement of evolutionist, diffusionist and outmoded intellectualist theories by its own vivid explanations of practices and institutions in terms of their very contemporaneity, their very 'here-and-nowness'. Merging the temporal nearness of the present with the spatial nearness of presence, functional explanations proposed that cause and effect merged in an actuality of social existence. Hence the investigation of functional processes had to occur proximately in both spatial and temporal senses: in the 'here-and-now' of the investigator's research. When experience-based description and functional explanation were written up in the ethnographic present, a third 'now' – writerly and generic – was made the medium of a presentism that was simultaneously methodological and theoretical. The consistency of this high valuation of the 'here and now' elevates it, to my mind, beyond mere preference towards an aesthetic disposition characteristic of its time.

A preference for the 'here and now' was nowhere more obvious than in functional approaches to history itself. Malinowski's famous theory of mythical charters (1944: 111, 162-4) suggested that accounts of the origins and purposes of institutions had to be studied as justifications of a present order; charters were used in the present and should be studied and explained as such. For instance, in societies that conserved them to any depth, genealogies needed to be investigated in those contexts when people felt moved to bring them forward to support arguments, and their being so moved should be explained in terms of the interests, both personal and collective, that genealogical charters served. Evans-Pritchard for the Nuer (1940: 229-34) and such of his students as Laura and Paul Bohannan (1952, 1955) for Tiv and Emrys Peters (1960) for Bedouin demonstrated the power of this line of argument in explaining the invariant depth of genealogies despite the passage of time and generations. More generally, the argument was taken up to emphasise how far rhetorical uses of the past needed to be construed as the expression of identity interests in the present (whether of individuals or collectivities).

All this is well-worked ground, and my traversal of it hasn't involved new paths. My purpose is to spotlight just how recursively and insistently the intellectual strategies of modern social anthropology urge the present upon us. Self-consciously a modern intellectual movement, social anthropology researched into the present, explained in terms of the present, and wrote in its own specialized expansion and condensation of the present tense. A quality of 'now-ness' recommended whatever it touched; and 'pastness' seemed correspondingly unattractive. Those of us trained by the mid-century modernists probably absorbed presentism as we acquired a sense for the aesthetics of a properly proportioned anthropological argument.

Our editors' observation (James and Mills 2005) that there has been little dialogue between anthropological theories of time and history, applies especially to functional or charter theories of history. If history is to be understood only as a construction subservient to current interests, a more or less serviceable past designed for the present, then no theory about the passage of time is required. Value is attributed to a (rather one dimensional) 'pastness' existing entirely in the present.

All this emphasis on the present was not, as we know, unproblematic. Slightly amending Johannes Fabian's argument of the 1980s (1983, 1991) to my interests, I would argue that the tendency to use the present as an answer to all of anthropology's problems (whether of theory, method or genre) had the perverse effect, like a goodwill gesture over-used, of rendering all – and thereby no – ethnographic scenarios coeval. Writing in the ethnographic present, as has been amply demonstrated, compounded the problem of undiscriminating coevalness by conflating the 'now' of writing, with the various 'nows' of local research, whether reported events, recurrent processes, reconstructions of the eve of colonization and so forth. Functional anthropology deserves to lose credibility less on account of its arguments from effects, the usual villain of the piece, than on account of the unsustainable weight it places upon the idea of the present. Arguments from effect come in more and less justifiable forms, but a theory of history entirely invested in the present, and wholly devoid of reference to the passage of time, becomes unsustainable even in its own terms. If the present is baldly counterposed to the past, and attempts to narrate that past are only efforts to underwrite present interests, then it is difficult to understand how present interests could have any temporal trajectory that is not simply their own justification?

In short, radical presentism makes the present itself incomprehensible (and something we cannot understand can scarcely be asked to explain its own history). This said, it may seem surprising now to argue that this modernist theory has a future in social anthropology; however, I believe it raises interesting questions so long as it is treated not as a theory of either history or of time, but only as a theory of how some 'pastness' is transfigured for the 'now'. Fundamentally, this is a theory of identity transformation in need of temporal specification rather than a theory of history.

The most succinct, mid-century, expression of the operator imagined to animate such identity work – at least that I have come across – occurs in one of Franz Baermann Steiner's *Statements and essays,* the semi-private prequels to extended and considered statements he did not, for the most part, live to make.

> The chief sociological principle is probably this: that no individual can have a position [*eine Stelle*] without identifying himself with something, and there is no identification without transformation. The necessity for identification is primary. This is the chief difference between human and animal social forms. The 'I' of human society is at the apex of a triangle of which the other corners are called communication and identification. The sides [*Schenkel,* also thighs] adjacent to the I-point are called language and transformation [*Verwandlung*]. The circumscribing circle is 'society' – in its metaphysical sense. (based on Schüttpelz 2003: 44)

As Erhard Schüttpelz points out, Steiner's formulation maps a tension: in order to occupy a status there must be identification, but identification implies transformation. The image evoked by Steiner's prose recalls the most famous of Leonardo's 'measurement' drawings[1] of the proportions of the human figure (an illustration to the first chapter of the third book of Marcus Vitruvius Pollio's first century BC treatise *De architectura* that was rediscovered as an inspiration to the Italian Renaissance). The

---

1. Pen on paper, 34.3 x 24.5 cm, Venice, Accademia, No. 228, c.1492. Apparently the text Leonardo copied to accompany his original drawing did not include the sentences he illustrated: 'The navel is naturally placed in the centre of the human body, and if a circle be described of a man lying with his face upward and his hands and feet extended, it will touch his fingers and his toes. It is not alone by a circle that the human body is thus circumscribed, as may be seen by placing it within a square. For if we measure from the feet to the crown of the head, and then across the arms fully extended, we should find the latter measure equal to the former; so that the lines at right angles to each other enclosing the figure would form a square' (Vitruvius quoted by Ludwig Goldscheider 1945: Note 48, p. 29).

outstretched limbs of Leonardo's human figure touch the inner edge of the circle circumscribing him. This circle, Steiner tells us, is 'society', but not in its actuality (as described perhaps by Radcliffe-Brown [1952]) but in terms of its presence to the individual.

Schüttpelz notes that a second aphoristic statement, following directly upon it in Steiner's notebooks, seems to extend the same train of thought:

No transformation is conceivable without previous identification. The goal of transformation is thus communicable, lies within language. The process of trans-formation is only indirectly language-related – through the goal towards which it points but which does not interpret it. The mythical occurrence is a transforma-tion that is wholly expressible through identifications; thus it is comprehensible through language. As such it is not irrational, rather the series of mythic trans-formations are the quasi-rational organizing principles of all non-communicable series, that is the whole chaotic transformative potentiality of the human universe. (Schüttpelz 2003: 45)

So far as can be ascertained in the present state of research, Steiner's only explicit development of the concept of transformation[2] occurs in his lectures on taboo during a discussion of Arnold van Gennep's *rites de passage*. This suggests that Steiner imported into his native German philosophical references a cluster of French-language sociological ideas that make up – as our editors' Introduction notes (James and Mills 2005) – one of the informing images of mid-century British social anthropol-ogy. Identification is treated as a status (thus communicable), whereas movement between status positions, or more precisely the state of be-ing in movement between them, cannot be expressed propositionally (and may be apprehended only through evocation of the experience of liminal excursus, or by analogy with the effects of mythological opera-tors – functions that Steiner himself seems forced to conjure up visu-ally). Steiner adds two unusual elements to this sophisticated but also typical, quintessentially mid-century, British social anthropological analy-sis: these concern positionality and movement (the second envisaged as distinct operations of detachment and attachment). From others of his writings it is clear that Steiner habitually considered individuals (whether persons or societies) as composite, thus potentially conflictual entities. This is entirely consistent with the sense of restless instability between identification and transformation in Steiner's aphorism. Transformation

---

2. To judge both from Schüttpelz's perusal of the unpublished aphorisms and from the index to Adler and Fardon's (1999) edition of Steiner's selected writings.

necessitates identification, but identification in its turn entails transformation. In short, identities are in constant movement within the human universe's 'chaotic transformative potentiality', which we may take as a summation of all the finally inexpressible processes of being in movement between momentarily determinable positions. If the image of triangle within circle is indeed meant to suggest such hermetic devices as Leonardo's implausibly proportioned encircled human figure – as well as the cabbalist literature of the renaissance, and the generative and combinatorial operators of the aphoristic tradition[3] – then we should envisage it not as static but as spinning in that chaos of transformative energy to which Steiner refers. Perhaps Steiner intended another parallel here to Leonardo's derivation (via Vitruvius) of man-made architectural symmetries from the given potentialities of the human form (see *Figure 7.1*).

If the reader is able to accept my proposition that Steiner's idiosyncratic imagery nonetheless encapsulates much of the essential mood of mid-century social anthropological thought, then it is worth posing once more the problem of the notorious absence of a historical dimension. And, in terms of Steiner's imagery, it would seem that the problem arises because individuals in movement between positions are envisaged to be outside structural determination and therefore in a state that may only be evoked – diagrammatically or perhaps by analogy with myth. While finding Steiner's identity operator a fertile thought object, I see no reason why some effort cannot be made to specify its operations temporally – even in terms of a strong benchmark conception of historical time, such as that proposed by Georg Simmel.

In the 1916 essay translated as on 'The problem of historical time', Georg Simmel (1980: 127-44) provides an ambitious standard. For an 'item' to qualify as historical for Simmel: it ought both to be fully understandable to us, and to be uniquely located in a temporal frame. The two criteria should intermesh such that it is on the basis of our understanding that we realize the item could not be located temporally other than

---

3. Jeremy Adler and I discuss the notion of what H.G. Adler called a 'universal mathesis' in Steiner's work in our Introduction the first volume of Steiner's selected works (1999 I: 36, 48-9). The translation presented here of 'The chief sociological principle…' benefits from Erhard Schüttpelz's research on Steiner's original manuscripts. Obscurities that Adler and I were unable to resolve in our earlier translation (Steiner 1999 II: 240) had their source in (reasoned but probably erroneous) transcription decisions made in H.G. Adler's typescript from which we worked.

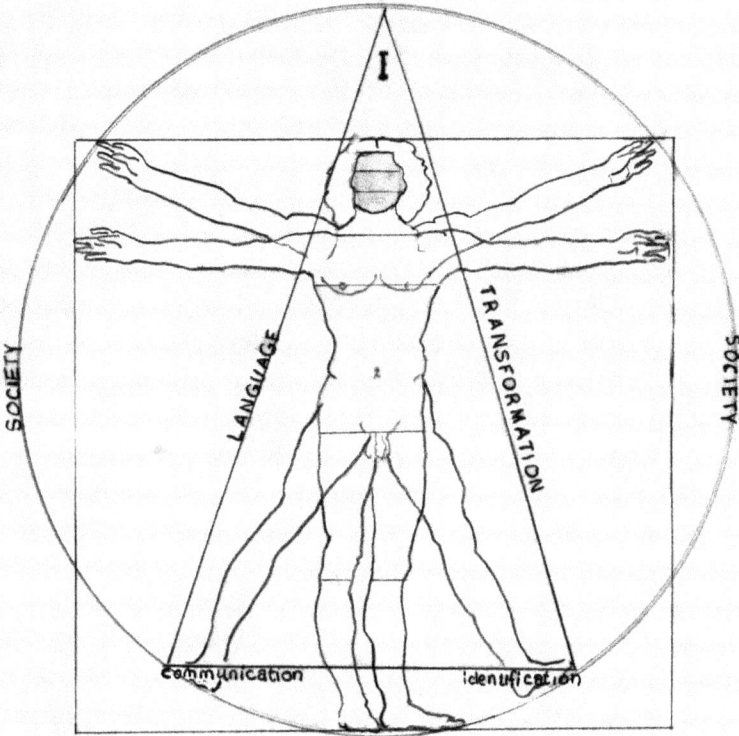

Figure 7.1. Steiner's operator superimposed on Leonardo's measurement drawing

in the position – relative to other items – it in fact occupies. His own summary at this point in his argument reads:

> ... from the fact that an item has a *temporal status*, it does not follow that it is historical. And from the fact that this item is *understood*, it does not follow that it is historical. Suppose, however, that both of these conditions are satisfied. An item is historical when it is temporalized on the basis of an atemporal interpretation. In principle, this criterion for historicity can be satisfied only if interpretation embraces the totality of contents. This is because the single item can really be understood only in its relationship to the absolute totality. It follows that in this context temporalization can only mean location within a specific temporal frame. (ibid.: 1980: 131, added emphases)

Continuing, Simmel explains why 'temporalization' is so important to the understanding of events.

> This logical consequence is based on the following two considerations. First if temporalization is based on the total process, then every event can have only one

unique location that cannot be exchanged with any other. Second, interpretation is possible only given the relatively precise determination of time. It is not possible to understand an item simply by ascribing a general temporal location to it. To ascribe a general temporal location to an item is simply a way of saying that the event in question really happened. And that is precisely what cannot be achieved by interpretation. (ibid)

Simmel's requirements to cross the threshold of historicity may be unfeasibly high in many cases but, as such, they usefully highlight just how far short of a theory of history modern social anthropology's account of the uses of the past fell. Modern social anthropology revealed ways that 'past-ness' was mobilized in present processes of identification and transformation. Explanatory weight fell (as it did iteratively) upon the present: deployment of the past made sense in terms of its impact now. The social anthropologists' account ignored both of Simmel's threshold criteria of historicity: the past was not (in some cases, anthropologists believed, could not be) temporally specified, and there was no attempt to understand the past 'item' other than in terms of its present use. It hardly needs to be added that achieving the two-pronged criterion of uniquely placing the past event temporally in terms of our understanding of it, could not be addressed at all. Instead, to return to my opening, explanatory weight was thrust onto the present as the context in which to explain how recollections of the past were transacted. However, to repeat what now should seem only mildly paradoxical, this hectic and reiterative presentism ended by having no account of why the present was as it was, or – and this is fundamentally damaging – any way of delimiting what 'present' designated. This became abundantly clear when commentators attempted to define any consistent temporality to the written 'ethnographic present'.[4] Mid-century anthropology, in short, was not predisposed to see the present as the product of the past, hence – despite the intentions of many of its practitioners – its apolitical character as a theoretical project. I expressly say 'as a theoretical project' since social anthropology in practice had a redeeming characteristic: the experience of ethnographic actualities usually prompted writers to go beyond what we are able to read retrospectively into the theoretical pronouncements of their times. Ethnographic experience

---

4. Within an extensive debate, see Davis 1992 and Sinclair 1993.

as corrective to anthropological precept would, however, be another paper on the same subject.[5] Here, I have been concerned instead with what, following Fredric Jameson (1981), might be called the generative political unconscious of anthropological precept.

To recap: what looked like mid-twentieth-century social anthropology's contribution to the study of history was nothing of the sort. Rather, it was a demonstration that all contemporary individual and collective identifications had recourse to the past. Effective in a crude kind of way in dealing with contemporary uses of the past, and important as a methodological caution against naïve derivation of history from present sources, social anthropology's 'identity operator' drew from notions current in turn of the century French-language sociology – including van Gennep's – the precept that resting points in identification had a propositionality that processes of transformation between identities did not (a harbinger of V.W. Turner's more thoroughgoing sense of the necessity of liminality to change). Steiner's originality within his circle – even if he didn't follow it through – was to produce a formulation that implicitly challenged the possibility of a distinction between identity and identity transformation by showing the two to be mutually entailed. I think these remain fertile ideas, and I want now to explore them in a direction Wendy James anticipates in her discussion of Marcel Mauss's rather hesitant relation to time and history in Africa. His difficulty, as James sees it in introducing her subject, is that the ideas of the *Année sociologique* school rested heavily on a distinction between archaic and modern time that could at least *seem* to be made to work better in the Arctic or Australia than it could in Africa. 'The distinction between "traditional" and "modern" time ... collapses into the history which has produced it: in particular, the history of the concepts of modernity and progress themselves, and in the special case of anthropology, the colonial encounter' (James 1998: 226).

The counterpoising of the traditional with the modem is a feature of widespread contemporary African sensibility that itself, as James suggests more generally, is a product of a particular historical process rather than the shape that history has taken. Evaluations like traditional versus modern assume some life of their own in so far as they come to inflect

---

5. Lyn Shumaker's recent account of research at the Rhodes-Livingstone Institute in Northern Rhodesia (2001) shows just how far precept and practice might diverge.

human agency by becoming part of its context. Ethnicity in Africa has been a striking example of the simultaneous changes in item and context that makes identity transformation so difficult to express in terms that are clear without being oversimplifications. Our problem is that changes over time occur both in the 'figure' (say, a particular ethnicity) and in the 'ground' (current anticipations of ethnicity as a type of difference) (Fardon 1996b, 1999a Chapters 5 and 6 in this volume, 1999b). To take up James's comment on the significance of colonialism: colonial administration, based on colonial presuppositions about difference, acted upon both ethnicity as ground and ethnicities as figures. Often it could affect the latter indirectly: where local administrative practices were mediated through already dominant ethnicities, less powerful ethnicities were obliged to resort to a kind of catching up exercise by carrying out identity work in a changing context that, while generally unfavourable to them, nonetheless offered the possibility of an emergent rights discourse related to affirmations of distinct identity. Analytic arguments as to whether ethnicities were, or were not, invented or constructed or however made up – or whether they either did, or did not, have histories – do considerable injustice to both the modulations between mutually implicated fields and figures in these historical processes of change and to the increasingly undecidable status of quite what should be construed local and what imported in such processes. Following Simmel, we need to temporalize these processes, such that the terms in which we understand them simultaneously fix them as having to have occurred at one time rather than another. Here I find it helpful to explore these issues in the light of some rather literal fields and figures: in this case images of tigers, how they were framed, and quite what they are doing in a trope-filled, African palace.

Tiger in an African palace

The existence of tigers in Africa has engaged some notable minds. Nelson Mandela and his prison companions' celebrated debate raised some germane points.

> One subject we harkened back to again and again was whether there were tigers in Africa. Some argued that although it was popularly assumed that tigers lived in Africa, this was a myth and that they were native to Asia and the Indian subcontinent. Africa had leopards in abundance, but no tigers. The other side argued that tigers were native to Africa and some still lived there. Some claimed to have seen with their own eyes this most powerful and beautiful of cats in the jungles of Africa.

I maintained that while there were no tigers to be found in contemporary Africa, there was a Xhosa word for tiger, a word different from the one for leopard, and that if the word existed in our language, the creature must once have existed in Africa. (Mandela 1994: 511)[6]

There is some truth in most of the views expressed here. There are archaeological traces of tigers north of the Sahara (Wilson 1995: 537); tigers have entered African English via translation of local terms, so that tiger masquerades are reported from southern Nigeria (Oha 2001); nowadays there are football teams called 'The Tigers' – notably the national team of the Central African Republic (Royer 2002: 462); and numerous products are tiger branded.[7] As some listeners asked at the conference in Arusha, why are tigers in Africa more problematic than, say, the tigers that a particular brand of petrol promised to put in European petrol tanks, or the lions of European heraldry, or indeed the British annexation of Tippoo's mechanical tiger from India that now occupies a prominent spot in the Victoria and Albert Museum in London (Karp and Kratz 2000)? No reason at all, of course, except that in the African case – or at least the particular one to which I turn – it is possible to chart the stages of the tiger's introduction as a cultural item and, on this basis, to develop some more general points about the relation of imagery to identity.

This case study concerns what, in general terms, might be called a 'durbar' ceremony – if by that term we understand not just its Indian 'original' but a variety of local martial displays that were able to be incorporated into colonial 'ornamentalism'.[8] In the course of their north to south raiding before establishing the Bali chiefdoms in the Grassfields of present-day Cameroon, Chamba leaders had incorporated various peoples, and their Lela festival developed from earlier martial ritual to become an occasion for – among other things – this motley crew to

---

6. Gemetchu Megerssa was kind enough to point out that many of the questions I raised were prefigured in this excerpt. I have only subsequently come across Carmel Schrire's engaging lecture which uses the same device and quotation (Schrire 2002).

7. Thanks to Christine Stelzig's retentive memory for the historic reference and to David Pratten's advice on the interpretation of references to tiger masquerades in Nigeria.

8. I am indebted to Umar Buratai, who visited the University of London as an A.G. Leventis Fellow in autumn 2001, for conversations on this shared interest. The durbar itself might have served as well as the tiger for my example. Ornamentalism is, of course, the title of David Cannadine's account of British imperial ritual and display (2001).

pledge loyalty to their king. The ceremony crystallized into something recognizable as that performed today during the earliest years of German colonization of Kamerun, of which the chiefdom of Bali Nyonga was an important intermediary. In May 2001, when the opportunity arose to take part in a block seminar in Basel[9] where many of the most important early photographs of this event are housed in the mission archive, I was fascinated to see a video of the 1999 Lela taken by a Swiss cooperant, Andres Wanner. I have not myself seen Lela since 1984, so this is vicarious 'fieldwork' in the digital age. Much remained the same fifteen years on, but among the things that had changed was a mural depicting a tiger painted on a bright red background behind the King's throne in the palace forecourt, an area that accommodated much of the activity of the Lela celebration. Why a tiger in an African tropical kingdom? The lions and elephant to either side of the tiger were at first sight less incongruous, but this was misleading since they transpired to share much of their inspiration with the tiger. Finding a still image and some information about all this involved me in more digital-age research. Days before the conference, scouring the internet more in desperation than expectation, I found myself indebted to a site belonging to Peter Sengbusch, a biologist based at the University of Hamburg, who had posted photographs taken in 1997 on his website, Afrika-online (see *Figure 7.6*).[10] Further enquiry to Ted Johnson, proprietor of a Bali Nyonga website and an American volunteer who worked with coffee cooperatives in the early 1990s, provided the information that the murals had been undertaken in 1993-4 by David Louis Musi. Musi, who had died some time in 2000, had been a schoolteacher and the town's leading electric guitarist as well as an artist and carver.[11] His services had been engaged during palace improvements undertaken at the behest of the reigning monarch, HRH

---

9. I am grateful to Paul Jenkins for adding this invitation to his other kindnesses (including permission to reproduce photographs from the collection of the Basel Mission Archive), and to the seminar participants for stimulating responses that I shall acknowledge more fully in a detailed account of Lela that is in preparation [subsequently Fardon 2006]. Here, I want to acknowledge two participants particularly: Ernst Elsenhans and Hans-Peter Straumann who sent me photographs after the seminar two of which appear here.

10. At the time of writing, there are three colour photographs of the Bali Nyonga palace at http://www.biologie.uni-hamburg.de/b-online/afrika/kamemn/bali.htm

11. At the time of writing, his photograph appears at http://www.bamenda.org/ted/drmoses/crydie/musi.jpg

Figure 7.2. The Palace of Bali Nyonga (1997) © Peter v. Sengbusch

Figure 7.3. Treasure displayed at the 1908 Lela. Basel E-30.27.003

Fon Dr Ganyonga III, who succeeded to his father's throne in 1985.[12]
So we know when the tiger – and the elephant and lions – were painted
as a palace mural, but we are none the wiser why a tiger.

A clue to the *proximate* origin of these images – and of their blue and
white patterned borders – comes in an early twentieth-century record
of the treasure displayed during Lela. In those days, fences encircling
the palace were renewed, and to the right of the entrance from the orientation of the exiting monarch – that is, in the position that the murals
now occupy – were hung cloths. In a photograph of the 1908 ceremony
we see a display of royal wealth including ivory horns, a throne placed
upon leopard and cow skins, a stool, statues, an umbrella, a fog horn and
cloths hung upon the palace fencing (*Figure 7.3*). Three layers of cloth
can be discerned: at the bottom are patterned blue and white cloths imported as part of the regional trade from either the Jukun to the west or,
more likely, the Ndop plains closer by. (The missionary Jakob Keller refers to them as *ndi ndob,* 1919: 65.) These types of prestige cloths predate
European colonization.[13] That a figurative cloth overlays these becomes
clearer in a photograph taken in either 1909 or 1910 to which I turn
shortly. The topmost layer of cloth in the 1908 display consists of two
simulacra of leopard skins. To the best of my knowledge, these fabrics
are not recorded as reappearing at later Lela (but the record is uneven,
so this absence of evidence is not evidence that they were never used
again); and it is readily apparent that they are not displayed for want
of real leopard skins (since some skins lie upon the ground). It looks
more as if we are dealing with a decorative aesthetic that finds cloth appropriate for hangings and skins for footings. The middle layer of cloth
is visible in a (somewhat blurred and crudely retouched) photograph

---

12. At the time of writing, photographs of the cry die of Galega II and the installation
of Ganyonga III were to be found on the website of the Bali Cultural Association of
the USA: http://www.bca-usa.org/bea/galega.html

13. E-30.27.003 is one of a series of photographs of the 1908 ceremony in the Basel
Mission Archive. The circumstances under which they were taken can be reconstructed
with a high degree of likelihood and seem to rest on the simultaneous presence in Bali
of the German museum ethnologist, Bernhard Ankermann, the missionary and coun-
sellor to the Bali chief, Ferdinand Ernst, and the trainee missionary, Jonathan Striebel,
who was responsible for most of the photographs finding their to way to Switzerland
along with his written account. A fuller account of these circumstances will appear in
a *Festschrift* for Paul Jenkins (Fardon 2004).

Figure 7.4. Treasure displayed at the 1909 or 1910 Lela. Basel E-30.27.008

that comes from the Lela of either 1909 or 1910 (*Figure 7.4*).[14] Three animals may be discerned with difficulty: clearest is an elephant in the centre of the photograph, to the viewer's right is a standing lion, and to the left a tiger. The animals are abundantly clear in a colour photograph taken over a half century later, in 1963, showing that one of the cloths (the elephant), all of which had a red background, was by that time patched (*Figure 7.9*).[15] Another dozen years on, the cloths were again

14. Basel E-30.27.008 is attributed to Clara Schultze-Reinhardt who was in Bali during the month of Lela only in 1909 and 1910. An interesting feature of this photograph is that the lion to the viewer's right appears to be facing left. Since the lion panels otherwise always appear facing right, this suggests the panels to have been reversible (Keller, as mentioned earlier, suggests the figures were woven). Close inspection of later photographs suggest that the panels may subsequently have been backed with a blue material, so they were no longer reversible.

15. A series of photographs was taken by Hans-Peter Straumann when he was a teacher in Bali Nyonga. These have been copied for the Basel archive and are used here with permission. A roughly contemporaneous history of Bali compiled by the Headmaster of the Cameroon Protestant College, Bamenda, refers to 'large red cloth draperies with elephants and tigers pictured on them' used during Lela (1971, originally 1965: 18). The survival of cloth for long periods is apparently not unusual: a photograph of

photographed by the curator and ethnographer Hans-Joachim Koloss. One of Koloss's photographs reveals for the first time that there were actually three lion panels, although apparently only one each of tiger and elephant (and the elephant panel has the patch apparent in 1963; *Figure 7.10*). Despite lion and elephant being African mammals, it seems likely that all three creatures were originally of exotic inspiration: the elephant is a small-eared Indian example and, given that it clearly belongs to a set including the tiger and elephant, the lion is likely to have been Asian-derived as well. The earliest definite textual reference to these animal cloths occurs in the description that the missionary Jakob Keller published in 1919, although it is based on information he collected before the First World War: he mentions 'European carpets/tapestries with woven animal figures' *('europäische Teppische mit eingewebten Tierfiguren'*, 1919: 65). Max Esser who visited Bali Nyonga in 1896 had referred to the King having a costly carpet spread before his ivory throne (Chilver and Röschenthaler 2001: 82), but this might or might not have been the hangings in the photographs of which we know.

Where might the hangings have come from? Since Jakob Keller does not state that they were a missionary gift, they are likely to have come via Bali's other contacts with the coast; perhaps they were the gift of a trader, or of one of the labour recruiters on behalf of the coastal plantations who visited in Bali in the decade around the turn of the nineteenth century between the closure of the first German military station and the establishment of a missionary presence. Most likely European-manufactured but of Indian inspiration, extensive enquiries of British, Dutch and German museums have not – as yet – pinned down their provenance.[16]

---

his 1940 installation shows the mid-century Fon of Bali Nyonga wearing – apparently in pristine condition – a robe that his father used decades earlier (Basel E30.85.215).
16. For their attempts to clarify this question, sincere thanks are due in the UK to Rosemary Crill and Deborah Swallow of the Victoria and Albert Museum, June Hill of the Bankfield Museum, and John Picton at SOAS; in Germany to Brigitte Tietzel of the Deutsches Textil Museum in Krefeld, Heide Nixdorf (Professorin Kulturgeschichte der Textilien) of the University of Dortmund, and to Hans-Joachim Koloss and Christine Stelzig of the Ethnologisches Museum, Berlin; in the Netherlands to Annemieke Hogervorst of the Gemeentemuseum, Helmond, and Pieter ter Keurs of the Rijksmuseum voor Volkenkunde, Leiden; in the USA to Lisa Aronson of Skidmore College, Saratoga Springs. Vibha Arora, Oxford, suggests a possible origin in Western India for these cloths. [See also my Introduction to this volume pp. 16-17.]

Figure 7.5. HRH Fon Galega II during Lela in 1963. Basel E-30.27.008
© Hans-Peter Straumann

Figure 7.6. Treasure displayed at the 1975 Lela © Hans-Joachim Koloss

The animal tapestries are not particularly exotic in the context of the Bali palace treasures: the inventory of 1908 encompasses items like the matting fences that are locally argued to be of northern origin (like the Chamba leadership), prestige items local to the Grassfields (wooden stools and a throne copying Grassfield style), as well as a variety of European imports (including glassware, pottery and a ship's foghorn – the last already present by the time of Esser's visit, as perhaps were our draperies). However, the animal panels have left an enduring trace. Presumably – since I have not had the opportunity to enquire into this on the spot – when David Louis Musi undertook the palace murals at the behest of his relatively recently installed Fon, he was under instructions to take inspiration from the animal panels. Interestingly enough, he positioned the tiger panel behind the throne, retaining its red background and adding an oliphant and a calabash (presumably for transporting palm wine). He added a couple of other panels too: one depicting a double gong like that the Fon strikes at Lela, and another with a pair of fighting warriors, presumably a reminder that the Bali had fought their way to their present kingdom However, most of the decoration derives from the early twentieth-century cloth images. The lion panels were doubled and placed at either end of the display wall (which may reflect an actual disposition of cloths at some Lela, given that photographic evidence suggests the lion panels to be the only cloths of which the Bali Fon had more than one example). A single elephant panel has been retained, and the elephant depicted remains the small-eared Indian variety (although its head is partly obscured in *Figure 7.2* by the pronged posts which are a part of the *lela* apparatus, this feature is clearly visible from other photographs not reproduced here). Is it accidental that the 'indigenous' animals – elephant and lion – have been given a relatively naturalistic background of sky and grass, while the tiger alone has retained the scarlet backdrop of its cloth version? The prestige cloths that hung behind the imported animal cloths in the photographs from 1908-10 have morphed into decorative borders painted around the panels of the mural.

My final piece of photographic evidence – at least for now – dates from 2002, and I owe it to Ernst Elsenhans who visited Bali in August that year. Elsenhans's photographs show that the external murals were still intact, although peeling, and that the fabric panels were pinned up in the hall of the palace, looking rather threadbare given that they must

Figure 7.7. The throne dais of HRH Fon Dr Ganyonga III (2002) © Ernst Elsenhans

be around a hundred years old. New to the photographic record is a tiger panel behind the Fon's throne within the palace (*Figure 7.7*). Framed by a border inspired by indigo cloth patterns, a powerful and markedly naturalistic tiger – which certainly looks as if it had been taken from an original source other than the cloth – bares its teeth behind the throne dais. A winged crown is painted directly above the Fon's throne, itself a compelling exercise in the accumulation of symbols of power. The whole assemblage – but particularly the tiger – seems to speak to the renewal of power of chiefship, including the power to exercise violence, at the close of the twentieth century not just in Cameroon, but in many African countries where 'modern' state institutions are locally weak.

So much for proximate origins of the animal images but, following Nelson Mandela's lead, presumably other ideas paved the path to their acceptance: a noisy, oliphant-using ceremonial culture readily accommodated a ship's foghorn, and the kingly attributes of the leopard must have provided a welcoming niche for the import of what – with apologies to Wole Soyinka – we could call symbolic tigritude. Perhaps there always is some sense in which a new idea is already there in the environment that receives it, that is to say in the abilities people have to forge continuities.

Treasures and translations

My brief example has traced how some past treasures have been re-evoked in the service of contemporary identifications. The vagaries of my own 'research' through old photographs and texts, internet and e-mail, conversations and letters of enquiry seems to mirror with respect to its accidental progress, something in the processes of transfer occurring more than a century ago. Materials were imported into Bali and redeployed, figures have literally (in the case of the local patterned cloths) become frames. The reworking of treasures bears a close resemblance to the reworking of identities: change occurs subtly and simultaneously in figure and ground. Similarity is produced over time in terms of a project that is driven (but not entirely guided) by local perceptions of means and ends. When Paul Bohannan – who had skilfully edited Steiner's papers on economics after his death – came to use some of Steiner's ideas to explore his own ethnography, he decided to change a term that was quite telling in Steiner's original usage. Bohannan (1955) wrote of conversion when goods from one sphere of exchange (say subsistence goods) were traded for goods of another sphere (say prestige goods). Bohannan wanted to draw attention to the transaction itself. Steiner seems more explicitly to have been concerned with questions of value, and he referred not to conversion but 'translation'. Something was translated into a treasure when it brought to mind for people the memorably intensive effort that had gone into creating or acquiring it. Like identities, treasures were conceivable only in terms of their having a past. Modernist social anthropology did all its explaining – as I emphasised at the outset – in terms of the present. But throwing so much weight upon the present is problematic, not least because for most people, most of the time, it is the present that is full of uncertainties and problems, and the past that seems a source of stability. The audacity of modernist social anthropology's approach was to eschew the popular view and seek resolution where there is typically instability – in the present. I do not think this modernist insight is entirely exhausted, but neither do I feel that it is wholly sustainable. A modest proposal to extend its working life would involve historicizing those mutually entailed processes of identification and transformation of which Steiner spoke in his aphorism. Contrary to his words, this would entail a close investigation of identifications as processes in time in order to ask about the conditions under which mementoes of memorably intensive time are objectified, reified and even fetishized. Identity work, I would suggest, has much in common with the creation (and indeed loss) of value by treasured objects. Both involve an investment of labour that must be studied historically; both treasures and identities are subject to temporal resignification; both may lose as well as gain value; both are materialized in ways that may resist or subvert people's attempts to annex or use them in particular ways. A labour theory of value necessarily begs questions of history in ways that an exchange theory (rooting value entirely in the present) need not. Presentism, in this respect, relies heavily on an exchange theory of value, whereas a labour theory of value recognizes that present value is not autonomous of past labour.

ACKNOWLEDGEMENTS

Specific acknowledgements may be found in notes, but I want to thank the British Academy and Research Committee of the School of Oriental and African Studies for making possible my attendance at the ASA Conference in Arusha, and the audience to this paper, given as a plenary lecture, for their astute questions and amused generosity towards the near invisibility of tigers in the illustrative material I managed to find by the time of the event. Johannes Fabian and Sjaak van der Geest suggested specific references which I have been glad to follow up.

Chapter 8

COSMOPOLITAN NATIONS, NATIONAL COSMOPOLITANS

Conviviality begins at home: a ceremony

During a return visit to Ganye[1] (capital of the chiefdom of the same name in Adamawa, Nigeria's easternmost middle-belt state on its border with Cameroon), one of the main topics of daily conversation among Chamba, the majority population, was the precise date their reigning traditional chief (the *Gangwari* of Ganye) would formally receive his First Class Staff of Office from the Lamido of Adamawa, a Fulani?[2] Along with two other non-Fulani[3] chiefs, the Bachama *Hama* of Numan, and the Bata *Hama* of Demsa, the *Gangwari* of Ganye had seen his chiefdom elevated from second-class to first-class status by the Governor of Adamawa State in December 2004. His would be the last of the three ratification ceremonies to be held.

An installation ceremony is a complex and expensive undertaking: invitations must be sent in ample time to be certain the most important dignitaries, Cameroonian as well as Nigerian, may be present; accommodation and food has to be prepared, ceremonial spaces upgraded,

---

1. I carried out research in this area regularly between 1976 and 1990 but had not returned between then and a month-long visit in January 2006. I am grateful for small grants from the Central Research Fund of the University of London and the School of Oriental and African Studies which assisted my passage. An even briefer revisit to the *fondom* of Bali Nyonga in Cameroon at the turn of 2004-5 furnishes a very brief comparative observation later in this chapter.
2. In the event this happened on 18 February 2006, a couple of weeks after I had returned home. Strictly, installation is by the Governor, but local discussion tends to present the relationship as one involving traditional rulers rather than transient political figures.
3. I use Fulani rather than Fulbe in this chapter since all my references are to Fulani in Nigeria where this version of the ethnic term is in use.

and a variety of what the programme calls 'cultural dances' arranged for the entertainment of the distinguished visitors. All this demanded an organizing committee well in excess of a hundred people. The dignitaries must be seated according to fine gradations of precedence – the most important at the front – in rows under an awning sheltered from the sun, on one side of a large plaza (Gangwari Square in Ganye), the other three sides of which would be lined by the throng of standing spectators. Before and after the big day, a variety of publications need to be put in hand: a full-colour programme, with a history of the kingdom, biography of the *Gangwari*, order of events and portraits of the main protagonists; and a souvenir brochure and calendar, with more portraits of the main actors, sponsored pages from well-wishers that also emphasise their own contributions to the chiefdom as elected representatives or officials, as well as a photographic record of the events on the day of the 'Official Presentation of First Class Staff of Office'.

Continuing in this vein would add another account to many writings that have explored the modernity of invented tradition, and the prominent role played by neo-traditional chiefs in the politics of contemporary West African nation states. Given the subject of our volume, however, I need to start where such analyses typically end. Readers have become accustomed to such, only superficially, paradoxical counterposings of modernity and tradition. Tradition is important to contemporary ethnic identities in several ways: it gives identities expression and value, making them presently comprehensible and worthwhile both to their members and to outsiders; and this expression is also instrumental in the more narrowly immediate sense of facilitating an interlacing of political interests at local and national levels. Ethnicities cannot be conjured out of nothing: the past of any identity has to be expressed in its present. Hence, it is not just unparadoxical but inevitable that such events are appeals to tradition in urgently contemporary contexts. Taking this as given, my interest here concerns the relation between another two apparently counterposed terms: intensely rooted identity (simultaneously modern *and* traditional) and cosmopolitanism. Can one come to the second through the first, or are they necessarily antithetical? And how does globalization enter this picture?

One of the several reasons given by the chief for the delay in seeking a date for his installation ceremony from the Governor concerned the poor quality of mobile telephone service in his capital. Ganye was

Figure 8.1. Gangwari Presentation. Courtesy of HRH Alhaji Umar A. Sanda

served by Mtel, the mobile telephone subsidiary of the Nigerian statal provider Nitel, but intermittently and with an unreliability to be relied upon. Mtel never seemed to work after dark, something local opinion, whether with technical insight I cannot judge, attributed to the evening boosting from a nearby relay station of the signal of the Adamawa Broadcasting Corporation, the only TV channel available locally without satellite subscription. In a few days during my visit, Glo, by consensus Nigeria's most dynamic provider of Global Systems of Mobile Communications (GSMC), had their mast up and running: there was a brisk business for SIM card salesmen as people either switched to, or added, this more expensive but also more reliable provider, and the Chief of Ganye sought a date for his installation ceremony, confident that his visitors would not be rendered incommunicado from their pressing concerns elsewhere in Nigeria, which is also to say, confident that his own capital would not strike these visitors as a 'bush' (or might I say an uncosmopolitan?) place.

Despite an immense oil income during several postcolonial decades (or because of it, in the view of those who argue that mineral wealth may be a curse for developing economies), Nigeria's infrastructure has grown very unevenly; and Ganye's is in some respects, for instance roads, not much better than it was thirty years ago. In fairness, it should be said that particular roads have been upgraded, but 'no condition', as the tried and tested Nigerian idiom has it, 'is permanent': tarred but unmaintained roads soon become less motorable than they were in the first place. The mobile communications industry has been an exception to the hesitant trend in other sectors.[4] Nigeria is touted as home to the world's fastest growing mobile communications industry. Five years after the onset of deregulation in 2001, when Nigeria apparently had 450,000 functioning land lines (and quite what, or when, 'functioning' means in this context is open to argument), mobile telephone ownership had risen to sixteen million. Glo alone claimed to have attracted five million subscribers in the two years to January 2006, and Ganye was

---

4. Radio has been another exception thanks to a similar combination of deregulation, technological innovation and potential profitability (though the profits are less readily harvested from users in this case). In thinking about language policy, broadcasting and now majority/minority relations in African states, I am indebted to many years of collaboration with my SOAS colleague Graham Furniss (see, Fardon and Furniss 1994, 2000).

among 30 towns connected to the Glo network during just two weeks at the beginning of that year.[5] As any visitor to West Africa pre- and post-GSMC will attest, the difference this technology has made to people's notions of accessibility, punctuality and communicability has been unprecedented, as if some sections of the population had been waiting for the technology that would let them, when it suited their purposes, get off what Anglophone West Africans call 'African time' for particular purposes. The attitude may not persist, but it is anticipated not just that mobile phones will be switched on, but that answering them will take precedence over whatever else is in hand. Not only can some matters, particularly those involving trusted interlocutors, now be transacted virtually, but arrangements that once took weeks to make as messages were sent back and forth by pedestrian, or at best motorized, word of mouth can now be made in minutes. Hence, returning to our subject, an event can now follow hard on the heels of its date being chosen.

There was a second reason for the *Gangwari*'s delay in asking that a date be fixed for his installation. Despite its remoteness from Nigerian centres of power, Ganye chiefdom happens to include the homes of two of Nigeria's most powerful men: Vice-President Abubakar Atiku, and the influential politician and business magnate, Bamanga Tukur, son of the Fulani who presided over Chamba administration from the mid-1930s to mid-1950s. Although neither of these men's fathers was Chamba, both have been given titles on *Gangwari*'s traditional council. It would have been unthinkable to fix the date of the installation before ensuring the presence of the Nigerian Vice-President as guest of honour, and the Vice-President's diary was filled well ahead of time, not least thanks to the wrangle over the constitution, and the limitation of any presidency to two terms of office between himself and President Obasanjo, which had preoccupied Nigerian news media. National electoral politics and Global Satellite Mobile Communications, souvenir brochures and

---

5. These figures are from www.mobileafrica.net and need to be treated with some caution: all Nigerian mobile telephone services are 'pre-pay' or 'pay as you go', and telephone numbers for which no credit is received have their right to receive calls blocked after a period that varies between providers. Where service is patchy, phone users who rely on remaining connected need more than one handset, or a handset adapted to take multiple SIM cards. This reasoning suggests there are likely to be fewer telephone users than there are telephone numbers. Against this, individuals' phones are rarely denied to needful kin or friends who have no phone of their own.

cultural dances, these are just a few of the considerations bearing upon the public celebration of a first-class staff of office, itself of course a colonial introduction.

The internal diversity of contemporary African states has most often been discussed in terms of its deviance from European, or European-settler, norms. Top-down discussions of African statehood typically begin from the fact that contemporary state boundaries were imposed by European fiat with only the most occasional attention to pre-existing ethnic resemblances. The step from this truth to the view that most of Africa's state problems stem from the heterogeneity of their populations is sometimes made too quickly. Somalia and Rwanda have not been advertisements for the virtues of a closer fit either between state and preexisting nation, or between postcolonial and precolonial state boundaries. For their part, investigators looking at matters from the bottom-up have been struck by the consolidation under colonial and postcolonial governments of whatever ethnic identity they have been studying, and they have provided numerous excellent case studies showing how present identities have been teased from past resemblances under conditions conducive to this way of envisaging collective claims on state resources. Fewer studies have analysed the multi-ethnic, and usually multi-faith, national cultures emergent from the interplay of ethnicities defining themselves in some respects contrapuntally, that is to say playing on the terms of their differences from other ethnicities within the nation. Counterpoint has involved a high degree of stereotyping of more or less familiar others, and occasionally it has led to extreme violence. However, it has not been demonstrated that, relative to their internal diversity, African states have been more prone to violence than the history of consolidating nation states globally might lead us to anticipate. More or less lasting accommodations have been reached between diverse elements; pluralistic habits of language use have been arrived at practically, and sometimes recognized *post hoc* in planning documents; access to media has been shared. From all of this, a variety of majority and minority practices and opinions has crystallized. While ethnicity is prominent, these are not simply ethnic cultures; they involve considerations of social standing, wealth, education, region and religion. Rather than being stable and easy to define, they tend to be called forth in relation to particular issues and events. By being called forth often, and with reasonable reliability, a set of practices and opinions becomes more visible, which in turn may encourage emulation and adherence, or op-position, or schism, or all three simultaneously. This complexity is par-ticularly challenging for the resource-poor minorities, whose main asset may consist in their ability to put on a show of public solidarity.

Very few Chamba from Ganye chiefdom live outside Nigeria; slightly more have either travelled abroad (particularly for pilgrimage to Mecca or Jerusalem) or studied abroad. However, Nigeria is a big and popu-lous place. No one is sure of its exact population; estimation is made contentious by matters of taxation and election which predictably pull population returns in opposite directions. Another attempt to count the population is imminent but, in the meantime, observers bandy around figures in the region of 120 to 135 million, meaning that Nigerians make up more than half and perhaps as much as two-thirds of all West Africans (depending on various assumptions about which countries are consid-ered West African and what their populations might be). Chamba try to argue up their own numbers to around half a million, most of whom live within Adamawa State, but including communities mixed and scat-tered in neighbouring Taraba State to the west (not counting Chamba to the east in Cameroon). Leaving aside serious quibbles about the basis of ethnicity, in the roughest of terms Chamba make up between one-third and two-fifths of one per cent of the population of Nigeria. Given this status as one of the country's middling-size minorities (in a smaller West African nation they might have been calling the shots), Chamba can move around a good deal and live in Nigeria's larger cities among people unlike themselves, without ever leaving their country. Unlike interna-tional emigration, national migration is very substantial. Poster-sized an-nual almanacs produced in many of the university and commercial cities of Nigeria line up their Chamba residents: larger photos of dignitaries, placed towards the top and centre, preside over thumbnail portraits of Chamba members of local student or cultural associations. The enthusi-astic uptake of computer software supporting photographs and artwork has encouraged far more organizations than previously to produce not just almanacs, but ornate invitations, announcements and condolences, drawing on both national and international ideas of appropriate design.

Most literature on cosmopolitanism assumes that cosmopolitan senti-ments are, if not antithetical to, then certainly in tension with the na-tionalism, or 'beyond' the nation (Cheah and Robbins 1998; Archibugi 2003). This strikes me as privileging a particular experience of the nation,

pre-eminently that of Europe's language majorities and their settler societies. Particularly if you belong to a minority ethnic group nationally, a
cosmopolitan sensibility, in so far as the term is understood to apply to
a capacity to reach beyond cultural difference – and not only the cultural
differences of people outside your own nation – is necessary to feel any
sense of belonging to your own nationalist project. Yet cosmopolitanism is usually presented as transcendent of nationalism, an aspiration
to internationalism or transnationalism. Like many such, this argument
rests uncomfortably on the assumption and implicit narrative it claims
to refute. Nations did not become diverse only through receiving culturally distinctive immigrants; in a loose sense, all were cosmopolitan at
their inception and some did not, or have not yet, undergone the nation-
building processes which for a time effaced some of the differences
within older, mainly European, states. Even discounting immigration
from other countries, Nigeria is in this sense a cosmopolitan nation. The
proliferation of almanacs strikes me as a slight, but nevertheless interesting, imaginative representation of Chamba in the enormous nation
to which they belong: successful or aspirational in these distant places,
but claiming ethnic loyalty and pride. *Pen leuka be nokin Samba,* or 'I am
proud to be Chamba', as the bumper sticker of the Chamba Progressive
Union, Jos Chapter, proclaims bilingually (*Figure 8.2*).[6]

Members of the Progressive Union (and of other Cultural Associations)
in major Nigerian towns display their ethnic pride for the same reason
that the Chamba of Ganye prove their modernity: they have been, in
their own eyes – which reflect the views of some Nigerian majorities –
disparaged and marginalized. Becoming more cosmopolitan involves a
coming to terms with the evaluation of differences within the nation,
particularly between themselves and their principle contrapuntal other
(the Fulani) but also with other majorities. Doing this requires them
also to address the differences, especially those between Muslims and
Christians, which potentially threaten their own peace.

This leads me to some misgivings about the proposal that cosmopolitanism might serve as a defining trope of anthropology as a discipline

---

6. Jos, which once had a reputation as a peaceful middle-belt city, has become increasingly fractious in the past decade, especially in relations between predominantly
Christian locals and Muslim, predominantly Hausa, incomers. A bumper sticker pro-
claiming Chamba identity might also be a passport out of the blood-lettings these have
visited on one another (on this, see Higazi 2007).

Figure 8.2. Chamba Progressive Union bumper sticker. Courtesy Steve Simon Samleukenni

(see Rapport 2006). Cosmopolitanism, it seems to me, is no less a loaded focus in the twenty-first century than ethnic authenticity was in the twentieth century. Belonging to a national state dominated by a few regional majorities (matters of power and culture, rather than just numbers), Chamba need to appear both authentic and modern. But this is a reflection of weakness as much as strength: they know that others in the nation-state exercise more cultural clout than they do (over language policy, education, broadcasting, national spectacles, and so forth), and that the same people are in all likelihood better connected than they are in cosmopolitan terms (both nationally and internationally). Chamba, in turn, exercise more power and are better connected than some micro-minorities. Their ethnic identity provides the most important ground of their encapsulation within the nation-state: as individual voters they count for very little, even during civilian transitions between regimes. Consciousness of this ethnic identity has grown alongside the kinds of cosmopolitanism that are products of technological globalization (mobile telephones and computer graphics, above, being instances).

When I first visited Ganye in 1976, only a small fraction of the elite, who were all older than me, spoke some English (the official Nigerian language), and my Chamba was the more serviceable medium of communication for many of our relations. Now many people younger than me, including women, very few of whom spoke English in 1976, speak English much better than I speak Chamba. They learnt it at school from an early age, and employed that language-learning to get educated, listen to the radio, read English-language Nigerian newspapers, communicate with travellers (including some Nigerians, like Igbo, who may not have learnt Hausa), and so on. Even more Chamba speak very serviceable Hausa (the northern Nigerian national language); again, more than when I visited first. Fewer, however, speak Fulfulde, the language of the old Adamawa Emirate. This simply corresponds to Hausa's cultural dominance in northern Nigeria. Matters could have been different, as is evident from the dominance of Fulfulde in those parts of the Adamawa Emirate (including Chamba populations) that now belong to Cameroon. My (not systematically tested) hunch is that fewer Chamba nowadays speak the languages of their non-Fulani neighbours than was once the case.[7] Most Chamba, Verre, Mumuye, Bachama, or Koma have the option of speaking to one another in Hausa or English.

Do these changing linguistic and, one could demonstrate also, cultural capacities imply that people are becoming more cosmopolitan in outlook, or are they simply being connected more closely to global concerns and adjusting their behaviour and alliances to try to prosper?

Encapsulation and identity – history

Chamba have been confronted with efforts, serially, to incorporate them into a Fulani Muslim empire, a German empire, a British colonial mandate and trusteeship, and a succession of independent Nigerian governments, both military- and civilian-run (and the two are not mutually exclusive in practice). It has fallen largely to Chamba elites to try to derive value of different kinds (economic, political, symbolic) from their relations with others whose identities (more properly, trajectories of identity, since flux has been the rule) differ from their own. We might like to call these efforts cosmopolitanization to add moral mission to what the Africanist literature generally calls ethnic brokerage or suchlike. Benefits have percolated to non-elite Chamba to the extent that they have been able to curb elite self-interest (by pressing moral or material claims on them). It would be premature and dangerous for Chamba of the Ganye paramountcy to start relying too much on the kindness of the strangers who make up their huge and diverse national state. Their historic experience has been of degrees of marginality in terms of rights

7. With the single exception of Chamba Leko in Nigeria, who usually have a functional grasp of Chamba Daka, the majority Chamba language, Chambaness overrides language difference, but at the cost of Chamba Leko learning the majority Chamba language.

granted, and peripherality in terms of access to them: these degrees, as everywhere, varied with status, but even the best-connected have been far from secure in their relative privilege.

Several writers have suggested phases in globalization as the extension and overall connectivity of its technologies have deepened (e.g. Mignolo 2002: 157 – 'a set of designs to manage the world'). They write about this, as it were, from the world's point of view. The ethnographer's contribution is made distinctive by reversing the optic, to ask how the wider world seems to those becoming caught up increasingly within it. Although I do not pursue it here, this approach would be just as germane to looking at the 'packaging' of the world for the information-rich (Calhoun 2003: 107). I want, very briefly, to provide a context to local globalization in the last quarter millennium for the Chamba case, and to ask how this might be related to the extension of their projects for 'conviviality' (Mignolo 2002).[8]

In the mid-eighteenth century most Chamba[9] would have lived in sizeable chiefdoms around the mid-point of what is now the Nigeria-Cameroon border. Their immediate neighbours were much like themselves, and the suppositions about the world they shared allowed a lively trade in cults and cult performances, alongside ties based on co-residence, clan- and ethnic-based relations of privileged insult, intermarriage, and so forth. Chamba were usually self-sufficient in staple foods, although there are indications of droughts in the second half of the eighteenth century. Apart from such small stock as chickens, goats and sheep, Chamba may have kept dwarf cattle and ponies. In these respects, their communities were probably self-sufficient too. Their cosmology – a grand term I use because it resonates with the likely limits of their cosmopolitanism at that time – predicated a distant creator god and an array of more locally rooted and more immediate powers: an underworld from which the dead affected the lives of the living, forces of the wild including malevolent animals, witches, seers and shape-changers.

---

8. Although ideally it would be even-handed to do so, it is impossible, in the current state of our knowledge, to characterize a Chamba half millennium corresponding to the creation of the northern circum-Atlantic part of the world system.

9. I ask the reader to hear, because it would be unreadable if I wrote it on each occurrence that, given the recent crystallization of current ethnic identities, by 'Chamba' I mean the people who would be Chamba by the time of twentieth-century written records.

Technologies of offering, ordeal, and cultic performance allied to the expulsion or killing of people who posed supernatural dangers to the community (whether or not they intended to do so) provided a degree of control over these immediately present, super-human powers, and there were also means of reparation for human damage (by theft, killing, adultery, and so forth). God was invoked but did not receive sacrifice.

Chamba would have been aware of various types of people unlike themselves: to the north they presumably knew of the powerful Muslim empire of Bornu, and they would have been familiar with predominantly Hausa traders whose routes crossed Chambaland. Fulani graziers with their herds of zebu cattle and smallstock also traversed Chambaland on seasonal migrations and, in all probability, some settled in small villages. To the south, Chamba may have heard of European traders far away at the coast who brought trade goods and collected slaves. The epicentre of the European slave trade had been moving towards the area due south of Chamba. However, Chamba probably sensed the power of both the Europeans and the Kanuri of Bornu only indirectly, while the Fulani herders were vulnerable and so acted as clients. The most immediate social experience would have been small in scale and extension, but minutely differentiated in terms of kin, clan, ethnicity, dialect and language, and rooted super-human powers. In short, Chamba individuals and groups were themselves at the centre of complex social landscapes of difference.

The nineteenth century saw this situation change entirely. Chambaland was largely overrun by the easternmost emirate of the Sokoto Caliphate – at the beginning of the twentieth century the most populous political entity in Africa. Numerous Chamba Leko-speaking chiefdoms disappeared as their members set off south and southwest to escape Fulani domination and to profit from the disruptions of Fulani state-building. Other Chamba retreated into the hills and mountains that nullified the advantages of Fulani cavalry. Those left in the plains had to find some kind of, doubtless changing, *modus vivendi* with the ascendant Fulani powers in whose eyes they were, more often than not, pagans and slaves and racially inferior. In the course of a century, those Chamba who did not emigrate entirely found their status changed – in very crude terms – from being at the centre of their own universe to living on the margins of a Muslim and, in terms of its dominant stratum, ethnically Fulani state to which they were significant only as a resource. A minority of

Chamba clients were able to derive value from this wider world, but only at the cost of collusion and exploitation of their fellow Chamba. Early Chamba experience of Islam was as a religion of ethnically distinct conquerors: chiefs who allied with this outside power were often required, at least nominally, to become Muslims. Hence, Islam (in Chamba, praying to, or literally 'greeting or showing respect to God') was seen as an aspect of Fulani identity (to become Muslim was to 'become Fulani'). A further century has done little to dissipate the legacy of rancour and distrust to which this gave rise between Chamba and Fulani as categories, and among Chamba themselves (though not, it needs to be added, always to the exclusion of cordial relations between some Chamba and Fulani as individuals).

Conquest of the Sokoto Caliphate by European imperial powers did not immediately make a substantial change to relations between Chamba and Fulani. Whatever their principled views on the topic, all three European powers involved (Britain, Germany and France) had little option other than to resort to indirect rule through Fulani chiefs. The Europeans found Chamba in the state to which the Fulani consigned them and this, allied to the Europeans' own perceptions of relative superiority among Africans, meant that early colonial rule was experienced by Chamba as at best a rearrangement, at worst a reinforcement, of Fulani dominance. It was not until the inter-war period that the British seriously addressed dismantling an administration that used Fulani intermediaries to deal with Chamba communities, and began to replace it with territorially and ethnically based local administrative units with headmen drawn from the majority ethnic group. The development of an ethnically based administration, drawing in small-scale on those same assumptions (of language, culture, shared history, and continuous identity, as arguments for autonomy) that underlay nationalist arguments,[10] coincided with intensification of two other globalizing influences.

Most of Chambaland was missionized relatively late, Lutheran Protestants (initially a New Zealand couple, later Norwegians) arriving from the mid-1920s, and Irish Roman Catholics a couple of decades later. The absence of Anglican, or indeed English, missionaries created

---

10. These assumptions also underlay an emergent sense of the person with the consequence that the self-evidence of ethnic identity received corroborative echoes both from the encompassing nationalist process and from the encompassed making of modern, ethnic and national subjects, who were also members of salvationist religions.

a distance between European colonial power and its associated religions that had not been the case for the Fulani Emirate and Islam in the nineteenth century. Simultaneously, conversion to Islam (which had scarcely occurred beyond nominal chiefly conversions during the nineteenth-century jihads) increased. Historic Chamba religion remained predominant for the first half of the twentieth century but declined thereafter, its performances becoming largely folkloristic by the end of the century (albeit some of its presuppositions, notably concerning witchcraft, continued to be entertained). Chamba religious affiliations were set upon a path that is still obvious: whether Chamba Christians are Lutheran Protestant or Roman Catholics may be predicted with a high degree of accuracy on the basis of their present or historic family residence: western Chamba tend to be Protestants, and eastern and southern Chamba are predominantly Catholics, a distribution that follows from the division of Chambaland between missionary interests on the Nigerian side of the border. Muslims are found all over Chambaland, but they especially predominate where no Christian mission was established. So far, other churches have remained very minor players and, according to local testimony, are largely confined to Ganye town where their congregations are predominantly non-Chamba.

The late colonial period[11] thus introduced Chamba to a set of assumptions concerning identity, autonomy and self-government, shared by both colonial and national regimes, as well as to the two major religious currents of Nigeria. The combination did not sit all that easily. Nigeria's religious geography is complex looked at in all its details, but a fundamental tension between a North that looks across the Sahara desert to the Muslim world, and a South which looks across the Atlantic to the Christian world, has centuries of precedent behind it (and is shared by many larger coastal states of West Africa). A campaign to islamize Northern Nigeria was waged in the first decade of Independence. More recently, the activities of religious fundamentalists in both camps, and the contest between the Nigerian Constitution and Sharia Law have served to exacerbate tensions (Paden 2005; Ostien, Nasir and Kogelmann 2005). Chamba in Ganye hold strongly, though it is difficult to know how anyone might check their assertions, that they are evenly

---

11. Itself a retarded affair because Ganye Chamba were in the Mandated and later Trust Territories created from German Kamerun, hence outside the main thrust of colonial development.

split between Muslims and Christians. The predominance of either religion would upset a delicate balance because, over and above these religious differences, which are common within families, there is a general insistence that where politics is concerned they are all Chamba and have to stick together. This would be a less sweeping commitment were it not also remarked frequently that in Nigeria everything is politics.

It was not until the British were close to leaving the Trust Territory that a further concerted effort was made to address the problems of Chamba administration. During the 1930s a Subordinate Native Authority had been stitched together that consisted of a few Chamba chiefdoms which had survived the nineteenth century, and a swath of smaller communities in the plains between the two major mountain ranges that border what is now the Ganye chiefdom to the west and east. Chamba and Fulani had become more mixed in this central plain than elsewhere, and the entire area was constituted as a single district headed by a Fulani who also acted as Wakilin Chamba (he was the father of the prominent businessman and politician mentioned earlier), effectively presiding over the Chamba Native Authority as a whole.

By the mid-1950s discontent against what they portrayed as Fulani domination was given voice by young Chamba Protestants. Largely as a result of their having raised the profile of the problem, the British moved the administrative centre of the Chamba Native Authority from Jada, a place founded by Fulani incomers, a few miles south to Ganye, which is said to have been the site of a small market but was otherwise hardly populated.

In 1961, the Northern Trust Territory joined Nigeria, which had gained independence the previous year, and a block of offices was buih in Ganye ('The Native Authority Offices. A gift of the people of the United Kingdom to the people of Chamba'; two textually equivalent 'peoples' related through gift exchange as the plaque commemorating their opening that year avows, *Figure 8.3*). Control over local administration there would become a focus of a Chamba/ Fulani rivalry that took a variety of forms: writing petitions, seeking offices of the different kinds that local administration seemed to have an inexhaustible capacity to generate, and occasional violence.

In 1967, the Fulani scored a symbolic victory when they petitioned successfully for the Chamba Native Authority to be renamed Ganye Native Authority. A rotational presidency of the Native Authority Council was brought in at the same time, so that the District Heads, Chamba and Fulani, took turns to preside over meetings. However, an eruption of violence in 1971, precipitated by disputed successions in two districts, revealed the inadequacy of this arrangement. In response to what became known as the 'Leko riots', named after the Chamba of one administrative area (Leko District) taking direct action against the installation of a Fulani District Head on the retirement of his Chamba predecessor, the State Governor set up a Commission of Enquiry. It was the recommendation of the enquiry that a paramount chiefship be created in Ganye. A complex election process was set in train, and a forty-year-old. Catholic-educated Muslim, an ex-teacher and veterinary officer, was approved as Chief (*Sarkin,* Hausa) of Ganye in 1972, formally receiving his Third-Class Staff of Office two years later. This was upgraded to a Second-Class Staff in 1982, and ceremonially bestowed the following year. On his death in 2000, his son was elected his successor and, although the position remains officially elective, it will become increasingly difficult to disentangle the resources of the chiefship from those of the family that has now held that office for more than thirty years.

Since its creation, the chiefship has been one of the few constants of Chamba organization, though it also has not gone uncontested, notably by Fulani petitioners variously demanding (in English): the removal of the incumbent, the division of the chiefdom, or for the chief to be prevented from titling himself *Gangwari* and be obliged to revert to the Hausa title *Sarkin,* on the basis that use of a Chamba term is discriminatory against future Fulani candidates. All of these petitions, according to Chamba in Ganye, have needed to be refuted actively because Fulani are better connected than Chamba at statal and federal levels of government, and who knows what might come to pass otherwise – for everything, recall, is politics.

While the chiefship has been a constant for a large part of the forty-five years since the Chamba joined an independent Nigeria, other administrative and electoral arrangements have changed with a frequency that precludes summary here. The country has lurched between civilian and military regimes, often accompanied by creation of states: their number currently stands at 36 (Chamba have successively belonged to Sardauna Province, North-Eastem State, Gongola State and Adamawa State). Native Authorities have become Local Government Authorities, and these have been created and dissolved, sub-divided and redrawn

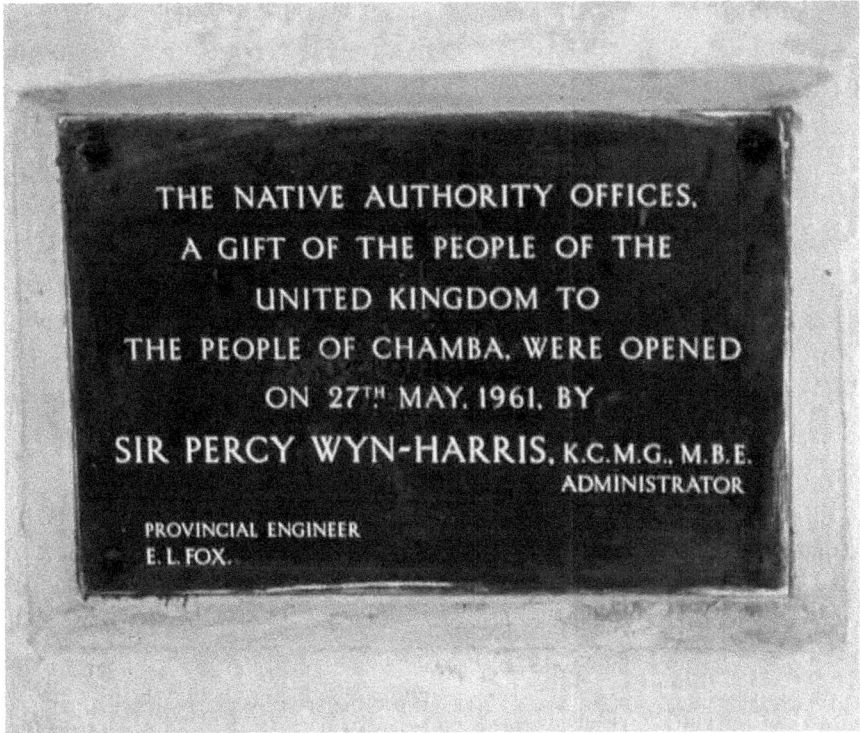

THE NATIVE AUTHORITY OFFICES,
A GIFT OF THE PEOPLE OF THE
UNITED KINGDOM TO
THE PEOPLE OF CHAMBA. WERE OPENED
ON 27ᵀᴴ MAY. 1961. BY
SIR PERCY WYN-HARRIS, K.C.M.G., M.B.E.
ADMINISTRATOR

PROVINCIAL ENGINEER
E. L. FOX.

Figure 8.3. Native Authority Offices Plaque. Photograph Richard Fardon

with little respite. This volatility has been more than matched by the creation and suppression of political parties that have managed both to be new and to have recognizable antecedents in past parties. And every time the political game has been redefined, Chamba have not had a choice whether to participate, both to protect their position vis-à-vis the Fulani, and because political office has been the most common, in fact for Chamba almost sole, route to personal wealth. Each change has required a refashioning of networks of influence, an undertaking that demands the investment of time, as well as the raising and expenditure of financial resources. This process has been not just repeated but inflated: most simply in monetary terms, but also in the numbers of states, local government areas, special development areas, and chiefdoms, and hence the number and rank of their elected and appointed political functionaries (notably, therefore, excepting those state employees most practically involved in the provision of welfare, education and physical infrastructure).

Chamba have been both citizens and subjects for much of the past four-and-a-half decades, at least when military governments have not held electoral processes entirely in abeyance. Because the Christians predominated among the first Chamba to be educated, there was a tendency for them also to predominate among those elected to offices. All occupants of 'traditional' offices are expected to be Muslims, and there are well-known cases of Christians having converted to Islam shortly before being appointed to some rung of the chiefdom's administration. Christian and Muslim interests have to be kept in some kind of balance in the interests of Chamba retaining ethnic solidarity. Seen from this perspective, there are not two systems of government but only one that happens to operate through two related branches with slightly different protocols, and the more durable of these, which seems capable of surviving transitions between national regimes, is called 'traditional' although it is actually a postcolonial introduction in an invented, syncretized traditional idiom. Moreover, it is not clear that one part of the system is more responsive or representative than the other. The Paramount Chief has to emerge from an electoral process, and he surrounds himself with a Council drawn representatively from those considered successful and influential in the chiefdom. In appointing District Heads (all 18 of whom currently have the honorific title Alhaji, indicating pilgrimage to Mecca), he has to gauge what will be acceptable to those they govern, and he knows that the precedents are plentiful for unpopular appointees to destabilize their own communities.

It is a moot point whether the elected officials are more accountable than the Paramount Chief. Quite how particular candidates for election emerge as such is often unclear to those invited to vote for them, who are left to assume some behind-the-scenes stitch-up. Arguments about ethnic turn-taking are widely imputed and surface explicitly as arguments for candidates. When one political party is ascendant, which is the present case, the candidate for that party inevitably emerges with a popular mandate. Hence the obscure process of candidate selection is more important than the more public process of election, as people are well aware. Federal and statal representatives are likely to spend much of their time respectively in the federal and statal capitals (Yola and Abuja); even local councillors may not always be accessible to their electorates, particularly if they combine elected office with a job elsewhere in the country. When there is a crisis, it is to the Chief that people turn for leadership and reconciliation.[12]

Chamba are politically more experienced than they were thirty years ago, but so are Nigerians generally. Their language repertoires have changed. Chamba identity has self-consciously been maintained in the face of their division between world religions, which is difficult because Muslim identities have typically been seen as supportive of the Northern Nigerian status quo, while Christian identities have as typically been cast as more radical, particularly those of the Protestants who challenged the British to reform the system of colonial administration they considered biased. The Bachama, another of the people who saw their Chief ascend to first-class paramountcy in 2006, are almost uniformly Lutherans and regard Chamba Muslims as an anomaly among two peoples whose solidarity rests in part on a shared history of resistance to incorporation in the Adamawa Emirate. Does any of this suggest Chamba have become more cosmopolitan in recent decades? Does the question in fact illuminate anything much of this process beyond changes in the fashionable concerns of academics?

Cosmopolitan sleights

Immigrant minorities in older nation-states are often thought to be more cosmopolitan in outlook than the majority population among whom they live: a minority may have international links not simply with a previous homeland but throughout a diaspora from that homeland; members of the minority may have settled in more or less concentrated areas throughout large parts of their new homeland; their favoured economic niches may draw upon their national and international connections, and upon linguistic and cultural skills that allow them to function in several national contexts; their marriage patterns may both tie them into overseas and local networks, as well as predominantly reproducing their own identity through a high rate of endogamy. Granted, few minorities exactly fit all these criteria, we might think of this kind of diasporic minority as an ideal type, and one that many anthropologists would be willing to see as cosmopolitan both in its orientation and in its practices. Leaving aside 'internationalism', all these features might apply

---

12. This was very evident during protests against police brutality that occurred during my visit in January 2006 and eventuated in a contingent of Nigeria's unloved Mobile Police being sent into Ganye.

equally to encapsulated minorities, particularly those in newer nation-states (such as Nigeria). Chamba, for instance, have a high degree of linkage in their Nigerian diaspora, but most also remain tied to their home places; there is a high degree of multilingualism and, while marriage is predominantly to other Chamba, many who have worked or studied outside their homeland married spouses of different ethnicity. Unlike ideal typical international cosmopolitans, however, Chamba, like other Nigerian minorities, have some local place within the nation-state where they are at home as a majority.

There is an extensive literature on West Africa dealing with home-town associations through which migrants stay in touch with projects at home, and these incorporate international migrants in much the same way as national migrants. Though Nigerian Chamba associations are not particularly active in this regard, the Bali Chamba of the Grassfields of Cameroon (some of whose founders left Chambaland as raiders in the nineteenth century, see Fardon 2006) have extensive associations both in the USA and in the UK which fund projects at home. It was in the town of Bali that I heard the only reference to 'cosmopolitans', using that term, while thinking about the subject of this chapter. This was in a comment made by the local mayor to the effect that 'cosmopolitans' were much appreciated for their financial contribution to their home town, but they had to realize they were not always in the best position to decide local priorities.

Although I do not have space to develop the argument here, Bali demonstrates just how dissimilar two related cases can be. Unlike Ganye, Bali is a precolonial *fondom* (kingdom), related to four other intrusive kingdoms in the Cameroon Grassfields. Its alliances tend to be with other kingdoms in the Anglophone region of Cameroon. Unlike Chamba, the Bali population is almost entirely Christian (though of differing denominations) and, in another striking contrast, customary religion linked to the palace is publicly prominent. The differences between the two places could be developed at length, but are introduced here as a caution against generalizations about the ways that national encapsulation functions.

Finally in this section, I want to remark how it appears to be the case that behaviours judged 'cosmopolitan', on the part of some internationalized minorities, are seen instead as 'extraverted' or 'inauthentic' on the part of African minorities. How far is cosmopolitanism in the eye of the beholder? And does that eye see all cases in the same light? How do beholders know cosmopolitanism when they see it? And, what is their interest in seeing it? I don't mean to pursue an argument that reduces interest in talking about cosmopolitanism to the interests of people who believe themselves to be cosmopolitans. Nevertheless, thinking through the concerns of minority peoples in heterogeneous nations does predispose attention to the effects that majorities and their interests (in different senses of this term) can cause, even, perhaps especially, unwittingly. The 'sleight' of this section's title, according to the dictionary definitions, can have relatively approving senses of skilfulness or cleverness, but these characteristics shade into a knack or trick, and this adroitness in turn spills into morally ambiguous areas of artifice, ruse or cunning. The homophonous verb to 'slight', meaning to take at little value, or betray indifference towards, has no etymological connection with 'sleight', but I cannot help hearing a potential for 'slight' lurking in 'sleight'. What, I wonder, is the effect of an increasing interest in cosmopolitanism on (those rendered thereby) the uncosmopolitans, or the aspirant cosmopolitans? Are the uncosmopolitans for cosmopolitans akin to what the uncivilized used to be in the eyes of those who thought themselves civilized? Because cosmopolitanism classifies (and as Bourdieu might have reminded us, classifies the classifiers), ignoring the vexed issue of its definition serves to naturalize it.

Commentators seem to agree both that they know cosmopolitanism when they see it and that it is very difficult to put a finger on quite how this happens. The editors of two recent collections of papers try different strategies to get around the problem. Stephen Vertovec and Robin Cohen (2002) helpfully disentangle six 'perspectives' on cosmopolitanism, without committing themselves either to the argument that these are perspectives on the same object seen from different vantages, or to the proposition that every aspect of the object thus envisioned might not be called something else chosen from the ample vocabulary of escape from hypertrophied identity categories (transnationalism, globalization, diaspora, creolization, hybridity, transculturation…). While grateful for their careful literature review, this reader is left unsure whether they are proposing a polythetic delineation of cosmopolitanism, or listing rather different concerns that simply happen to be included in some uses of the term.

Sheldon Pollock, Homi K. Bhabha, Carol A. Breckenridge and Dipesh Chakrabarty devote the first paragraph of their editorial introduction to explaining why, because cosmopolitanism is yet to come, we do not know what it currently is, and cannot therefore say where it came from. Moreover, it must 'always escape positive and definite specification, precisely because specifying cosmopolitanism positively and definitely is an uncosmopolitan thing to do' (Breckenridge et al. 2002:1). While wanting to sympathize with a project that wants to be so resolutely non-exclusive, arcane non-definition does threaten to defeat its own inclusive intentions by excluding those who simply lack prior knowledge that would allow them to begin to understand what this undefinable project might be. To be on board the cosmopolitan project, to put it crudely, you have to have been on board already.[13]

Kwame Anthony Appiah's urbane and witty account of cosmopolitan ethics in a 'world of strangers' clearly addresses those already on board. I agree with most that he says, but then my profile closely fits his intended audience. I ought to be part of his 'we'. Appiah argues that cosmopolitanism requires a conversation, interpreted in broad terms, between those who hold differing values, not so they come to agree on those values, but so they can achieve ways of practical coexistence. Extreme cultural relativism is no help here, since it precludes conversation (2006: 14, 57, 70-1, 85). His definition of cosmopolitanism varies from a minimal commitment to mutual obligation and respect for difference between humans (2006: xv), to a more elaborated commitment to fallibilism (recognizing the limits to one's certainties) and pluralism (2006: 144) Throughout he emphasises practices and the facts of a shrinking and culturally interpenetrating world in which being a non-cosmopolitan requires unrelenting vigilance. Cosmopolitanism is a normal condition. We are less different from one another than some like to suggest. Because he draws upon his autobiography, Appiah addresses an (elite) triangular cosmopolitanism (American, British and Asante) which sits within a history of Atlantic globalization. He might also have asked about Ghanaian conviviality, between coastal, central Akan, and northern peoples who differ widely and have historic antagonisms that so far

---

13. I moderate my own erstwhile enthusiasm for polythetic definitions in this context: polythetic definition illuminates the use of complex terms in an ethnographic sense, but this may be less insightful for those who are not users and hence cannot perform the auto-ethnography required.

have been restrained by relatively durable compromise in a half century of postcolonial history.

A philosopher appealing to practice is, as Appiah recognizes, in danger of putting himself out of business. His conclusion is called 'kindness to strangers' which echoes Kant. But with a change of preposition might also echo Tennessee Williams's Blanche DuBois in *A Streetcar Named Desire*, who claimed always to have relied on the kindness 'of strangers'. (Blanche, we may also recall, traded favours to strangers for their help, and the devaluation of her favours with age is a large part of the plot of the play.) We may become better cosmopolitans, Appiah concludes, by giving up a sum of money small enough not to trouble most Westerners which will nonetheless be large enough to alleviate basic poverty globally. It sounds like a win-win situation, but what does it make of the world's Blanche DuBoises, those who receive strangers' beneficence? Do they become more cosmopolitan in receiving our handouts? Or, will they be cosmopolitans only once they too give? And, are their problems simply a matter of our wealth? In part they certainly are, but wealth transfer and a regard for both cultural pluralism and every culture's plurality misses the connections between economy, practice and that variable degree of extension in the world we tend to recognize as being cosmopolitan or not. Appealing to practice in this fashion actually avoids most practical conundrums because it is devoid of curiosity about the social circumstances under which conversation occurs. When is it reasonable to anticipate people will embrace fallibilism and pluralism? When, most basically, can they afford to do so?

Anthropologists cannot leave the question of practice in quite such abstract terms as philosophers. We need to reinstate some of the sociologics between the philosophical-cum-cultural and political-cum-policy poles towards which much of the debate on cosmopolitanism tends to gravitate, and which are only apparently reconciled when conclusions about the one (say, policy) are drawn directly from the other (say, partial cultural relativism of some stripe). In order to do these things, we cannot allow the meanings of cosmopolitanism to bend so conveniently, since in recruiting a cosmopolitan 'we' on such various grounds, a non-cosmopolitan or uncosmopolitan 'they' is precipitated as a problematic object, and this implies a solution that asks them all to cross the floor to our cosmopolitan camp. Yet, even in principle, anthropologists know that is not how segmentary political processes work and, in practice, as I argued above, the vagueness of cosmopolitanism's definition has the effect of excluding some people's behaviour more because of the context in which they act than because of what they do.

What would be the potential effects of anthropologists framing their interests in terms of cosmopolitanism? Such a shift would certainly be in the spirit of anthropological *bouleversement*: anthropologists, one conventionally progressive version of disciplinary history tells us, were once predominantly interested in exotic places, now they also work at home; once they worked in few field sites over a career, now some undertake multi-sited fieldwork to triangulate extensive social processes from the outset of their research careers; that is, supposing they still privilege fieldwork, for anthropologists now use all kinds of materials not just to supplement fieldwork but as the primary focus of study. Why not complete the process of uprooting ethnography by making study of cosmopolitans or cosmopolitanism exemplary? Of course, the conventional history has been overstated here for effect (and brevity), and I agree with most of the arguments that have broadened the scope of anthropology. But I worry about their, probably unintended, aggregate effects. By doing one thing, we choose not to do others. In an intellectual landscape that is increasingly inter- and post-disciplinary (a single market place in which barriers to trade have been dismantled), if anthropologists choose to do what other (usually more powerful) disciplines also do, there is little likelihood of those other disciplines interesting themselves in the range of societies that used to be anthropology's hallmark. Hence my worry about 'cosmopolitanism' is not just that it seems to precipitate a category of the uncosmopolitan on grounds that take no account of the social logics of action, but that it may make uncosmopolitan enquiry unattractive to prospective researchers.

Ulrich Beck, presumably without meaning to do so, demonstrates what I have in mind when he writes that, 'Identity denies ambivalence, pins things down and attempts to draw boundaries in a process of cosmopolitanization that suspends and blurs boundaries. There is a corresponding nostalgia on the part of social scientists (not forgetting anthropologists) for an ordered world of clear boundaries and the associated social categories' (Beck 2002: 81). The scholarship here is careless for one so eminent, but also indicative in its assumption that evidence would be unnecessary: who are these anthropologists nostalgic for clear boundaries and social categories? The guilty go unnamed; as well they might.[14] What is studied has been conflated with how that study takes place. Throughout my career, anthropologists – particularly those who have been read widely – have indeed studied how people essentialize their identities and naturalize their social classifications, but to study such processes is neither to endorse them, nor to bemoan their loss where they have been undermined. Rather than berating forebears, I prefer to take seriously the contrapuntal sense of cosmopolitanism and its antonyms to which Beck also points when he writes that identity 'pin[s] things down' – indeed, how could it be identity if it did not? Even the identity of 'cosmopolitan' has the effect of trying, however evasively, to pin down something that otherwise very different people or practices share. If the idea of cosmopolitanism had no intention to pin anything down, why would commentators worry whether defining cosmopolitanism was itself uncosmopolitan? In reality, pinning down most identities is not so easy; it calls for vigilant and unrelenting work, and this is because the social worlds in which most of us live – not being total institutions – are criss-crossed by currents that both call forth and repudiate essentialized identities. *Pace* Beck, identities have as much to do with the creation of ambivalence as its denial: if there were no identities then what would people be ambivalent about? People with strong local identities, like Chamba in Nigeria, are rendered uncosmopolitan on account of their shared identity, without pausing to ask about the sociologics of that identity: which minimally would have to include the minority position in a multi-ethnic national state of people who nevertheless constitute a local majority, or the internal tensions between faith communities among them that ethnicity has to try, quite self-consciously, to trump.

Peripheral citizenship in practice

Most of this chapter has concerned the circumstances local to Chamba communities in Nigeria and Cameroon. So in conclusion I want to broaden my comments from this case to a wider sense of peripheral citizenship and do so in the interest of the project of cosmopolitanism. I appreciate the social sciences' current concern with cosmopolitanism as

14. While not wanting to leave myself open to the charge I just levelled at the eminent professor, neither do I want to clutter this chapter with references to an elderly literature some of which I surveyed twenty years ago (Fardon 1987a, Chapter 3 in this volume).

an attempt to highlight efforts at securing conviviality, including global justice and human rights, made in the face of trajectories of cultural, economic and political differentiation under contexts of globalization. However, processes of conviviality and differentiation have been concurrent, even mutually entailed, by the wider connections which fostered both. Privileging one as the transcendence of the other, as Beck does, also privileges its proponents, those in a position to propose it. How wide a project of conviviality might be anticipated of peripheral citizens under marginalized circumstances? Cosmopolitans, whether in outlook or in practice, usually need to have resolved their national role in one way or another: either secured their share of the national cake, or given it up as a bad job and invested in the outside. Those who have given up on their nation-states may be economic migrants (from the fabulously rich to the indigent), or illegal aliens and refugees, respectively the flotsam and jetsam of globalization.

Chamba in Ganye have an unresolved relation to their national state about which they need to be constantly vigilant. The identity underwriting their claims in the sub-national area in which they can construct themselves as a majority is the most cogent argument they have for their national position. Chamba neotraditionalism in ethnicity and in chiefship sits in a Nigerian world of ethnic claims, and Chamba anticipate that others will have similar identities to underpin their rights. The assertion of ethnicity is simultaneously a claim to statal and federal resources; in this sense, ethnicity involves a commitment to the national state as quartermaster. 'Traditional' chiefship must both participate in this agonistic jousting and stand slightly to one side of it, rising above sectional struggles and persisting beyond the party interests that are their vehicle.

Ethnicity, most fundamentally for Chamba, and at least for the present, trumps religion: the more confessional identities have become polarized (and this process has been accelerated by the globalizing projects of both Christians and Muslims), the more Chamba have been inclined to play down religious differences. Quite how resilient this ethnicizing response to religious polarization will remain is difficult to predict. There is ambivalence among some Chamba about an ethnic project that subordinates religious differences – particularly if one confessional identity seems regularly disadvantaged by it. Clearly, this fragile play of circumstances is not reducible to the kind of antinomian contest between cosmopolitanization and the essentialization of identities that Ulrich Beck suggests as a master process. Indeed, such a formulation would entirely fail to recognize the difficulties of constructing ethnic conviviality in a 'cosmopolitan' yet religiously riven nation. Granted the dangers inherent in an ethnic project, it would still be unjust to portray those struggling to contain religious polarization and contest historic marginality simply as obstacles to cosmopolitanization because their sole instrument for doing this involved identity politics.

Advocates of cosmopolitanism seek to make the world a better place. To argue that humans are a single species, that cultures are not essences, that loyalties may be complex, that responsibilities for one another do not end at national boundaries, and so forth. Who, among those addressed, would argue? But who is addressed? And under what circumstances are those addressed in a position to concur? Ethnographers have been the main specialists in the knowledge economy asking – on the basis of experience – how this all looks from the other end of the telescope. Without such investigations, cosmopolitanism risks being, by sleight not by intention, another way of excluding and disparaging others. The 'traditionalism' of marginalized ethnic subjects in Nigeria results from processes of globalization and from currents of cosmopolitanization as they are played out nationally and experienced locally through divisive world religious affiliations and the opportunities for hegemony offered to majorities by universal 'democratic' processes. Cultural relativism is untenable as a presupposition of cosmopolitanism, as Kwame Anthony Appiah argues, not just because extreme relativism would mean people had nothing to say to one another, but because cultured lives are *already* relative to one another historically and presently (Kahn 2003: 411). While the philosophical argument is unimpeachable in principle, it is irrelevant to the world as it exists. Worse, arguments about cultural relativism produce a Manichaean outlook. Here I want to return to Appiah's advocacy of cosmopolitan charity in conclusion.

The year 2005 witnessed a series of, what I applaud as having been, genuinely cosmopolitan initiatives. The publication of *Our Common Interest: Report of the Commission for Africa* in March that year was a landmark event, its impact reinforced by Bob Geldof's initiatives as author, television documentary-maker and concertmaster. It in no way diminishes this effort to use it as an example of the desire both to be deferential towards cultural difference and remain appalled by some of the behaviour carried out in the name of identities defined culturally. This shows up in the *Report* as a fretful switching between singular and plural, adding and removing the qualification 'African':

> Different cultures manifest their ideas of political and economic freedom in very different ways. For this reason the Commission decided to consider the issue of culture before embarking on political and economic analysis. By culture we are talking about far more than literature, music, dance, art, sculpture, theatre, film and sport. All of these, of course, are for any social group part of its shared joy in the business of being alive. But culture is more than the arts. It is about shared patterns of identity. It is about how social values are transmitted and individuals are made to be part of a society. Culture is how the past interacts with the future. (Commission for Africa 2005: 30)

> One commonly held fallacy about culture is that it is the expression of unchanging tradition. Those who hold this view usually see African cultures as regressive and tribal and therefore inimical to development. African culture, they often say, is an irrational force that generates inertia and economic backwardness. This is contrary to the evidence. History shows African cultures to have been tremendously adaptive, absorbing a wide range of outside influences, and impositions, as well as finding ways to survive often difficult natural, environmental and social conditions. (Commission for Africa 2005: 31)

These summarized thoughts (and their expansion in pp. 121-32 of the *Report's* main text) are clearly meant well; their respect for cultural difference, and emphasis on the need for dialogue (which I have not quoted) would presumably make them cosmopolitan in Kwame Anthony Appiah's terms. But like many propositions about culture, they quickly become perplexing. In the first paragraph, cultures are taken as foundational realities: able to 'manifest their ideas of political and economic freedom'; being 'about shared patterns of identity'; being 'how the past interacts with the future'. But, this version of African cultures does indeed lend itself to being construed in terms of a multiplicity of ethnic possessions, particularly when, out of proper deference to the immense variety of African societies, the *Report* insists on pluralizing 'cultures'. As Sir Bob puts it succinctly in his own book, 'Talking about tribalism makes Africans sound backward' (Geldof 2005: 235), yet the Commission does choose to start with cultures when talking about Africa.

The second paragraph I quoted tackles this point head on, refuting unnamed critics and arguing that African cultures have simultaneously absorbed outside influences (outside what one wonders?) while finding ways to survive a variety of difficult conditions. Is it not people who survive difficulties? Or is this a variation on the selfish gene: people being the medium through which cultures survive? This begins to sound more essentialist than the notion it was designed to refute. In terms of the likely impact of the Commission for Africa's report, I don't believe that the sort of confusions about the notion of culture likely to be picked up by a nit-picking academic matter much. The incoherence is not the authors' fault but symptomatic of the ambivalent role played by the ambitious idea of culture itself.

My detailed ethnographic example has worked some well-worn themes in the recent ethnography of Africa: that the invention of tradition involves a mixture of self-conscious motivations in addition to the taken-for-grantedness of some aspects of the past; that the increasing prominence of chiefship in contemporary Africa responds to present as well as past politics; that the apparent distinction between citizens and subjects in African societies is largely chimerical: for where both chiefs and elected representatives are found, their activities will have been interlaced in all manner of complicated ways. The social logics of identification have to be understood in terms of such factors and not, in the terms of the *Report of the Commission for Africa,* as a prior state of culture somehow expressing itself through people's values, however much this understanding is founded in a liberal sense of cultural relativism. Chamba emphasis on their ethnic identity, the importance they attribute to their paramount chiefship, their attempts to play down religious divisions among themselves while living in a country that is increasingly becoming polarized on religious grounds, developed in a context of political and economic peripherality. Identity is the vehicle of their interest in belonging to the culturally diverse and unequal national state that is contemporary, cosmopolitan Nigeria.

Philosophical and policy arguments about cosmopolitanism per se, different though they may seem – and indeed are – in many ways, share a tendency to talk about cultures in ways that dislocate them from their social and political contexts. That they tend to ignore the social grounds of their own enunciation should, therefore, not come as a surprise. Social anthropologists may play a role in identifying the social logics of projects of conviviality of ethnographic subjects, whether these subjects are distinguished philosophers and sociologists, or politicians in the 'West', or peripheral citizens and subjects of African states. Current discussions of cosmopolitanism, I have suggested, remain indebted to their roots in European assumptions about the role of cultural homogeneity in the nation (the same assumptions that were exported to settler colonies in the Americas, Antipodes and parts of Africa with the imposition for longer or shorter periods of systems of racial segregation for indigenous or enslaved peoples). West Africa hardly saw settler colonialism. Its racial segregation was restricted to small groups of agents of colonialism (administrative, commercial, religious, and so forth) who were themselves not of single purpose. West Africa's efforts to actualize nation-states (created neither by local domination, on the model of European states, nor by immigrant domination, on the model of settler colonies) involve forms of national cosmopolitanism that are unprecedented in their complexity.

BIBLIOGRAPHY

Abubakar, Sa'ad (1977) *The Lamibe of Fombina. A political history of Adamawa 1809-190*, Zaria: Ahmadu Bello University and Oxford University Press.

Adler, Alfred (1982) *La mort est le masque du roi. La royauté sacrée des Moundang du Tchad*, Paris: Payot.

Adler, Jeremy and Richard Fardon (1999) 'Orientpolitik, value, and civilisation: the anthropological thought of Franz Baermann Steiner', Introduction to Jeremy Adler and Richard Fardon (eds) *Franz Baermann Steiner Selected Writings*, Volume II, Oxford: Berghahn.

Adler, Jeremy and Richard Fardon (eds) (1999) *Franz Baermann Steiner Selected Writings*, 2 Volumes, Oxford: Berghahn.

Akiga, Sai (1939) *Akiga's Story. The Tiv tribe as seen by one of its members*, translated and annotated by Rupert East, London: Oxford University Press for the International African Institute.

— (1954) 'The "descent" of the Tiv from Ibenda Hill', translated by Paul Bohannan, *Africa* 24: 295-310.

ALCAM (1983) *Atlas linguistique du Cameroun - inventaire préliminaire*, DGRST: Yaoundé.

Amadiume, Ifi (1987a) *Afrikan Matriarchal Foundations: the Igbo case*, London: Karnak.

— (1987b) *Male Daughters, Female Husbands: gender and sex in an African society*, London: Zed.

Amselle, J.-L. (1985) 'Ethnies et espaces: pour une anthropologie topologique', in Amselle, J.-L. and E. M'Bokolo (eds) *Au coeur de l'ethnie: ethnies, tribalisme et état en Afrique*, Paris Editions de la découverte/ textes à l'appui, pp. 11-48.

— (1990) *Logiques métisses: anthropologie de l'identité en Afrique et ailleurs*, Paris: Editions Payot.

Amselle, J.-L. and E. M'Bokolo (eds) (1985) *Au coeur de l'ethnie: ethnies, tribalisme et état en Afrique*, Paris Editions de la découverte/ textes à l'appui.

Anderson, B. (1991) (originally 1983) *Imagined Communities: reflections on the origin and spread of nationalism* (revised edition), London: Verso.

Appiah, Kwame Anthony (1992) *In My Father's House. Africa in the philosophy of culture*, London: Methuen.

— (2006) *Cosmopolitanism: ethics in a world of strangers*, New York and London: W.W. Norton.

Archibugi, Daniele (ed.) (2003) *Debating Cosmopolitics*, London and New York: Verso.

Ardener, Edwin (1974) 'Social anthropology and population', in H. P. Parry (ed.) *Population and its Problems*, Oxford: Clarendon.

Armstrong, R. G. (1955) 'Igala- and Idoma-speaking peoples', in D. Forde, P. Brown and R. G. Armstrong, *Peoples of the Niger-Benue Confluence*, Ethnographic Survey of Africa, West Africa, Part X, London: International African Institute.

Article 19 (1996) *Broadcasting Genocide: censorship, propaganda and state-sponsored violence in Rwanda 1990-94*, London: International Centre against Censorship.

Article 19 and Index on Censorship (1995) *Who Rules the Airwaves: broadcasting in Africa*, London: International Centre against Censorship.

Austen, R. (1992) 'Tradition, invention and history: the case of the Ngondo (Cameroon)', *Cahiers d'études africaines* 126, XXXII(2): 285-309.

Azonga, T.M. (1993a) 'Walking a tight rope', *West Africa* 17-23 May, pp. 814-15.

— (1993b) 'Fru Ndi states his case', *West Africa* 14-20 June, pp. 997-98.

Barley, Nigel (1983) *Symbolic Structures. An exploration of the culture of the Dowayos*, Cambridge and Paris: Cambridge University Press and Editions de la Maison des Sciences de l'Homme.

Barnes, R.H. (1984) *Two Crows Denies It. A history of the controversy in Omaha sociology*, Lincoln and London: University of Nebraska Press.

Barth, Fredrik (1969a) 'Introduction', to his *Ethnic Groups and Boundaries: the social organisation of culture difference,* London: Allen and Unwin.

— (1969b) 'Pathan identity and its maintenance', in his *Ethnic Groups and Boundaries: the social organisation of culture difference*, London: Allen and Unwin.

Baumann, H. and L. Vajda (1959) 'Bernhard Ankermann's völkerkundliche Aufzeichnungen im Grasland von Kamerun 1907-9' (including letter from Adolf Vielhauer to Ankermann of 22 November 1910 pp. 271-76) *Baessler Archiv* (NF) 7(2): 217-317.

Bayart, J.-F. (1979) *L'Etat au Cameroun*, Paris: Presses de la Fondation National des Sciences Politiques.

— (1993) (originally 1989) *The State in Africa: the politics of the belly*, Harlow: Longman.

Bazin, J. (1985) 'A chacun son Bambara', in Amselle, J.-L. and E. M'Bokolo (eds) (1985) *Au coeur de l'ethnie: ethnies, tribalisme et état en Afrique*, Paris Editions de la découverte/ textes à l'appui, pp. 87-127.

Beck, Ulrich (2002) 'The cosmopolitan perspective: sociology in the second age of modernity', in Steven Vertovec and Robin Cohen (eds) *Conceiving Cosmopolitanism: theory, context, and practice*, Oxford: Oxford University Press, pp. 61-85.

Beidelman, T.O. (1967) *The Matrilineal Peoples of Eastern Tanzania*, D. Forde (ed.), Ethnographic Survey of East Africa, Part XVI, London: International African Institute.

Bennett, P. (1983) 'Adamawa-Eastern: problems and prospects', in I. R. Dihoff (ed.) *Current Approaches to African Linguistics*, Dordrecht: Foris.

Berns, Marla C., Richard Fardon and Sidney Littlefield Kasfir (eds) (2011) *Central Nigeria Unmasked: arts of the Benue River Valley*, Los Angeles: Fowler Museum at UCLA.

Bhabha, H.K. (1990) (ed.) *Nation and Narration*, London and New York: Routledge.

Bloch, Maurice (1990) 'What goes without saying: the conceptualization of Zafimaniry society', in Adam Kuper (ed.) *Conceptualizing Society*, European Association of Social Anthropologists, London: Routledge.

Bohannan, Laura (1952) 'A genealogical charter', *Africa* 22: 301-15.

— (1958) 'Political aspects of Tiv social organisation', in J. Middleton and D. Tait (eds) *Tribes without Rulers*, London: Routledge & Kegan Paul.

— (1960) 'The frightened witch', in J. Casagrande (ed.), *The Company of Man*, New York: Harper.

Bohannan, L. and P. (1953, 1969) *The Tiv of Central Nigeria*, Ethnographic Survey of Africa, West Africa Part VIII, London: International African Institute.

Bohannan, Paul (1954a) *Tiv Farm and Settlement*, London: HMSO.

— (1954b) 'The migration and expansion of the Tiv', *Africa* 24: 2-16.

— (1955) 'Some principles of exchange and investment among the Tiv', *American Anthropologist* 58: 60-9.

— (1957) *Justice and Judgement amongst the Tiv*, London: Oxford University Press for the International African Institute.

— (1958) 'Extra-processual events in Tiv political institutions', *American Anthropologist* 60: 1-12.

— (1965) 'The Tiv of Nigeria', in J. L. Gibbs (ed.), *Twelve African Tribes*, New York: Holt Rinehart & Winston.

Bohannan, P. and L. (1968) *Tiv Economy*, Evanston: Northwestern University Press.

Bowen, Elenore Smith (1955) *Return to Laughter*, New York: Harper.

Boyd, Raymond (1989) 'Adamawa-Ubangi, John Bendor-Samuel (ed.) *The Niger-Congo Languages*, Lanham, New York and London: Summer Institute of Linguistics, pp. 178-215.

Boyd, Raymond and Richard Fardon (2014) 'Naming powers: Hausa *tsafi* and Tiv *tsav*', *Journal of African Cultural Studies* 26(1): 1-23.

Brain, Robert (1972) *Bangwa Kinship and Marriage*, London: Cambridge University Press.

— (1981) 'The Fontem-Bangwa: a western Bamileke group', in Claude Tardits (ed.) *Contribution de la Recherche Ethnologique à l'histoire des Civilisations du Cameroun*, Paris: Editions du CNRS.

Breckenridge, Carol A., Sheldon Pollock, Homi K. Bhabha and Dipesh Chakrabarty (eds) (2002) *Cosmopolitanism*, Durham/London: Duke University Press.

Brenner, Louis (ed.) (1993) *Muslim Identity and Social Change in Sub-Saharan Africa*, London: Hurst and Company.

Breton, Roland (1981) *Les Ethnies. Que sais-Je?*, Paris: Presses Universitaires de France.

'Buea Declaration' [1993] issued by the *All Anglophone Conference* held at Buea on 2nd and 3rd April, 1993.

Burnham, Philip (1980) *Opportunity and Constraint in a Savanna Society*, London and New York: Academic Press.

— (1990) 'Stratégie d'alliance et formation des groups chez les Gbaya du Cameroun', in Françoise Héritier and Elisabeth Copet-Rougier (eds) *Les Complexités de l'alliance, systèmes semi-complexes*, Volume 1, Paris: Archives Contemporaines, Collection Ordres Sociaux.

— (1991) 'L'ethnie, la religion et l'Etat: le rôle des Peuls dans la vie politique et sociale du Nord-Cameroun', *Journal des Africanistes* 61: 73-102.

— (1996) *The Politics of Cultural Difference in Northern Cameroon*, Edinburgh: Edinburgh University Press for the International African Institute.

Burnham, Philip and Last, Murray (1994) 'From pastoralist to politician: the problem of a Fulbe "aristocracy"', *Cahiers d'études africaines*, 133-35, XXXIV (1-3): 313-57.

Calhoun, Craig (2003) 'The class consciousness of frequent travellers: towards a critique of actually existing cosmopolitanisms', in Daniele Archibugi (ed.) *Debating Cosmopolitics*, London: Verso, pp. 86-116.

Calvino, Italo (1978) *The Castle of the Crossed Destinies*, London: Pan Books.

Cameroon Protestant College (C. E. G.) (1971 [1965]) *Bali History*, mimeographed, CPC: Bamenda, Cameroon (copy in Basel Mission Archive).

Cannadine, David (2001) *Ornamentalism: how the British saw their Empire*, London: Allen Lane.

Cheah, Pheng and Bruce Robbins (eds) (1998) *Cosmopolitics: thinking and feeling beyond the nation*, Minneapolis: University of Minnesota Press.

Chilver, E.M. (1963) 'Native Administration in the West Central Cameroons 1902-1954', in K. Robinson and F. Madden (eds) *Essays in Imperial Government presented to Margery Perham*, Oxford: Basil Blackwell.

— [1964; revised 1970] *Historical Notes on the Bali Chiefdoms of the Cameroons Grassfields* (Two Reports to the Bali Historical Society, Report 1 *Origins, Migration and composition*. Report 2 *The Bali-Chamba of Bamenda: settlement and composition*). Cyclostyle: privately circulated.

— (1966) *Zintgraff's Explorations in Bamenda, Adamawa and the Benue Lands 1889-1892*, Buea, Cameroon: Government Printer. (Previously circulated privately in 1961).

— (1967) 'Paramountcy and protection in the Cameroons: the Bali and the Germans, 1889-1913' in P Gifford and W.R. Louis (eds) *Britain and Germany in Africa: imperial rivalry and colonial rule*, New Haven: Yale University Press.

Chilver, E.M. and P.M. Kaberry (1965) 'Sources of the nineteenth-century slave trade: the Cameroons Highlands', *Journal of African History* 6(1): 117-20.

— (1968) *Traditional Bamenda. The pre-colonial history and ethnography of the Bamenda Grassfields*, Ministry of Primary Education and Social Welfare and West Cameroon Antiquities Commission, Buea: Government Printer.

Chilver, E.M. and Ute Röschenthaler (eds) (2001) *Cameroon's Tycoon: Max Esser's expedition and its consequences*, Oxford: Berghahn Cameroon Studies, Vol. 3.

Chrétien, J.-P. and Prunier, G. (eds) (1989) *Les ethnies ont une histoire*, Paris: Editions Karthala.

Clifford, James (1980) 'Review of *Orientalism* by E. W. Said', *History and Theory* 2: 204-23.

Cohen, Abner (1969) *Custom and Politics in Urban Africa. A study of Hausa migrants in Yoruba towns*, Berkeley and Los Angeles: University of California Press.

— (1981) *The Politics of Elite Culture. Explorations in the dramaturgy of power in a modern African society*, Berkeley: University of California Press.

Cohen, Ronald (1978) 'Ethnicity: problem and focus in anthropology', *Annual Review of Anthropology* 1: 379-403.

— (1980) 'The natural history of hierarchy: a case study', in G. M. Brittan and R. Cohen (eds) *Hierarchy and Society*, Philadelphia: Institute for the Study of Human Issues.

Cohen, R. and J. Middleton (1971) 'Introduction', to their (eds) *From Tribe to Nation in Africa*, Scranton, New Jersey: Chandler.

Commission for Africa (2005) *Our Common Interest: report of the Commission for Africa*, London: Commission for Africa.

Copet-Rougier, Elisabeth (1980) 'Mariage et incest. L'endogamie dans une société à fortes prohibitions matrimoniales', *Bulletin de la Societé d'Anthropologie du sud-ouest*, 15(1): 13-53.

— (1985) 'Contrôle masculine, exclusivité feminine dans une societé patrilinéaire', in J.C. Barbier (ed.) *Femmes du Cameroun*, Paris: Cameroun.

Coquery-Vidrovitch, Catherine (1983) 'A propos des racines historiques du pouvoir: Chefferie » et « Tribalisme », in *Les Pouvoirs Africains* Special Issue *Pouvoirs* 25: 51-62.

Cruise O'Brien, Donal B. (1991) 'The show of state in a neo-colonial twilight: Francophone Africa', in J. Manor (ed.) *Rethinking Third World Politics*, London and New York: Longman Group, pp. 145-65.

Davidson, Basil (1992) *The Black Man's Burden: Africa and the curse of the nation-state*, London: James Currey.

Davis, John (1992) 'Tense in ethnography: some practical considerations', in Judith Okely and Helen Callaway (eds) *Anthropology and Autobiography*, ASA Monograph 29, London and New York: Routledge.

Dorward, D. C. (1969) 'The development of the British colonial administration among the Tiv, 1900-49', *African Affairs* 68: 316-33.

— [1971] 'A Political and Social History of the Tiv People of Northern Nigeria, 1900-39', University of London, Ph.D. thesis.

— (1974) 'Ethnography and administration. A study of Anglo-Tiv "working misunderstanding"', *Journal of African History* 15: 457-77.

Douglas, Mary (1996) *Thought Styles*, London: Sage.

Douglas, Mary and David Hull (eds) (1992) *How Classification Works: Nelson Goodman among the social sciences*, Edinburgh: Edinburgh University Press.

Downes, R. M. (1933) *The Tiv Tribe*, Kaduna: Government Printer.

— (1971) *Tiv Religion*, Ibadan: Ibadan University Press.

Dugast, I. (1953) 'Banen, Bafia and Balom', in *Peoples of the Central Cameroons*, Ethnographic Survey of Africa, West Africa Part IX. London: International African Institute.

Edwards, A. C. (1983) 'Seeing, believing, doing: the Tiv understanding of power',
  Anthropos 78(3-4): 359-80.
— (1984) 'On the non-existence of an ancestor cult among the Tiv', *Anthropos*
  79: 77-112.
— (nd) 'The Tiv people of Nigeria', unpublished typescript.
Ekeh, P.P. (1990) 'Social anthropology and two contrasting uses of tribalism in
  Africa', *Comparative Studies of Society and History* 32(4): 660-700.
Ellis, J.M. (1989) *Against Deconstruction*, Princeton: Princeton University Press.
Epstein, A. L. (1978) *Ethos and Identity: three studies in ethnicity*, London: Tavistock.
Eriksen, T.H. (1993) *Ethnicity and Nationalism: anthropological perspectives*, London and
  Boulder, Colorado: Pluto Press.
Evans-Pritchard, E. E. (1940) *The Nuer: a description of the modes of livelihood and political
  institutions of a Nilotic people*, Oxford: Clarendon Press.
— (1951) *Kinship and Marriage among the Nuer*, Oxford: Clarendon Press.
Fabian, Johannes (1983) *Time and the Other: how anthropology makes its object*, New York:
  Columbia University Press.
— (1991) *Time and the Work of Anthropology: critical essays*, Reading: Harwood.
Fardon, Richard [1980] 'The Chamba', 2 volumes, University of London PhD Thesis.
— (1983) 'A chronology of pre-colonial Chamba history', *Paideuma* 29: 67-92.
— (1984) 'Sisters, wives, wards and daughters: a transformational analysis of the
  political organization of the Tiv and their neighbours', Part I 'The Tiv', *Africa*
  54(4): 2-21. [Reprinted here in Chapter 1]
— (1985a) 'Sisters, wives, wards and daughters: a transformational analysis
  of the political organization of the Tiv and their neighbours', Part II 'The
  transformations', *Africa* 55(1): 77-91. [Reprinted here in Chapter 1]
— (1985b) 'Secrecy and sociability: two problems of Chamba knowledge', in Richard
  Fardon (ed.) *Power and Knowledge*, Edinburgh: Scottish Academic Press.
— [1986] 'Report on ethnographic and historical researches amongst the Pere of
  North Cameroon', Yaoundé, MESRES: Institut des Sciences Humaines, Garoua.
  [Revised as (1999) 'Pere and Chamba: a report on comparative researches in
  Adamawa, North Cameroon', *Ngaoundere-Anthropos* IV: 5-52.]
— (1987a) '"African ethnogenesis": limits to the comparability of ethnic
  phenomena', in Holy Ladislav (ed.) *Comparative Anthropology*, Oxford: Blackwell,
  pp. 168-88. [Reprinted here as Chapter 2]
— (1987b) 'History, ethnicity and pageantry: the 1987 ASA', *Anthropology Today* 3(3):
  15-17.
— (1988a) *Raiders and Refugees: trends in Chamba political development 1750 to 1950*,
  Washington: Smithsonian Series in Ethnographic Enquiry.
— (1988b) 'The creation of peripheral places: an example, a history and a
  comparison', in P. Geschiere and P. Könings (eds) *The Political Economy of
  Cameroon: historical perspectives* (Volume 2), Leiden: African Studies Centre,
  pp. 757-77.
— (1990) *Between God, the Dead and the Wild: Chamba interpretations of religion and ritual*,
  Edinburgh University Press for the International African Institute.
— (1995) 'Counterworks', in Richard Fardon (ed.) *Counterworks: managing the diversity
  of knowledge*, London: Routledge, pp. 1-22.

— (1996a) 'Covering ethnicity? Or, ethnicity as coverage?', *Contemporary Politics* 2(1): 153-8.

— (1996b) '"Crossed Destinies": the entangled histories of West African ethnic and national identities', in Louise de la Gorgendière, Kenneth King and Sarah Vaughan (eds), *Ethnicity in Africa: roots, meanings and implications* (Proceedings of the 1995 Conference of the Centre of African Studies), Edinburgh: University of Edinburgh, pp. 117-46. [Reprinted here as Chapter 5]

— (1996c) 'The person, ethnicity and the problem of "identity" in West Africa', in Ian Fowler and David Zeitlyn (eds), *African Crossroads: intersections between history and anthropology in Cameroon* (Cameroon Studies Vol. 2), Oxford: Berghahn, pp. 17-44. [Reprinted here as Chapter 4]

— (1999a) 'Ethnic pervasion', in Tim Allen and Jean Seaton (eds) *The Media in Conflict: war reporting and representations of ethnic violence*, London: Zed, pp. 64-80. [Reprinted here as Chapter 6]

— (1999b) *Contrast and Comparison: notes from a middle-belt, West African practice*, (Inaugural Lecture, May 1998), London: SOAS (University of London).

— (2004) 'The ethnologist and the missionaries: recording the 1908 Lela in Bali Nyonga', in Michael Albrecht, Veit Arlt, Barbara Müller and Jürg Schneider (eds) *Getting Pictures Right*, Köln: Rüdiger Köppe Verlag, pp. 75-97.

— (2006) *Lela in Bali: history through ceremony in Cameroon*, Oxford: Berghahn, Cameroon Studies 7.

— (2007) *Fusions: masquerades and thought style east of the Niger-Benue confluence, West Africa*, London: Saffron.

Fardon, Richard and Graham Furniss (1994a) 'Frontiers and boundaries: African languages as political environment', in Richard Fardon and Graham Furniss (eds) *African Languages, Development and the State*, London: Routledge.

Fardon, Richard and Furniss, Graham (eds) (1994b) *African Languages, Development and the State*, London: Routledge.

— (2000) *African Broadcast Culture: radio in transition*, Oxford: James Currey; Westport, Connecticut: Praeger; Harare: Baobab; Cape Town: David Philip.

Fardon, Richard and Christine Stelzig (2005) *From Column to Volume: formal innovation in Chamba statuary*, London: Saffron.

Fohtung, M.G. (1992) 'Self-portrait of a Cameroonian, taken down by Peter Kalle Njie and edited by E.M. Chilver', published version of *Portrait of a Cameroonian: an Autobiography of Maxwell Gabana Fohtung*, cyclostyled for private circulation 1962, *Paideuma* 38: 219-48.

Fortes, Meyer (1945) *The Dynamics of Clanship among the Tallensi*, London: Oxford University Press.

Fremantle, J. M. (1922) *Gazetteer of Muri Province*, London: Waterlow and Sons.

Friedman, Jonathan (1979) *System, Structure, and Contradiction in the Evolution of 'Asiatic' Social Formations*, Copenhagen: National Museum of Denmark.

Frobenius, Leo (1913) *Und Afrika Sprach*, Volume 3, Berlin: Vita Deutsches Verlagshaus.

— (1925) *Dichten und Denken im Sudan: Volksmärchen und Volksdichtungen im Sudan*, Volume 5, Jena: Eugen Diederichs.

Gaillard, P. (1992) 'Pluralisme et régionalisme dans la politique camerounaise', *Afrique 2000* 11: 97-109

Gandonu, A. (1978) 'Nigeria's 250 ethnic groups: realities and assumptions', in R. E. Holloman and S. A. Arutinov (eds) *Perspectives on Ethnicity*, The Hague: Mouton.

Garbosa II B.S. (Gara of Donga) c.1956. *Labarun Chambawa da al'amurransu* and *Salsalar sarakunan Donga*, Nigeria: Privately published.

Gates, Henry Louis (1995) *Colored People. A memoir of a West Virginia boyhood*, Harmondsworth: Viking/Penguin.

Geldof, Bob (2005) *Geldof in Africa*, London: Century.

Gellner, Ernest (1983) *Nations and Nationalism*, Oxford: Blackwell.

Glazer, N. and D. Moynihan (1975) 'Introduction', to *Ethnicity: theory and experience*, Cambridge, Mass. and London: Harvard University Press.

Gluckman, Max (1940) 'The analysis of a social situation in modern Zululand', *African Studies* 14: 1-30; 147-74.

Godelier, Maurice (1977) 'The concept of "tribe": a crisis involving merely a concept or the empirical foundations of anthropology itself', in his *Perspectives in Marxist Anthropology*, Cambridge: Cambridge University Press.

Goldscheider, Ludwig (1945) *Leonardo da Vinci*, Oxford and London: Phaidon Press.

Goodman, Nelson (1992) 'Seven Strictures on Similarity', reprinted in Mary Douglas and David Hull (eds) *How Classification Works: Nelson Goodman among the social sciences*, Edinburgh: Edinburgh University Press, pp. 13-24.

Goody, J.R. (1971) *Technology, Tradition and the State in Africa*, London: Oxford University Press for the International African Institute.

Graeber, David (2011) *Debt: the first 5,000 years*, Brooklyn, New York: Melville House.

Gufler, Hermann (2003) *Affliction and Moral Order: Conversations in Yambaland (Cameroon)*, Canterbury: Centre for Social Anthropology and Computing, CSAC Monographs 18.

Gunn, Harold D. (1954) *Pagan Peoples of the Central Area of Northern Nigeria*, Ethnographic Survey of Africa, West Africa Part XII, London: International African Institute.

Hacking, Ian (1990) *The Taming of Chance*, Cambridge: Cambridge University Press.

— (1992) 'World-making by kind-making: child abuse for example', in Mary Douglas and David Hull (eds), *How Classification Works: Nelson Goodman among the social sciences*, Edinburgh: Edinburgh University Press, pp. 180-238.

— (1997) 'Taking bad arguments seriously', *London Review of Books*, 21 August, Vol. 19, No. 16, pp. 14-16.

Hawkesworth, E.G. [1926] *Assessment Report on the Bafut Tribal Area of the Bamenda Division*.

Héritier, Françoise (1977) 'L'identité Samo', in Claude Lévi-Strauss (ed.) *L'identité: séminaire dirigé par Claude Lévi-Strauss*, Paris: Grasset.

— (1981) *L'exercice de la parenté*, Paris: EHESS-Le Seuil-Gallimard.

Héritier-Augé, Françoise and Elisabeth Copet-Rougier (eds) (1990-94) *Les complexités de l'alliance*, Paris: Editions des archives contemporaines, 4 volumes.

Higazi, Adam (2007) 'Violence urbaine et politique à Jos (Nigeria), de la période colonial aux élections de 2007', *Politique Africaine* (Special Issue, *Le Nigeria sous Obasanjo: violences et démocratie*, June) 106: 69-91.

Hobsbawm, Eric (1962) *The Age of Revolution, 1789-1848*, London: Abacus.
— (1994) *The Age of Extremes: the short twentieth century, 1914-1991*, London: Michael Joseph.
Hobsbawm, E. and Ranger, T. (eds) (1983) *The Invention of Tradition*, Cambridge: Cambridge University Press.
Holy, Ladislav. (1979) 'Introduction' to L. Holy (ed.) *Segmentary Lineage Systems Reconsidered*, Belfast: Queen's University Papers in Social Anthropology, 4.
Holy, Ladislav and Milan Stuchlik (1983) *Actions, Norms and Representations: foundations of anthropological inquiry*, Cambridge: Cambridge University Press.
Hopkins, Keith (1973) *An Economic History of West Africa*, London: Longman.
Horton, Robin (1961) 'Destiny and the unconscious in West Africa', *Africa* 31: 110-6.
— (1983) 'Social psychologies: African and Western', 'Introduction' to Meyer Fortes *Oedipus and Job in West African Religion*, Cambridge: Cambridge University Press.
Hunt, W.E. [1925] *An Assessment Report on the Bali clan in the Bamenda Division of Cameroons Province*.
Hurault, Jean (1962) *La Structure sociale des Bamileke*, Paris: Mouton.
Isajiw, W. W. (1974) 'Definitions of ethnicity', *Ethnicity* 1: 111-24.
Jackson, Michael (1989) *Paths Towards a Clearing: radical empiricism and ethnographic enquiry*, African Systems of Thought Series, Bloomington: Indiana University Press.
James, W. R. (1975) 'Sister-exchange marriage', *Scientific American* 223(6): 84-94.
— (1979) '*Kwanim Pa. The making of the Uduk people*, Oxford: Clarendon Press.
— (1998) 'Mauss in Africa: on time, history and polities', in Wendy James and N.J. Allen (eds) *Marcel Mauss. A centenary tribute*, Oxford and New York: Berghahn.
— (2012) 'A tetradic starting point for skewing? Marriage as a generational contract: reflections on sister-exchange in Africa', in Thomas R. Trautmann and Peter M. Whiteley (eds) *Crow-Omaha: new light on a classic problem of kinship analysis*, Arizona: Amerind Studies in Anthropology, Arizona University Press, pp. 135-52.
James, Wendy and David Mills (2005) 'Introduction: from representation to action in the flow of time', in their (eds) *The Qualities of Time: anthropological approaches*, Oxford and New York: Berg, ASA Monographs 41, pp. 1-15.
Jameson, Fredric (1981) *The Political Unconscious. Narrative as socially symbolic act*, London: Methuen.
Jeffreys, M. D. W. (1962a) 'The Wiya tribe', *African Studies* 21(1-2): 83-104, 174-222.
— (1962b) 'Isaac Fielding Pefok, B.E.M: a Brief Autobiography', *The Nigerian Field* 27(2): 81-90.
— (1962c) 'Some notes on the customs of the Grassfields Bali of Northwestern Cameroon', *Afrika und Übersee* 46(3): 161-8.
Kaberry, P.M. and E.M. Chilver (1961) 'An outline of the traditional political system of Bali-Nyonga, Southern Cameroons', *Africa* 31(4): 355-71.
Kaehler-Meyer, E. (1953) 'Sprachenproben aus der Landschaft Mbembe im Bezirk Bamenda, Kamerun', *Afrika und Übersee* 37(4): 109-18.
Kahn, Joel (2003) 'Anthropology as cosmopolitan practice?', *Anthropological Theory* 3(4): 403-15.
Karp, Ivan (1978) 'New Guinea Models in the African Savannah', *Africa* 48(1): 1-16.

Karp, Ivan and Corinne Kratz (2000) 'Reflections on the fate of Tippoo's Tiger: defining cultures through public display', in Elizabeth Hallam and Brian V.Street (eds) *Cultural Encounters: representing otherness*, London and New York: Routledge.

Kastfelt, N. (1994) *Religion and Politics in Nigeria: a study in Middle Belt Christianity*, London and New York: British Academic Press.

Kedourie, E. (1960) *Nationalism*, London: Hutchinson.

Keller, Jakob (1919) 'Das Lelafest in Bali', *Der Evangelische Heidenbote*, Juni: 63-66, Juli: 78-81, Oktober: 116-18.

Köbben, A. (1967) 'Why exceptions? The logic of cross-cultural analysis', *Current Anthropology* 8: 3-19.

— (1970) 'Comparativists and non-comparativists in anthropology', in R. Naroll and R. Cohen (eds) *A Handbook of Method in Cultural Anthropology*, New York: Columbia University Press.

Kopytoff, Igor (1971) 'Ancestors as elders', *Africa* 41: 129-42.

— (1981) 'Aghem ethnogenesis and the Grassfields ecumene', in Claude Tardits (ed.) *Contribution de la Recherche Ethnologique à l'Histoire des Civilisations du Cameroun*, Paris: Editions du CNRS.

— (1987) 'The internal African frontier: the making of African political culture', in Igor Kopytoff (ed.) *The African Frontier: the reproduction of traditional African societies*, Bloomington: Indiana University Press.

Kopytoff, I. and S. Miers (1977) 'African "slavery" as an institution of marginality', in I. Kopytoff and S. Miers (eds) *Slavery in Africa: historical and anthropological perspectives*, Madison: University of Wisconsin Press.

Kuper, Leo (1977) *The Pity of It All: polarisation of racial and ethnic relations*, London: Duckworth.

Lancaster, C. S. (1974) 'Ethnic identity, history and "tribe" in the Middle Zambezi Valley', Special number on *Uses of Ethnohistory in Ethnographic Analysis*, *American Ethnologist* 1: 707-30.

Law, Robin (1976) 'Horses, firearms and political power in pre-colonial West Africa', *Past and Present* 72: 112-32.

— (1978) 'Slaves, trade and taxes: the material basis of political power in precolonial West Africa', *Research in Economic Anthropology* 1: 27-52.

Leach, E. R. (1954) *Political Systems of Highland Burma*, London: Athlone.

Lembezat, Bertrand (1961) *Les populations païennes du Nord-Cameroun et de l'Adamaoua*, Paris: Presses Universitaires de France.

Lévi-Strauss, Claude (1966) 'The future of kinship studies', *Proceedings of the Royal Anthropological Institute*, pp. 13-21.

— (1969) 'Preface to the second Edition', of *The Elementary Structures of Kinship*, translated by J.H. Bell, J.R. von Sturmer and Rodney Needham, London: Eyre and Spottiswoode.

Lilley, E.S. [1921] 'Historical and ethnographic notes on the Chamba people of Dakka', Nigerian National Archives Kaduna, Yola Profile, File J8 The Chamba.

Macleod, Olive (1912; facsimile reprint 1971) *Chiefs and Cities of Central Africa. Across Lake Chad by way of British, French, and German Territories*, Freeport, New York: Books for Libraries Press.

McKnight, David (1967) 'Extra-descent group ancestor cults in African Societies', *Africa* 37(1): 1-21.

Mazrui, A. and M. Tidy (1984) *Nationalism and New States in Africa*, Nairobi, Ibadan, London: Heinemann.

Malinowksi, Bronislaw (1944) *A Scientific Theory of Culture and Other Essays*, Chapel Hill: University of North Carolina Press.

Mandela, Nelson (1994) *Long Walk to Freedom*, London: Little, Brown & Co.

Meek, C. K. (1925) *The Northern Tribes of Nigeria. An ethnographical account of the Northern Provinces of Nigeria together with a report on the 1921 Decennial Census*, London: Oxford University Press.

— (1931) *Tribal Studies in Northern Nigeria*, London: Kegan Paul, Trench and Trubner.

— (1936) 'Marriage by exchange in Nigeria. A disappearing institution', *Africa* 9: 64-74.

Meillassoux, Claude (1981; originally 1975) *Maidens, Meal and Money: capitalism and the domestic community*, Cambridge: Cambridge University Press.

Mignolo, Walter D. (2002) 'The many faces of cosmo-polis: border thinking and critical cosmopolitanism', in Carol A. Breckenridge, Sheldon Pollock, Homi K. Bhabha and Dipesh Chakrabarty (eds) *Cosmopolitanism*, Durham: Duke University Press, pp. 157-88.

Mitchell, J. C. (1956) *The Kalela Dance: aspects of social relationships among urban Africans*, Rhodes Livingstone Papers No. 27. Manchester: Manchester University Press.

Mohammadou, Eldridge (1978) *Les royaumes foulbé du plateau de l'Adamaoua au XIX siècle*, Tokyo: Institute for the Study of the Languages and Cultures of Africa and Asia.

— (1983) *Peuples et royaumes du Foumbina*, Yaoundé: Centre de recherches et d'études Anthropologiques.

— [1984] *Ethiopiens du Nord-Cameroun. Etude du Leo Frobenius,* Garoua: Institut des Sciences Humaines. Subsequently published as (1987) *Peuples et sociétés du Nord-Cameroun*, (A translation of the chapters of Frobenius 1925 *Dichten und Denken im Sudan*, concerned with Cameroon.) Stuttgart: Franz Steiner.

Moisel, Max (1908) 'Zur Geschichte vom Bali und Bamum', *Globus* 93: 117-20.

Muller, Jean-Claude (1982) *Du Bon Usage, du sexe et du marriage: structures matri-moniales du haut plateau nigerien*, Paris: Harmattan.

Nadel, S. F. (1935) 'Nupe state and community', *Africa* 8: 257-303.

Nairn, Tom (1977) *The Break-up of Britain*, London: Verso.

Naroll, R. (1964) 'Ethnic unit classification', *Current Anthropology* 5: 283-91.

— (1970) 'The culture bearing unit in cross-cultural studies', in R. Naroll and R. Cohen (eds) *A Handbook of Method in Cultural Anthropology*, New York: Columbia University Press.

Needham, Rodney (1975) 'Polythetic classification: convergence and consequences', *Man* NS 10: 347-69.

Ngome, V.E. (1993) 'Anglophobia', *Focus on Africa* 4(3): 27-29.

Nietzsche, F. (1977) *A Nietzsche Reader*, R. J. Hollingsworth (ed.), Harmondsworth: Penguin.

Nkwi, Paul and Jean-Pierre Warnier (1982) *Elements for a History of the Western Grassfields*, Yaoundé: Publication of the Department of Sociology, University of Yaoundé.

Nyamndi, N.B. (1988) *The Bali Chamba of Cameroon: a political history*, Paris: Editions Cape.

Oha, Obododimma (2001) 'Mmanwu Awusa: masquerading the Hausa Muslim in Igbo tiger performance', in *Africa at the Crossroads: Complex Political Emergencies in the 21st Century*, UNESCO/ENA: Most Ethno-Net Africa Publications, (www.unesco.org/most/crossroadsoha.htm).

Okamura, Jonathan (1981) 'Situational ethnicity', *Ethnic and Racial Studies* 4: 452-65.

Orwell, George (originally 1940, 1970) 'Inside the Whale', in Sonia Orwell and Ian Angus (eds), *The Collected Essays, Journalism and Letters of George Orwell*, Vol. 1 *An Age Like This*, Harmondsworth: Penguin, pp. 540-77.

Ostien, Philip, Jamila M. Nasir and Franz Kogelmann (2005) *Comparative Perspectives on Shari'ah in Nigeria*, Ibadan: Spectrum Books.

Paden, John N. (2005) *Muslim Civic Cultures and Conflict Resolution: the challenge of democratic federalism in Nigeria*, Washington DC: Brookings Institution Press.

Palmié, Stephan (1995) 'African frontiers in the Americas?', in Wim Hoogbergen (ed.) *Born out of Resistance*, Utrecht: ISOR Publications, pp. 286-300.

Panos Institute (1993) *Radio Pluralism in West Africa: a survey conducted by the Panos Institute and l'Union de Journalistes d'Afrique de l'Ouest*, Paris: Institut Panos and L'Harmattan.

Peter, Emrys L. (1960), 'The proliferation of segments in the lineage of the Bedouins of Cyrenaica', *Journal of the Royal Anthropological Institute* 90: 29-53.

— (1967) 'Some structural aspects of the feud among the camel-herding Bedouin of Cyrenaica', *Africa* 37: 261-82.

Pontié, G. (1984) 'Les sociétés païennes', in Jean Boutrais (ed.) *Le Nord du Cameroun. Des hommes, une region*, Paris: ORSTOM.

Prunier, Gerard (1995) *The Rwanda Crisis 1959-1994. History of a genocide*, London: Hurst and Company.

Quayson, A. (1994) 'Unthinkable Nigeriana', in G. Gbadamosi and A. Quayson *Redrawing the Map: two African journeys*, Cambridge: Prickly Pear Press.

Radcliffe Brown, A. R. (1952) *Structure and Function in Primitive Society*, London: Cohen and West.

Ranger, Terence (1982) 'Race and tribe in Southern Africa: European ideas and African acceptance', in R. Ross (ed.) *Racism and Colonialism*, Leiden: Nijhoff.

— (1983) 'The invention of tradition in colonial Africa', in E. Hobsbawm and T. Ranger (eds) *The Invention of Tradition*, Cambridge: Cambridge University Press.

— (1993) 'The invention of tradition revisited: the case of colonial Africa', in Terence Ranger and Oluferni Vaughan (eds) *Legitimacy and the State in Twentieth-Century Africa*, Basingstoke: Macmillan (in association with St Antony's College, Oxford), pp. 62-111.

Rapport, Nigel (2006) 'Anthropology as cosmopolitan study', *Anthropology Today* February 22(1): 23.

Rée, Jonathan (1992) 'Internationality', *Radical Philosophy* 60 (Spring): 3-11.

Rehfisch, F. (1960) 'The dynamics of multilineality on the Mambila plateau', *Africa* 30: 246-60.

— (1962) 'Competitive gift exchange among the Mambila', *Cahiers d'Etudes Africaines* 3(9): 91-103.

— (1969) 'Death, dreams and the ancestors in the Mambila culture', in M. Douglas and P. Kaberry (eds), *Man in Africa*, London: Tavistock.

— (1972) *The Social Structure of a Mambila Village*, Occasional Paper No. 2, Zaria: Ahmadu Bello University Press.

Richards, Paul (1992) 'Landscapes of dissent - Ikale and Ilaje Country 1870-1950', in J.F. Ade Ajayi and J.D.Y. Peel (eds) *Peoples and Empires in African History: essays in memory of Michael Crowder*, London: Longman.

— (1996) *Fighting for the Rainforest: war, youth and resources in Sierra Leone*, Oxford and Portsmouth, NH: the International African Institute in association with James Currey and Heinemann.

Riches, David (1979) 'On the presentation of the Tiv segmentary lineage system, or, speculations on Tiv social organisation', in Ladislav Holy (ed.) *Segmentary Lineage Systems Reconsidered*, Belfast: Queen's University Papers in Social Anthropology, 4.

Royer, Patrick (2002) 'The spirit of competition: *wak* and sport in Burkina Faso', *Africa* 72(3): 464-83.

Said, Edward (1993) *Culture and Imperialism*, London: Chatto and Windus.

Schilder, K. (1993) 'Local rulers in North Cameroon. The interplay of politics and conversion', in K. Schilder and W. van Binsbergen (eds) *Ethnicity in Africa*, Special Issue of *Afrika Focus*, 9(1-2): 43-72, Leiden: African Studies Centre.

Schilder, K. and van Binsbergen, W. (1993) 'Recent Dutch and Belgian approaches to ethnicity in Africa', Introduction to K. Schilder and W. van Binsbergen (eds) *Ethnicity in Africa*, Special Issue of *Afrika Focus,* 9(1-2), Leiden: African Studies Centre.

Schrire, Carmel (2002) *Tigers in Africa: stalking the past at the Cape of Good Hope*, Landsdowne, and Windhoek: LLAREC Series in Visual History, University of Cape Town Press.

Schumaker, Lyn (2001) *Africanizing Anthropology: fieldwork, networks, and the making of cultural knowledge in Central Africa*, Durham and London: Duke University Press.

Schüttpelz, Erhard (2003) 'Transformation and identification: Franz Baermann Steiner's "chief sociological principle"', in Jeremy Adler, Richard Fardon and Carol Tully (eds) *From Prague Poet to Oxford Anthropologist: Franz Baermann Steiner celebrated*, Munich: Judicium; London: Publications of the Institute of Germanic Studies (University of London School of Advanced Studies) 80.

Seton-Watson, H. (1977) *Nations and States. An enquiry into the origins of nations and the politics of nationalism*, London: Methuen.

Sharpe, B. (1986) 'Ethnography and a regional system: mental maps and the myth of states and tribes in North-Central Nigeria', *Critique of Anthropology* VI(3): 33-65.

Simmel, G. (1950) *The Sociology of Georg Simmel*, translated by K. H. Wolf, New York: Free Press.

— (1980) *Essays on Interpretation in Social Science*, edited and translated by Guy Oakes, Manchester: Manchester University Press.

Sinclair, Simon (1993) 'The present tense again', *Journal of the Anthropological Society of Oxford* 24(1): 33-48.

Siran, Jean-Louis (1981) 'Appellations et attitudes: le système de parenté Vouté', *L'Homme* 21(3): 39-60.

Smith, Anthony (1971) *Theories of Nationalism*, London: Duckworth.

— (1981) *The Ethnic Revival*, Cambridge: Cambridge University Press.

— (1983) *State and Nation in the Third World*, Brighton: Wheatsheaf Books.

Smith, M. G. (1956) 'On segmentary lineage systems', *Journal of the Royal Anthropological Institute* 86: 39-80.

— (1971) 'The institutional and political conditions of pluralism', and 'Some developments in the analytic framework of pluralism', in L. Kuper and M. G. Smith (eds) *Pluralism in Africa*, Berkeley: University of California Press.

— (1974) *Corporations and Society*, London: Duckworth.

— (1982) 'Ethnicity and ethnic groups in America: the view from Harvard', *Ethnic and Racial Studies* 5: 1-22.

Southall, Aidan (1970) 'The illusion of tribe', *Journal of African and Asian Studies* 5: 28-50.

— (1976) 'Nuer and Dinka are people: ecology, ethnicity and logical possibility', *Man* (N.S.) 11: 463-91.

Southwold, Martin (1978) 'Buddhism and the definition of religion', *Man* (N.S.) 13: 362-79.

Steiner, Franz Baermann (1956) 'Notes on Comparative Economics', *British Journal of Sociology* 5(2): 18-29.

— (1956) *Taboo*, Harmondsworth: Pelican/Penguin.

— (1999) *Franz Baermann Steiner - Selected Writings*, Volumes I and II, Jeremy Adler and Richard Fardon (eds), Oxford: Berghahn.

Strathern, Marilyn (1985) 'Kinship and economy: constitutive orders of a provisional kind', *American Ethnologist* 12: 191-209.

— (1988) *The Gender of the Gift: problems with women and problems with society in Melanesia*, Berkeley: University of California Press.

Strümpell, Karl (1910) 'Vergleichendes Wortzeichnis der Heidensprache Adamauas', *Zeitschrift für Ethnographie* 42: 444-88.

Takougang, J. (1993) 'The demise of Biya's New Deal in Cameroon, 1982-92', *Africa Insight* 23(2): 91-101.

Tardits, Claude (1970) 'Femmes à credit', in J. Pouillon and P. Miranda (eds), *Echanges et communications, Mélanges offerts à Claude Lévi-Strauss*, The Hague: Mouton.

— (1973) 'Parenté et pouvoir chez les Bamoum', *L'Homme* 13: 37-49.

— (1980) *Le Royaume bamoum*, Paris: Librarie Armand Colin.

Tardits, Claude (ed.) (1981) *Contribution de la recherche ethnologique à l'histoire des civilisations du Cameroun*, Paris: Editions du CNRS.

Terray, Emmanuel (1972; originally 1969) 'Historical materialism and segmentary lineage-based societies', in his *Marxism and 'Primitive' Societies: two studies*, New York: Monthly Review Press.

Thomas, N. (1994) *Colonialism's Culture: anthropology, travel and government*, Cambridge: Polity Press.

Titanji, V., M. Gwanfogbe, E. Nwana, G. Ndangam and A.S. Lima (eds) (1988) *An Introduction to the Study of Bali-Nyonga. A tribute to His Royal Highness Galega II, Traditional Ruler of Bali-Nyonga from 1940-1985*, Yaoundé: Stardust Printers.

Tonkin, Elizabeth (1985) 'Creating Kroomen: ethnic diversity, economic specialism and changing demand', in J. Stone (ed.) *Africa and the Sea*, Aberdeen: Aberdeen University African Studies Group.

Trautmann, Thomas R. and Peter M. Whiteley (2012) 'A classic problem', in Thomas R. Trautmann and Peter M. Whiteley (eds) *Crow-Omaha: new light on a classic problem of kinship analysis*, Arizona: Amerind Studies in Anthropology, Arizona University Press, pp. 1-27.

van den Berghe, P. (1981) *The Ethnic Phenomenon*, Amsterdam: Elsevier/North Holland.

van Binsbergen, Wim (1985) 'From tribe to ethnicity in Western Zambia: the unit of study as an ideological problem', in W. van Binsbergen and P. Geschiere (eds) *Old Modes of Production and Capitalist Encroachment*, London: Routledge and Kegan Paul.

van Gennep, Arnold (1960 [1909]) *The Rites of Passage*, London: Routledge and Kegan Paul.

Vertovec, Steven and Robin Cohen (eds) (2002) *Conceiving Cosmopolitanism: theory, context, and practice*, Oxford and New York: Oxford University Press.

Warnier, Jean-Pierre (1985) *Echanges, développement et hierarchies dans le Bamenda pré-colonial (Cameroun)*, Stuttgart: Franz Steiner.

— (1996/2012) 'Rebellion, defection and the position of male cadets: a neglected category (with an afterword)', in his *Cameroon Grassfields Civilization*, Bamenda, Cameroon: Langaa, pp. 109-18. Original version in Ian Fowler and David Zeitlyn (eds), *African Crossroads: intersections between history and anthropology in Cameroon* (Cameroon Studies Vol. 2), Oxford: Berghahn, pp. 115-24.

— (2007) *The Pot-King: the body and technologies of power*, Leiden: Brill; (2009) *Régner au Cameroun: le roi-pot*, Paris: Karthala (French version with new conclusion).

— (2012) *Cameroon Grassfields Civilization*, Cameroon: Langaa Press.

Warnock, Mary (1987) *Memory*, London: Faber.

Welch, T.G.B. [1935] 'Report on Chamba wife stealing', Nigerian National Archives Kaduna, Yola Profile, File 3058 Chamba Marriage (including letters on this subject).

Werbner, Richard (1977) 'Introduction', to Richard Werbner (ed.) *Regional Cults*, London: Academic Press.

— (1984) 'The Manchester School in Central Africa', *Annual Reviews in Anthropology* 13: 157-85.

— (1996) 'Multiple identities, plural arenas', in Richard Werbner and Terence Ranger (eds) *Postcolonial Identities in Africa*, London: Post-colonial Encounters, Zed Books, pp. 1-25.

Wilson, R.J.A. (1995) 'Carthaginian, Numidian, Roman', in Tom Phillips (ed.) *Africa: the Art of a Continent*, London: Royal Academy.

Young, Crawford (1976) *The Politics of Cultural Pluralism*, Madison: University of Wisconsin Press.

Zeitlyn, David (2005) *Words and Processes in Mambila Kinship: the theoretical importance of the complexity of everyday life*, Lanham: Lexington Books.

Zintgraff, Eugen (1895) *Nord-Kamerun*, Berlin: Paetel.

INDEX

www.ingramcontent.com/pod-product-compliance
Lightning Source LLC
Chambersburg PA
CBHW060029030426
42334CB00019B/2236